T0214820

Communications in Computer and Information Science   **647**

Commenced Publication in 2007
Founding and Former Series Editors:
Alfredo Cuzzocrea, Dominik Ślęzak, and Xiaokang Yang

More information about this series at http://www.springer.com/series/7899

Takashi Yoshino · Gwo-Dong Chen
Gustavo Zurita · Takaya Yuizono
Tomoo Inoue · Nelson Baloian (Eds.)

Collaboration Technologies and Social Computing

8th International Conference, CollabTech 2016
Kanazawa, Japan, September 14–16, 2016
Proceedings

 Springer

Editors
Takashi Yoshino
Wakayama University
Wakayama
Japan

Gwo-Dong Chen
National Central University
Taoyuan City
Taiwan

Gustavo Zurita
Department of Management Control
  and Information Systems
University of Chile
Santiago
Chile

Takaya Yuizono
Asahidai
JAIST
Nomi-shi
Japan

Tomoo Inoue
University of Tsukuba
Tsukuba
Japan

Nelson Baloian
University of Chile
Santiago
Chile

ISSN 1865-0929   ISSN 1865-0937   (electronic)
Communications in Computer and Information Science
ISBN 978-981-10-2617-1   ISBN 978-981-10-2618-8   (eBook)
DOI 10.1007/978-981-10-2618-8

Library of Congress Control Number: 2016950900

Printed on acid-free paper

This Springer imprint is published by Springer Nature
The registered company is Springer Science+Business Media Singapore Pte Ltd.

Preface

Message from the General Chairs

CollabTech 2016, the 8th International Conference on Collaboration Technologies, offered a unique forum for academics and practitioners to present and discuss innovative ideas, methods, or implementations related to collaboration technologies, which are greatly needed for various everyday collaboration activities owing to recent advances in networking, computing, and interaction technologies.

The previous CollabTech conferences were held in Tokyo in 2005, Tsukuba in 2006, Seoul in 2007, Wakayama in 2008, Sydney in 2009, Sapporo in 2012, and Santiago in 2014. Following the success of the joint organization with CRIWG in the last conference, CollabTech 2016 was co-located and organized with CRIWG 2016 again, but this time in Kanazawa, Japan. The CRIWG and CollabTech communities had similar research topics and goals, but had been geographically located in different regions. We believed this joint endeavor would provide an interesting opportunity to meet each other.

The success of the conference was largely due to the authors and presenters, as well as the Program Committee and the Conference Committee members, whose efforts made the conference possible. The success was also due to the SIG on Groupware and Network Services of the Information Processing Society of Japan, the SIG on Cyberspace of the Virtual Reality Society of Japan, and the SIG on Communication Enhancement of the Human Interface Society. The Japan Advanced Institute of Science and Technology (JAIST) and the Faculty of Library, Information and Media Science of the University of Tsukuba also gave us warm support. Ishikawa Prefecture, Kanazawa City, Support Center for Advanced Telecommunications Technology Research (SCAT), and Hitachi, Ltd. contributed financially to the success of the conference.

We are pleased that the conference was fruitful for all participants and played an important role in cultivating the community in this research field.

September 2016

Tomoo Inoue
Takaya Yuizono
Nelson Baloian

Message from the Program Chairs

After seven events of the International Conference on Collaboration Technologies series, we had the eighth edition (CollabTech 2016) in Kanazawa, Japan. The following topics on collaboration technologies were discussed:

– Cross-Cultural Collaboration
– Learning Support Systems
– Social Networking
– Rescue and Health Support
– Real and Virtual Collaboration

For this conference, we received 48 submissions (28 full papers, 20 work-in-progress papers) and assigned five reviewers per full paper or three reviewers per work-in-progress paper. As a result, we had 16 full papers and four work-in-progress papers. The acceptance rate was 42 %. Because of the high quality of the submissions, many excellent papers were not among those accepted. We hope that the detailed technical review comments we provided were helpful.

Without our distinguished Program Committee members, we could not have maintained our high standards. We truly appreciated their devotion. Finally, we hope that these proceedings serve as a reference for future researchers in this rapidly evolving field.

September 2016

Takashi Yoshino
Gwo-Dong Chen
Gustavo Zurita

Organization

Conference Co-chairs

Nelson Baloian	Universidad de Chile, Chile
Tomoo Inoue	University of Tsukuba, Japan
Takaya Yuizono	Japan Advanced Institute of Science and Technology, Japan

Program Co-chairs

Gwo-Dong Chen	National Central University, Taiwan
Takashi Yoshino	Wakayama University, Japan
Gustavo Zurita	Universidad de Chile, Chile

Financial Co-chairs

Shinkuro Honda	NTT, Japan
Kei Utsugi	Hitachi, Japan

Local Arrangements Co-chairs

Hideaki Kanai	Japan Advanced Institute of Science and Technology, Japan
Kazushi Nishimoto	Japan Advanced Institute of Science and Technology, Japan

Local Arrangements Members

Tessai Hayama	Kanazawa Institute of Technology, Japan
Atsuo Yoshitaka	Japan Advanced Institute of Science and Technology, Japan
Tomohito Yamamoto	Kanazawa Institute of Technology, Japan

Publication Chair

Junko Ichino	Kagawa University, Japan

Publicity Co-chairs

Yugo Hayashi	Ritsumeikan University, Japan
Masaki Omata	University of Yamanashi, Japan

Registration Chairs

Hidekazu Shiozawa Tamagawa University, Japan
Hironori Egi University of Electro-Communications, Japan

IPSJ SIG GN Liaison

Satoshi Ichimura Otsuma Women's University, Japan

VRSJ SIG CS Liaison

Kazuyuki Iso NTT, Japan

HIS SIG CE Liaison

Takashi Yoshino Wakayama University, Japan

Steering Committee

Hideaki Kuzuoka University of Tsukuba, Japan
Ken-ichi Okada Keio University, Japan
Jun Munemori Wakayama University, Japan
Minoru Kobayashi Meiji University, Japan
Hiroaki Ogata Kyushu University, Japan

Program Committee

Pedro Antunes Victoria University of Wellington, New Zealand
Luis Carriço University of Lisbon, Portugal
Maiga Chang Athabasca University, Canada
Hui Chun Chu Soochow University, Taiwan
Gj De Vreede University of South Florida, USA
Dominique Decouchant UAM Cuajimalpa, Mexico DF, Mexico - LIG de Grenoble, France
Yannis Dimitriadis University of Valladolid, Spain
Hironori Egi The University of Electro-Communications, Japan
Benjamim Fonseca UTAD/INESC TEC, Portugal
Kinya Fujita Tokyo University of Agrculture and Technology, Japan
Adam Giemza University of Duisburg-Essen, Germany
Atsuo Hazeyama Tokyo Gakugei University, Japan
Adam Hou NTHU, Taiwan
Gwo-Jen Hwang National Taiwan University of Science and Technology, Taiwan
Satoshi Ichimura Otsuma Women's University, Japan
Junko Ichino Kagawa University, Japan

Yutaka Ishii	Okayama Prefectural University, Japan
Kazuyuki Iso	NTT, Japan
Marc Jansen	University of Applied Sciences Ruhr West, Germany
Jongwon Kim	Gwangju Institute of Science and Technology, South Korea
Hyungseok Kim	Konkuk University, South Korea
Liang-Yi Li	National Central University, Taiwan
Chiu Pin Lin	National Hsinchu University of Education, Taiwan
Stephan Lukosch	Delft University of Technology, The Netherlands
Wolfram Luther	University of Duisburg-Essen, Germany
Sonia Mendoza	CINVESTAV-IPN, Mexico
Roc Meseguer	Universitat Politècnica de Catalunya, Spain
Kazuyoshi Murata	Aoyama Gakuin University, Japan
Hideyuki Nakanishi	Osaka University, Japan
Mamoun Nawahdah	Birzeit University, Palestine
Andres Neyem	Pontificia Universidad Católic de Chile, Chile
Cuong Nguyen	University of Nebraska at Omaha, USA
Masayuki Okamoto	Toshiba Corporation, Japan
Masaki Omata	University of Yamanashi, Japan
Nobuchika Sakata	Osaka University, Japan
Flavia Santoro	NP2Tec/UNIRIO, Brazil
Rodrigo Santos	Universidad Nacional del Sur - Bahía Blanca, Argentina
Yoshiaki Seki	NTT, Japan
Hidekazu Shiozawa	Tamagawa University, Japan
Marcus Specht	Open University of the Netherlands, The Netherlands
Chengzheng Sun	Nanyang Technological University, Singapore
Shin Takahashi	University of Tsukuba, Japan
Stefan Trausan-Matu	University Politehnica of Bucharest, Romania
Vaninha Vieira	Federal University of Bahia (UFBA), Brazil
Hao-Chuan Wang	National Tsing Hua University, Taiwan
Benjamin Weyers	RWTH Aachen University, Germany
Tomohito Yamamoto	Kanazawa Institute of Technology, Japan

A New You: From Augmented Reality to Augmented Human (Keynote Talk)

Jun Rekimoto

Interfaculty Initiative in Information Studies, The University of Tokyo,
7-3-1 Hongo, Bunkyo-ku, Tokyo 113-0033 Japan
Sony Computer Science Laboratories, Inc., 3-14-13 Higashigotanda,
Shinagawaku, Tokyo 141-0022 Japan
rekimoto@acm.org

Abstract. Traditionally, the field of human–computer interaction (HCI) was primarily concerned with designing and investigating interfaces between humans and machines. The primary concern of surface computing is also about designing better interfaces to information. However, with recent technological advances, the concept of enhancing, augmenting, or even re-designing humans themselves is becoming a very feasible and serious topic of scientific research as well as engineering development. *Augmented human* is a term that I use to refer to this overall research direction. Augmented human introduces a fundamental paradigm shift in HCI: from human–computer interaction to human–computer integration. In this talk, I will discuss rich possibilities and distinct challenges in enhancing human abilities. I will introduce recent projects conducted by our group including the design and applications of wearable eye sensing for augmenting our perception and memory abilities, design of flying cameras as our external eyes, a home appliance that can increase your happiness, an organic physical wall/window that dynamically mediates the environment, and an immersive human–human communication called "JackIn."

Keywords: Human Augmentation · Augmented Reality · Internet of Abilities · JackIn

ACM Classification Keywords: H.5.m. Information Interfaces and Presentation (e.g. HCI): Miscellaneous

Bio. Jun Rekimoto received his BASc, MSc, and PhD in information science from Tokyo Institute of Technology in 1984, 1986, and 1996, respectively. Since 1994 he has been working for Sony Computer Science Laboratories (Sony CSL). In 1999 he formed and directed the Interaction Laboratory within Sony CSL. Since 2007 he has been a professor in the Interfaculty Initiative in Information Studies at The University of Tokyo. Since 2011 he also has been Deputy Director of Sony CSL.

Rekimoto's research interests include human–computer interaction, computer-augmented environments, and computer-augmented human (human–computer integration). He invented various innovative interactive systems and sensing technologies, including NaviCam (a hand-held AR system), Pick-and-Drop (a direct-manipulation technique for inter-appliance computing), CyberCode (the world's first marker-based AR system), Augmented Surfaces, HoloWall, and SmartSkin (two earliest representations of multi-touch systems). He has published more than 100 articles in the area of human–computer interactions, including ACM SIGCHI, and UIST. He received the Multi-Media Grand Prix Technology Award from the Multi-Media Contents Association Japan in 1998, iF Interaction Design Award in 2000, the Japan Inter-Design Award in 2003, iF Communication Design Award in 2005, Good Design Best 100 Award in 2012, Japan Society for Software Science and Technology Fundamental Research Award in 2012, and ACM UIST Lasting Impact Award, Zoom Japon Les 50 qui font le Japon de demain in 2013. In 2007, he was also elected to the ACM SIGCHI Academy.

Contents

Twitter Bot for Activation of Online Discussion and Promotion of Understanding by Providing Related Articles

Shota Kusajima$^{(\boxtimes)}$ and Yasuyuki Sumi

Future University Hakodate, Hokkaido, Japan
s-kusajima@sumilab.org, sumi@acm.org

Abstract. Twitter has been used in academic conferences and study meetings as a means of debating announcements and sharing information, alongside a real presentation. This paper discusses activating online discussion on a Twitter timeline and promotion of understanding. Accordingly, we developed a Twitter bot which suggests related webpages via tweets. This paper describes the deployments of our bot in two types of meetings: lightning talk format and relaxed group meeting. We report whether it was capable of providing appropriate topics and users' reactions to the bot in these meetings.

Keywords: Twitter bot · Activation of discussion · Keyword extraction from timeline · Documents provision to timeline

1 Introduction

The spread of the Internet means that currently, in academic conferences and study meetings, some participants attend to a presentation while simultaneously looking up questions on the Internet and arguing with other participants online using Social Networking Services (SNS) [1]. However, the meeting or presentation progresses while participants search, and they may lose track of the meaning. If the meeting progresses while participants do not understand, they may not be able to understand the next topic and as a result it is difficult for new discussions to occur.

The purpose of this study is to take the hassle out of searching for more information during meetings, and to activate online discussion by providing participants with new awareness to promote understanding. Therefore, we developed a Twitter bot which provides related information to participants in an online discussion by tweeting in real time. First, the bot analyzes tweets in online discussion, then extracts a keyword which is determined to be at the center of the discussion. After this, the bot searches on websites to which papers have been published, as well as news sites, and finally provides search results for participants in the form of tweets.

Also, we operate this bot in academic conferences and study meetings. We survey how the bot affects online discussion by observing whether the bot tweets

© Springer Science+Business Media Singapore 2016
T. Yoshino et al. (Eds.): CollabTech 2016, CCIS 647, pp. 1–16, 2016.
DOI: 10.1007/978-981-10-2618-8_1

promote new discussion between participants and users' responses (reply, retweet, like) to the bot tweets.

By introducing this bot into online discussions and providing participants with related webpages in real time, we can enable participants to get more related information without taking time out from attending to presentations to make searches. Furthermore, we hope to see effects such as occurrence of new discussion between participants, resolution of questions, and promotion of understanding.

2   Related Research

2.1   Support of Group Discussion

The purpose of this study is to support group discussion in terms of activating discussion and promoting understanding in online group discussion. Two examples of similar studies are Sumi's "AIDE" [2] and Akagawa's "INGA" [3] systems.

"AIDE" is a real time electronic conference system which has a function for chat via a network. This system is able to promote cooperative thinking among participants by visualizing the interactive structure of discussion.

Also, "INGA" is a system for assisting in activation of research discussion and facilitation of knowledge inheritance among participants. This system uses a microphone to record participants' voices during a conference, and extracts some keywords from the contents of the statements. Participants are then able to check the keywords and search the electronic data of related conference documents. In addition, this system sends some appropriate documents to participants' tablet devices. Participants are able to take notes and share the contents with each other in real time. This system enables participants to cooperate in assessing the electronic data and sharing the knowledge among themselves.

AIDE and INGA are closed systems with limited users. In contrast, our experiment focuses on allowing anyone to easily take part in discussion by using Twitter, which is a generally wide-spread a forum for discussion.

2.2   Information Provision by Agents

In this study, the Twitter bot estimates the key topics of meetings and provides participants with related information. The Kitamura group conducted research on a cooperative information retrieval system [4] and a competitive information recommendation system [5] using multiple character agents, as systems in which agents other than the users provides information for the users. These systems require the learning, via interaction with agents, of information that users need, whereas our study, on the other hand, changes the target of topic estimation from an individual participant to an entire discussion, and provides participants with related information without having to have this information entered intentionally.

2.3   Using Twitter in Meetings

Studies relating to Twitter, a site which anyone can use easily, include "PPTwi" [6], developed by Kurihara, which is an add-in that allows alterations made beforehand in the 'notes' column of a Microsoft Powerpoint presentation to be automatically tweeted, "Vital Atlas" [7], developed by Takeuchi et al., which is a system to visualize the spread of information by recursively clustering tweets displayed in chronological order. Furthermore, there have been studies on visualizing the data on Twitter [8,9].

These systems merely present information that has been entered in advance or analyze tweets on a timeline, whereas our study aims to analyze tweets in real time and provide optimal contents for discussion participants.

Also, it is important for the promotion of discussion and understanding that Twitter bots provide related information to participants directly. Regarding research on Twitter bots, Yamada developed a Twitter bot called "Ronbutter" [10]. This system regularly searches CiNii for papers with relevant content, on the basis of trend information on Twitter, then tweets the search results to general users.

However, this system is not able to narrow down the subject of discussion because the information provided is trend information for the entirety of Twitter. In contrast, our study is limits the target of discussion to conferences and study meetings currently being conducted, extracts a central topic, and provides information suitable for that specific discussion.

2.4   Keyword Extraction in Online Meetings

In our study, it is necessary to extract an appropriate keyword from participants' tweets in order to select webpages strongly related to the contents of the discussion.

There are several techniques for extracting keywords from text. To take some existing algorithms, there are TF-IDF [11], Key Graph [12], machine learning by SVM [13], LDA [14], and DTM [15]. Also, there are studies which assume that a word with a high instantaneous burst degree is important [16]. Other studies use a web-page ranking algorithm [17] to determine the importance of words [18], and estimate a main topic [19]. Also, there has been a study on summarizing single documents by using lexical chains [20]. Based on this study, Hatori et al. use lexical chains to extract key sentences and topics from corpuses [21]. However, these techniques require other texts (corpuses), besides the text from which keywords are to be extracted, or are not suitable for operation in real-time. For this reason, these techniques are not suitable for our research, which requires the successive extraction of keywords from tweets.

3   A Bot to Support Discussion on Twitter

This chapter describes the flow of our system and the techniques used in the development. Figure 1 is a concept diagram of our system.

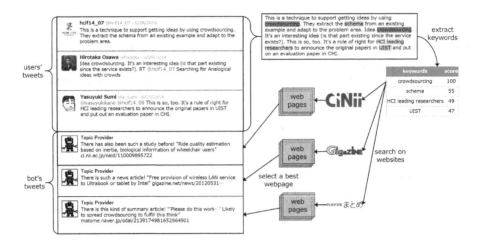

Fig. 1. Conceptual diagram

3.1 Overview of the Twitter Bot

In a meeting, Twitter is generally used with specific hash tags created for the meeting. Accordingly, the bot first searches Twitter for tweets which contain these hash tags, then stores the tweets in sequence. When a sufficient number of tweets have been saved, or a specified amount of time has passed, the bot extracts one keyword which is considered to be closely related to the meeting. Next, the bot uses the keyword to search within some websites to which papers are published, then finally tweets the titles and URLs of the webpages obtained as a result of the search, accompanied by the meeting-specific hash tags.

3.2 Keyword Extraction from Tweets

The first stage in this process is to obtain all the tweets which contain the specified hash tags, by using Streaming API. Streaming API is a form of API that can obtain tweets in real time via continuous HTTP connection. The second stage in the process is to continue storing tweets as text data, while removing excess information such as hash tags or URLs, until a certain amount has been stored. The final stage is to analyze the stored tweets and extract a keyword.

An appropriate timing for keyword extraction must be set depending on factors such as the number of participants and the presentation style of the meetings in which this system is used. For example, if a meeting is divided into a series of sessions, the bot will be set to select one keyword from all the tweets made during a single session and tweet the result at the end of the session. In other situations keyword extraction could be set to occur when a specified criterion is met, such as a certain period of time having passed, a certain number of characters having been used, or a certain number of tweets having been made.

Also, our system uses a text analysis API provided by Yahoo! JAPAN to extract a keyword. Using this API it is possible to analyze given texts and extract characteristic expressions (key-phrases) and their corresponding degrees of importance (score).

However, when using this API it is not uncommon for unknown words containing symbols or similar to be selected, leading to the extraction of a useless keyword. To avoid this, our system selects only the highest scoring keyword from among those that exist as titles of Japanese Wikipedia articles. A list of titles from Japanese Wikipedia is summarized and stored in the database in advance. Key-phrases are checked in order of score, beginning with the highest, until one is found that exists in the database.

3.3 Searching on Websites, and Tweets

Our Twitter bot searches on three websites: CiNii, Gigazine and NAVER matome. CiNii is an academic information database, Gigazine is a news site in blog format, and NAVER matome is a CGM-type web curation service. We decided these three websites to provide relevant past research papers from CiNii, and recent related topics from Gigazine or NAVER matome. When searching, the API provided by each website is used, or in the case of there being no provided API, the Bing Search API provided by Microsoft Azure is used.

Search results can be considered in order of relevance or date, but it is not guaranteed that the highest ranked website will be related to the content of the meeting. To resolve this issue, our system obtains a maximum of ten search results from each website in order of date, and selects the best webpage by using tf-idf [11] and cosine similarity estimation method [22] to determine the degree of similarity between the content of tweets made at the time of keyword extraction and the content of the webpages. The webpage with the highest degree of similarity is chosen as the best. By taking this approach, it is possible to select a webpage which is closer to the contents of the discussion, as this method does not depend solely on the highest scoring keyword, but also considers words which were not chosen as keywords yet which are nonetheless distinctive and relevant to the meeting.

After the webpages have been selected, the Twitter bot provides tweets including the titles and URLs of obtained webpages for users taking part in online discussion. This bot provides one tweet per website. If there are no search results, the bot does not tweet about the website. Also, if a useful keyword cannot be obtained, no search is carried out and the bot does not tweet.

4 Operational Experiment Conducted at a Lightning Talk Format Study Meeting, and Corresponding Considerations

We operated the Twitter Bot at "CHI study meeting 2015" which was held on June 27, 2015. This chapter describes the overview of the experiment, the results, and our considerations.

4.1 About "CHI Study Meeting 2015"

"CHI study meeting 2015" was a study meeting in which 485 papers presented at an academic conference, CHI 2015, were introduced in presentations of 30 seconds per paper. About 150 people participated in this meeting, and 49 people used Twitter during this meeting. Figure 2 is the overview of this meeting. This meeting was divided into 114 sessions consisting of three to six papers, and one person was responsible for one session and presented. This meeting was carried out at DMM.make AKIBA in Tokyo and Hokkaido University in Hokkaido. When a presentation was being made in one of the venues, the audio from the presentation, and the slides that were being used, were broadcast online in the another venue. Also, when each paper was presented, the title of the paper and an introduction of the contents, prepared by the presenter beforehand, were tweeted to a Twitter account specially created for the provision of information in this meeting.

Thus, we assumed that many of the participants used Twitter during the meeting, because the meeting was held in two different venues and Twitter was used to introduce papers.

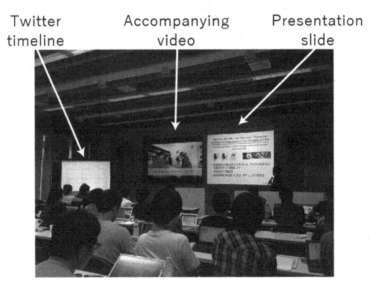

Fig. 2. Overview of lightning talk format study meeting, "CHI study meeting 2015"

4.2 Overview of the Experiment

In this experiment, tweets made over the course of one session were treated as one text, and analyzed, and a keyword was extracted. Next, a search was carried out in CiNii, Gigazine and NAVER matome. Finally, the Twitter bot tweeted at the end of each session. Besides this, participants took notes and tweeted their opinions on Twitter using a common hash tag.

Incidentally, it was stated in Sect. 3 that only the highest scoring keyword that existed as the title of a Japanese Wikipedia article would be selected, but this was not implemented in this particular experiment. We used the obtained keyword directly. Additionally, it was previously explained that the best webpage was selected by determining the degree of similarity to tweet content using tf-idf and cosine similarity estimation method, but this also was not implemented. The top-ranking webpage from among the search results was automatically selected.

4.3 Results of the Experiment

One of 114 sessions, we were able to extract a keyword in 100 sessions by excluding the sessions in which participants did not tweet. Also, out of those 100 sessions, we were able to obtain a keyword that could be considered useful in 47 sessions. In other sessions, common words such as "user" or "display", and words containing symbols were extracted.

Example of when appropriate webpages were provided. Table 1 shows an example of when the bot successfully extracted a useful keyword and provided appropriate webpages to participants in the meeting. "hcihokkaido" was an account created in order to provide the information of each paper's title and introduction of content, and "bot" was the Twitter bot that we made. Incidentally, all tweets contained a hash tag in the meeting, but it is omitted from the table, partly because it was not used to extract a keyword and also for the purpose of simplification.

In this section of the meeting, a finger-mounted device called "FingerReader", which assists visually impaired people to read sentences, was being presented. A keyword, "active reading", was successfully extracted and two related webpages provided.

Results obtained through the study meeting. We anticipated that participants would "like" some of the bot tweets and "re-tweet" them, or that new discussion would be generated as a result of the tweets. However, participants displayed almost no reaction to the bot during the meeting. Out of 233 bot tweets, only 7 tweets were reacted to by participants. Analysis of the timeline of the meeting reveals that out of a total of 342 tweets made by participants, only 18 tweets were replies to other participants or reference tweets. Figure 3 shows the tendency of the user's tweets.

4.4 Considerations

Regarding keyword extraction, less than half of all keywords selected could be considered useful. Accordingly, it is thought necessary not to simply use the Yahoo! JAPAN text analysis API, but also to contrive other methods of keyword extraction.

Table 1. Example of when appropriate information was provided (part of timeline of study meeting, translated from Japanese)

Username	Tweet
user01	UI of a belt is like "007"
hcihokkaido	RegionSpeak: Quick Comprehensive Spatial Descriptions of Complex Images for Blind Users http://t.co/OS6FVB0C2S
user02	I want to experience. https://t.co/rkSmh1G6eq
hcihokkaido	FingerReader: A Wearable Device to Explore Printed Text on the Go http://t.co/Cmec3onksU
hcihokkaido	Collaborative Accessibility: How Blind and Sighted Companions Co-CreateAccessible Home Spaces http://t.co/nQ9sFbakwQ
user03	@hcihokkaido Device to strengthen an active reading. It's good idea
bot	I search "active reading" in CiNii. Result: "On the Ambiguity of Sentences with Natural Language Quantifiers" http://t.co/ywcZX7y2fI
bot	I search "active reading" in Gigazine. Result: "Scientists revealed how brain wor···" http://t.co/qhKdBTOBSA

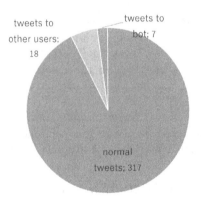

Fig. 3. Tendency of users' tweets

Furthermore, no significant participant reactions to the Twitter bot were observed in the lightning talk format study meeting. However, from analysis of the timeline it is evident that participants' purpose of using Twitter was to make memos rather than to hold discussion. It is thought that the reason for this may be that participants found it difficult to enter directly into online discussion with other participants who they did not know.

Concerning the reason that almost no reactions to the bot were observed, this is probably also because participants did not use Twitter to discuss with other participants but to take notes. Besides this, the bot tweets were monotonous, containing only titles and URLs. Evidently it is necessary to devise a way to make the wording of these tweets less monotonous.

5 Operational Experiment in Group Meetings

Taking into account the results from the lightning talk format study meeting, we devised new methods of keyword extraction and webpage selection, and operated the Twitter bot in study meetings in a laboratory. This chapter presents an overview of the experiment and some characteristic results.

5.1 Overview of the Experiment

In this experiment, 15 university students, 7 fourth-year students and 8 third-year students, participated in a meeting in which 4 of the fourth-year students made presentations to the other participants. The contents of the presentations were an overview of their current research, achievements and future prospects. The 15 participants all used Twitter to take notes and discuss, which compensated for the fact there was insufficient time taken for the question-and-answer session. One presenter was assigned 10 min to speak, and the meeting was held over approximately 40 min.

5.2 Results of the Experiment

The bot tweeted ten times, and five tweets were reacted (liked) to by users. This section presents some characteristic results along with the corresponding timelines.

Example of provision of appropriate webpages. Table 2 shows an example of when the bot successfully provided appropriate webpages for participants in this study meeting.

During the time that the tweets in Table 2 were being made, a study on activation of library usage through introducing a prisoner's base game was being presented. Figure 4 depicts the overview of the study meeting. The Twitter bot provided two webpages, one of which was a research paper about gamification in libraries, similar to the work being presented. This research paper was closely related to the contents of the meeting. Also, the presenter did not know of this paper and stated in the post-meeting questionnaire that it would be very useful as a piece of related research. This confirms that the bot was able to provide useful related information.

Table 3 shows the results of keyword extraction using the text analysis API provided by Yahoo! JAPAN. The highest scoring word was "gamification", and this word existed as the title of a Japanese Wikipedia article. Therefore, this word was selected as a keyword.

Also, Table 4 shows the results of searching for "gamification" within CiNii, and the calculation result of the cosine similarity between the webpages found

Table 2. Example of when appropriate information was provided (part of timeline of group meeting, translated from Japanese)

Username	Tweet
user12	This is a study about activation of library usage through gamification
user12	He wants people to use real-world libraries more
user12	By using prisoner's base game
user14	Using gamification to entice people in?
user03	Using library ⇔ Gamification
user04	'A chance encounter with books' has a nice ring to it doesn't it
user08	A study posting photos already exists
user12	At first users' objective is to play the game, but gradually, going to the library becomes their objective
user10	There is also this previous research. I didn't know about it
bot	There has also been such a study before! "Possibility of Gamification as an'escape game' in a university library" ci.nii.ac.jp/naid/120005588···
bot	There is this kind of summary article! "#Gamification Geeks 2015.12.08 :: iglobe Inc." matome.naver.jp/odai/214494283···
user01	The literature about escape games and library usage looks interesting!
user15	@user01 Is there such literature?
user01	@user15 It was shown a moment ago
user14	@user15 @user01 The provider tweeted it

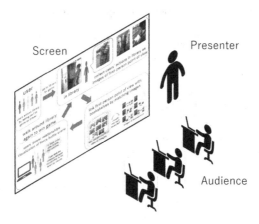

Fig. 4. Overview of group meeting, Example slide of work on "Library usage and Gamification"

Table 3. Results of keyword extraction (translated from Japanese)

Keyword	Score
Gamification	100
Library usage ⇔ gamification	44
Real-world	40
Prisoner's base	31
Game	26
Purpose	24
Previous research	22

Table 4. Results of search for "gamification" in CiNii and Cosine similarity between tweets and webpages (translated from Japanese)

Article Title	Cosine similarity
Design for W-DIARY, a diary-style-application for English word learning, with existing photos	0.0847
Demonstration of Character Rearing Game Application in Delay Tolerant Networks	0.057
Communication Support with Game-like Methods	0.0544
The possibilities of using gamification in information literacy education: examples from overseas libraries	0.0444
Effects of Gamification-Based Teaching Materials Designed for Japanese First Graders on Classrooms	0.0365
From NTT Data Technology using gamification and verification in the business field	0.0134
Possibility of Gamification as an 'escape game' in a university library	0.2426
Active Learning through Disoassion and Negotiation: Using University Education as Materials	0.012
Development and Practice of Gamified Coursework Design Framework (Paper on Educational Practice Research)	0.0509
Effects of Presenting Rank Order Generated from Subsets	0.0089

and the contents of tweets. From among 10 webpages obtained by searching, the bot was able to select a very closely related webpage about gamification in libraries. Therefore, it can be considered that calculating cosine similarity of content is a useful webpage selection technique.

Many participants were interested in this tweet, and five participants "liked" it. Besides this, several participants referred to the CiNii article and were able to obtain additional information, including the presenter ("user15"). Therefore, the result was useful in terms of providing new knowledge.

Example of failure to provide appropriate webpages. Table 5 shows an example of when the bot was not able to provide appropriate webpages.

Table 5. Example of when the bot failed to provide information (translated from Japanese)

Username	Tweet
user09	It looks interesting
user12	It's a book search based on individuals' reading experience
user03	Speaking of the universe... ☆
user12	Association is different for each person, so it refers to that
user06	The images are cute
user14	Apparently it's possible to obtain specialized search terms from the dictionary of a scholar in a specific field...
user08	This is good. It looks useful for when you don't have keyword to search by
user12	You can look at not only abstract but also professional ones
user05	I'd never have come up with that word...!
user15	I have heard of String theory, but what actually is it?
bot	There has also been such a study before! "Evolutionary learning of hysteresis neural networks" ci.nii.ac.jp/naid/400205244···
bot	There is such a news article! "'The steak at that time was delicious...' Greasy foods have..." gigazine.net/news/20090502···
user07	I want to eat steak

During the time when these tweets were being made, a presentation was being made about research on making associative dictionaries based on individuals' associations, and applying this to book searching. The keyword "association" was extracted. From CiNii the bot provided a paper about an evolutionary learning algorithm for hysteresis associative memory, based on greedy algorithm. On the other hand, from Gigazine the bot provided a useless article about the relationship between long-term memory and meals containing lipids. As these results demonstrate, even if a useful keyword is obtained the provided webpages will not necessarily be appropriate.

5.3   Considerations

The results of this experiment showed that participants discussed with each other freely in a study meeting among acquaintances. Also, that the method of webpage selection by calculating cosine similarity was a useful technique.

However, in the current method the bot tweeted about useless webpages, thus it is necessary to find methods to prevent the bot from tweeting in the case of a useless result, such as introducing a threshold of cosine similarity.

6   Continuous Use of the Twitter Bot

In the group discussion experiment described in this chapter, we were able to prompt participants to discuss and provide new information. Nevertheless, it is thought that because the participants were not yet accustomed to the bot, they did not check the bot tweets and the tweets did not tie in to their discussion. Therefore, we continuously operated the bot in an online group discussion and investigated the reactions of the participants. This chapter presents an overview of the experiment and characteristic results.

6.1   Overview of the Experiment

Out of the participants who took part in the group meeting described in Chap. 5, five participants discussed their individual graduation research, using Twitter.

In this experiment, the frequency of bot tweets was determined by the total number of characters of user tweets made thus far. In particular, useless information such as hash tags or URLs was removed from the participants' tweets, and the remaining data stored as text. When the number of characters of the text, which was converted to UTF-8, surpassed 2000, a keyword was extracted. The reason for using number of characters, rather than amount of time, to set keyword extraction frequency was that the discussion was not separated into sessions or fixed time slots. Also, the reason it was essential to convert the text to UTF-8 was that the Yahoo! JAPAN text analysis API requires search queries to be in UTF-8 format.

6.2   Results of the Experiment

In this meeting, the twitter bot tweeted eleven times, and six tweets were reacted (liked and retweeted) to by users. Besides there were many interactions between users, 28 tweets were replies in all 103 tweets.

Table 6 shows one of the characteristic timelines. At this time, participants were discussing a study conducted by "user04" on linking onomatopoeia and actions.

From this timeline, the keyword "onomatopoeia" was extracted and the bot was able to provide three webpages. One of these, an article from Gigazine, was closely related to the current discussion, so "user01" and "user05" reacted to it. In response to the reactions, "user04" explained to other participants the difference between the contents of the article and his own study.

6.3   Considerations

In this experiment, there were many exchanges of opinions between participants, and many remarks about the bot tweets, in contrast to the study meeting experiment detailed in Chap. 5. One reason for this difference may be that the second experiment centered on discussion in a small group. Additionally, it is thought

Table 6. Timeline when we continue to use Twitter bot (translated from Japanese)

Username	Tweet
user04	The thing that pains me. It's onomatopoeia
user01	Onomatopoeia
user02	What were the results of the onomatopoeia experiment in the end?
user05	I can't resist pronouncing "onomatopoeia"
user04	Onomatopoeia is tormenting me
user01	"Onomatopoeia" isn't on Wikipedia, but "Giseigo" is
user04	Changes were seen in the onomatopoeia of the same motions depending on environment
user04	The next thing is how to link it to the attributes of characters
user05	In line-of-sight measurement, the only thing I understood was that there's a difference in the length of time between when people are suffering and when they're not
user02	@user04 So did you finally calm down after all?
bot	There has also been such a study before! "Instruction on 'expression' of the child care and education content (expressive body movements)..." ci.nii.ac.jp/naid/400188785···
bot	There is such a news article! "Online dictionary that automatically collected examples of onomatopoeia..." gigazine.net/news/20080229···
bot	There is this is kind of summary article! "Twitter bots that you can't understand (Cuisine and Ingredients)" matome.naver.jp/odai/214089614···
user05	Ah, had it already been researched...?
user01	There is a dictionary of onomatopoeia!
user04	This only publishes examples, but my study analyzes actual movement data to determine whether you can really pronounce the sounds. Probably

that participants had become more accustomed to group discussion online than before, and had come to understand what kind of tweets the bot makes. Furthermore, this discussion was not separated into time slots, allowing participants to take the time to read the webpages provided by the bot. From these results, it is expected that if participants are accustomed to meetings of this format and are afforded time to read the webpages, promotion of understanding and the further development of discussion can be achieved.

Participants expressed the opinion that there was not time to read all the webpages provided by the bot. For them, three webpages per keyword are too many. Therefore, it is necessary to reduce the number of webpages presented at one time, or consider ways to allow participants to understand the content in a shorter period of time.

7 Conclusion

This study was carried out to develop a Twitter bot which provides related articles to participants in meetings in order to facilitate livelier discussion and promote understanding. The method used involved obtaining tweets during meetings and extracting a characteristic keyword. Using this keyword, the bot searched in several websites and selected one best webpage from each website by using the tf-idf and cosine similarity estimation method. Finally, the Twitter bot tweeted the titles and URLs of the webpages.

The bot was operated in various study meetings, to investigate whether it was able to provide appropriate webpages and affect online discussion. The results of the operating experiments reveal that there were a little effects in online meetings in which the participants did not know each other, and that participants used Twitter as a means to take notes rather than to discuss. On the other hand, our system was able to provide informations which the users prefer and the participants discussed actively and made new realizations as a result of the bot tweets.

Acknowledgements. We would like to thank participants of our experiments. The previous versions of the system shown in the paper have been developed by Takuya Fujitani and Ryo Tomiyama.

References

1. Denis, P., et al.: Twitter in academic events: a study of temporal usage, communication, sentimental and topical patterns in 16 computer science conferences. Comput. Commun. **73**, 301–314 (2016)
2. Sumi, Y., Nishimoto, K., Mase, K.: Facilitating human communications in personalized information spaces. In: AAAI 1996 Workshop on Internet-Based Information Systems (1996)
3. Akagawa, R., Takaya, Y.: Proposal and evaluation of a real-time conference support system "INGA" by reflection of phenomenal conference. IPSJ SIG Technical report 2013. 18, 1–8 (2013). (in Japanese)
4. Kitamura, Y., et al.: Multiple character-agents interface: an information integration platform where multiple agents and human user collaborate. In: Proceedings of the First International Joint Conference on Autonomous Agents and Multiagent Systems: Part 2. ACM (2002)
5. Kitamura, Y., Sakamoto, T., Tatsumi, S.: A competitive information recommendation system and its behavior. In: Klusch, M., Ossowski, S., Shehory, O. (eds.) CIA 2002. LNCS (LNAI), vol. 2446, pp. 138–151. Springer, Heidelberg (2002). doi:10.1007/3-540-45741-0_13
6. Kurihara, K.: PPTwi. https://sites.google.com/site/pptwiofficial/en.2016-04-18
7. T. Takeuchi, et al.: Visualization and classification of information spreading on Twitter. IEICE SIG Technical report (2010). (in Japanese)
8. Jussila, J., et al.: Information visualization of Twitter data for co-organizing conferences. In: Proceedings of International Conference on Making Sense of Converging Media. ACM (2013)

9. Maia, A., Cunha, T., Soares, C., Abreu, P.H.: TweeProfiles3: visualization of spatio-temporal patterns on Twitter. In: Rocha, Á., Correia, A.M., Adeli, H., Reis, L.S., Teixeira, M.M. (eds.) New Advances in Information Systems and Technologies. AISC, vol. 444, pp. 869–878. Springer, Switzerland (2016)

10. Yamada, T.: Ronbuntter. https://twitter.com/ronbuntter.2016-04-18

11. Salton, G., McGill, M.J.: Introduction to Modern Information Retrieval. McGraw-Hill, Inc., New York (1986)

12. Ohsawa, Y., Benson, N.E., Yachida, M.: KeyGraph: Automatic indexing by co-occurrence graph based on building construction metaphor. In: Proceedings of IEEE International Forum on Research and Technology Advances in Digital Libraries, ADL 1998. IEEE (1998)

13. Hirao, T., et al.: Extracting important sentences with support vector machines. In: Proceedings of the 19th International Conference on Computational Linguistics, vol. 1. Association for Computational Linguistics (2002)

14. Blei, D.M., Ng, A.Y., Jordan, M.I.: Latent dirichlet allocation. J. Mach. Learn. Res. **3**, 993–1022 (2003)

15. Blei, D.M., Lafferty, J.D.: Dynamic topic models. In: Proceedings of the 23rd International Conference on Machine Learning. ACM (2006)

16. Kleinberg, J.: Bursty and hierarchical structure in streams. Data Min. Knowl. Disc. **7**(4), 373–397 (2003)

17. Brin, S., Page, L.: The anatomy of a large-scale hypertextual web search engine. In: Seventh International World-Wide Web Conference (1998)

18. Wang, W., Do, D.B., Lin, X.: Term graph model for text classification. In: Li, X., Wang, S., Dong, Z.Y. (eds.) ADMA 2005. LNCS (LNAI), vol. 3584, pp. 19–30. Springer, Heidelberg (2005). doi:10.1007/11527503_5

19. Kubek, M., Unger, H.: Topic detection based on the PageRank's clustering property. IICS **11**, 139–148 (2011)

20. Ercan, G., Cicekli, I.: Using lexical chains for keyword extraction. Inf. Process. Manage. **43**(6), 1705–1714 (2007)

21. Hatori, J., Murakami, A., Tsujii, J.: Multi-topical discussion summarization using structured lexical chains and cue words. In: Gelbukh, A. (ed.) CICLing 2011, Part II. LNCS, vol. 6609, pp. 313–327. Springer, Heidelberg (2011). doi:10.1007/978-3-642-19437-5_26

22. Kita, K., Tsuda, K., Shishibori, M.: Information retrieval algorithms. Kyoritsu Shuppan (2002). (in Japanese)

Supporting Theatrical Performance Practice by Collaborating Real and Virtual Space

Mitsuki Shimada[1](✉), Takayoshi Takano[1], Hiroshi Shigeno[2], and Ken-ichi Okada[2]

[1] Graduate School of Science and Technology,
Keio University, 3-14-1 Hiyoshi Kohoku-ku, Yokohama, Kanagawa 223-8522, Japan
{shimada,takano}@mos.ics.keio.ac.jp
[2] Faculty of Science and Technology, Keio Univeristy,
3-14-1 Hiyoshi Kohoku-ku, Yokohama, Kanagawa 223-8522, Japan
{shigeno,okada}@mos.ics.keio.ac.jp

Abstract. In theater activities that are currently actively carried out, many of the theater organizations has been working with borrowed practice space and the actors have done theater activities while having another job. Therefore, the amount of practice time gathered a director and actors is limited. However, in order to carry out the practice with awareness of production and other actors, director and all actors must gather same place and make a practice based on the coaching of director. In this paper, we propose "Digital-Script" and theater practice support system. Digital-Script contains information that are important for production. Theatrical practice support system enables actors to practice performance in the situation that director or a part of actors cannot gather by using Digital Script. We evaluated the system by comparing the errors of subjects' performance who used theatrical practice support system and script visualization application.

Keywords: Theater activities · Production · Real space · Virtual space

1 Introduction

Theater activities are currently actively carried out as a part of arts. Theater organizations create products by director, actors and other many staffs through roughly divide in three practice steps, "Reading Script", "Standing Practice", and "Stage Rehearsal". Important factors of production coached by director are actor's standing position, head direction, movement, theatrical elocution, and action timing. actors acquire performance through practice with other actors and be coached by director. However, theater organizations cannot practice anytime because many of them does not have their own practice space and most actors have another job. In this paper, we propose "Digital-Script" and theater practice support system. Digital-Script contains important information of production. Theatrical practice system enables actors to practice with awareness of production and other actors in the situation that director or a part of

© Springer Science+Business Media Singapore 2016
T. Yoshino et al. (Eds.): CollabTech 2016, CCIS 647, pp. 17–30, 2016.
DOI: 10.1007/978-981-10-2618-8_2

actors cannot gather by using Digital-Script. Practice system supports practice by showing virtual actor that plays absent actor's role in monocular Head Mounted Display(HMD), and coaching automatically by detecting and comparing actor's movement with information contained in Digital-Script.

The rest of this paper is organized as follows: in Sect. 2, we describe theater activities, the work related to them. In Sect. 3, we explain the issues for theater activities and the requirements for solving them. Section 4, provides details of our proposal, and the evaluation experiment is explained in Sect. 5. Finally, in Sect. 6, we present our conclusion.

2   Theater Activities

Theater organizations create products by director, actors and other many staffs through roughly divide in three practice steps, "Read Scripts", "Standing Practice", and "Stage Rehearsal". "Standing Practice" is very important especially in three steps, and accounts for most of the period of the activity [1], so the quality of the product rely on standing practice. Standing practice is rarely done through to the end but mostly done several scenes repeatedly in a day and then director coaches. Table 1 shows the results of survey on efforts for theater quality improvement. It can be seen from Table 1 that many theater organizations encourage the voluntary practice of actors in order to improve the quality of theaters. Voluntary practice is very important and related deeply for the improvement of theater quality. In voluntary practice, learn by heart script or role making are mainly done and it is difficult for actors to practice standing position, head direction and timing of action because scripts only written in character.

Table 1. Activities of theater groups to enhance the quality of a theater [2]

Content	Propotion(%)
Left to voluntary practice of personal	57.3
Ensuring practice time for performances	80.5
Day-to-day training that do not lead directly to performances	37.8
Regularly special training that do not lead directly to performances	28.0
Encourage the performer's voluntary training by providing practice space	46.3
Others	7.3

2.1   Related Work

Studies that is about artistic activities are widely carried out in the past. Singh et al. enables dancers to practice independently with awareness of the instruction by enabling choreographers to add annotations to a video that records dancers' performance [3]. Oshita et al. made authoring system for video teaching materials about Noh play (Japanese traditional) [4]. They divided Noh motions in three elements (choreography, speech and locomotion) and visualize each element. Gandy et al. uses HMD for theater simulation. By using HMD, user can check stage environment from first-person view point but user cannot perceive the surroundings [5]. CAVE system that is omnidirectional display sometimes be used for study about theater production. Steptoe et al. use CAVE system for remote theatrical practice. By using CAVE system, user can perceive distance sense and positional relation [6]. Jacobson et al. and Cavazza et al. also uses CAVE system for theatrical practice [7,8]. CAVE system enables users to practice in virtual stage environment that is in real space. Omnidirectional display enables users to perceive stage environment from first-person view point same as HMD but the facility of the system is costly, so it is not easy to use. Rijsselbergen et al. and Zhang analyzes scripts by using natural language processing and visualizes the scripts which analyzed. There are some studies about creating scripts [9,10]. Szilas et al. made their original programming language to create scripts [11]. Hong et al. built interface that is used for creating scripts by using XML format [12]. Horiuchi et al. used tabletop interface to plan theatrical productions [13].

There are some studies on actors' voluntary practice [14,15]. These studies focus on important factors of production and enables actors to practice with awareness of these factors.

3   Support for Theatrical Creation

In this study, we propose "Digital-Script" which differ from usual script written only in characters contains actor's standing position on the stage, head direction that the actor should look and time information that actor should act. By using Digital-Script, we enables actors to practice with awareness of production and other actors that is difficult for practice using usual script.

3.1   Digital-Script

Factors of Production. Theatrical production has technical factor and actor's performance factors. Technical factors are such as sound effect, lighting effect, stage carpenter and stage design. When we focus on actor's performance factors, standing position, head direction and timing of actions are very important [16]. These factors determine the sight from audience and the flow of the theater. However, it is difficult for actors to practice in the situation that actors face each other or move while looking at other actor and cannot be coached on condition that the director or a part of actors is absent. Therefore, reflecting actor's performance factors to scripts is very important for theatrical practice that carried out by using a script.

Requirements for Scripts. A script is what represents story of the theater. It is difficult to perceive spatial environment such actors' standing position that changes with progress of a story because usual script is only written in character. In addition, if it is the famous script, such as a masterpiece, it also be performed many times by other theater organizations. If a script is performed by other theater organizations, productions are different each other because the staff who create the theater are different. Therefore, it is very difficult for actors to perceive the production that the director images. We propose "Digital-Script" that contains spatial information and time information. Spatial information are such as "where the actors are standing" and time information are such as "where the actors are looking". Spatial information is useful for actors to practice distance sense with other actors. Time information is useful for actors to practice the timing of actions. These two kinds of information represent production and important for practice. Digital-Script enables actors to share images of the theater by being shared. By adding production to script, actors who cannot be coached by the director because of economic, time and spatial constraints can perceive production. Further, since it is possible to make modifications to the production unlike such as recorded video, it is also possible to use information in the way appropriate for the production.

Requirements for Practice. Many theater organizations encourage actor's voluntary practice in order to improve the quality of play because of the cost of practice space and time. Therefore, by reproducing the coaching or act of the absent staff, we support actors' voluntary practice on the environment that a director or a actor is absent from the practice. The way to support voluntary practice in the situation that a director or a part of actors is absence is as follows.

- *Absent actor*: It is difficult to practice such as facing each other in the situation that the partner actor is absence because it cannot be perceived that where the partner is looking at or where the partner actor is. Therefore, we support actors' practice in the situation that a part of actors is absence by showing absent actor.
- *Coaching*: We support practice with awareness of production in a situation that the director is absence by focusing on actor's standing position and head direction. Standing position and head direction is very important for theater creation because these factors represent relationship between actors and determines theater progression. We focus on productions especially in spatial and time production and not mention theatrical elocutions or physical expressions. This is against that it is very difficult for directors to show what they image in an exactly way about such theatrical elocutions and physical expressions, and the purpose of voluntary practice is to acquire large scale performance such as standing position.

4   Digital-Script and Theatrical Practice System

We propose theatrical practice system. In this system, it is assumed a situation that is as follows.

- *Scripts that three actors appear*:
  We assumed a script for three performers and only two actors can join a practice. The script contains performances such as actors facing each other or move. We assumed this number of performers, because it is considered this system to be able to apply to other scripts which for more performers by increasing devices or detections if we can achieve in this number setting.
- *Practice space*: We assume practice space that about 4×4 meters wide and nothing in it. actors practice in the space. This area is derived from device but same as number of performers, if we can achieve proposal in this setting it is considered that this system is thought to be able to apply large area by improving device capacity.
- *Production in practice*: We do not deal with theatrical elocution, physical expressions and facial expressions because it is very difficult to express what the director wants in the exact way and we focus on large scale production. For the first step of practice, actors acquire standing position and head direction where they should look at.

4.1   Digital-Script Databse

Production information are managed in database implemented by MySQL. Figure 1 shows configuration of the Digital-Script database. Information stored in database in scene units. Scene data contains IDs, title of the script, title of the scene and actor data. actor data contains MOVE data that is about actor's position, SAY data that is about actor's speech and SEE data that is about head direction. Each of the data is as follows.

- *MOVE data*: MOVE data are about actor's standing position. It means actor's move to (x, y, z) coordinates during elapsed time (the origin is the begging of the scene) is t_1 sec to t_2 sec.
- *SEE data*: SEE data are about actor's head direction where the actor should look at. It means that the actor looks at the designated direction when the elapsed time get t sec. The direction where the actor should look at is designated by (x, y, z) coordinates.
- *SAY data*: SAY data are about actors' speech. It means that the actor utterance speech T when the elapsed time gets t sec.

4.2   Theatrical Practice System

We propose theaterical practice support system in the situation that a part of actors or the director cannot gather.

Approach. We support theatrical practice by supplementing the role of an actor or a director who is absent from practice. In this study, we assume that two actors join the practice, so it is necessary for those two actors to be able to

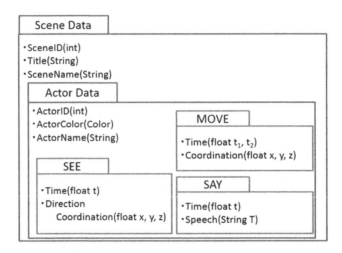

Fig. 1. Component of Digital-Script Database

recognize the partner actor who joins the practice and the actor who is absent from practice. Further, there is a problem that actors cannot to be coached. Therefore, the function to supplement absent actor's role and director's role is needed for theatrical system. Practice system supplements the role of absent actor by showing the actor who cannot gather while checking the actor in the space. User can check virtual actor that perform instead of absent actor with real actor by using monocular HMD. We realize theatrical practice with awareness of other actors by showing virtual actor. In addition, the system enables actors to practice with awareness of production by coaching them automatically along the production. The role of real space and virtual space is as follows.

- *Real space*: The space actors are present. Only the actors who join the practice perform in Real Space.
- *Virtual space*: Virtual space is the virtual environment built on the system. Virtual actor performs move and change head direction along with production information in database instead of absent actor. The standing position and point of view links user's position and head direction. The two actors gathering the practice are not showed in virtual space.

The actor who joins the practice recognizes real space in the eye that does not equip monocular HMD and virtual space through monocular HMD, so it is possible to recognize real actor and virtual actor simultaneously. In addition, the view point of the virtual space links the user's position and head direction in real space constantly. Users can check partner's performance and virtual actor's performance from any place as if the virtual actor really be there.

4.3   Implementation

Theatrical practice system is coded in C# and implemented in Unity that is often used for building 3D games. Virtual stage and virtual actor are made in Unity and showed in monocular HMD, and the view point in the virtual space moves according to user's movement. By using monocular HMD equipped with a gyro sensor and Microsoft Kinect that can detect user's position, user can view virtual space from the view that links their own movement. In the following, we describe the method of supporting practice, then describe system configuration.

Detection of Actor' Movement. The system detects user's standing position and head direction. The detected information is used for controlling view point camera what is in the virtual space. Figure 2 shows system configuration.

Method of Showing Virtual Space. In the virtual space, a virtual actor is shown and perform along with Digital-Script information. In virtual space, there is a view point camera and it moves virtual space linked with actor's real space movement. User can check virtual space intuitively because of the view point movement that links with actor's movement.

- *Position*: Kinect detects actor's standing position. Kinect can detect many body parts coordination but we only use head position and reflect the detected data to view point because it is enough for controlling view point camera. Head position is detected in three dimensions and reflect them constantly to view point. Therefore, actors can check virtual space from anywhere in real time.
- *Direction*: We use Vuzix M100 that is monocular HMD. The HMD equipped with gyro sensor. We get actor's head direction and reflect it to the view point direction. It is possible for users to see virtual space intuitively by reflecting their head direction constantly to view point.

4.4   Screen Displayed on HMD

Figure 3 shows what is displayed on HMD. Virtual actor, elapsed time and actor's speech is shown on the screen. Virtual actor is 3D model and performs such action like move or change head direction along with production in the database. Elapsed time is shown in second unit and constantly progress while the system is being played. actor's speech is colored and the color matches the virtual actor model's body color, so user can distinguish who should say the speech.

Practice Method Using the Theatrical Practice System. User equips the monocular HMD and starts the system. Figure 4 shows an image from user view point. The performance along with the theater flow in the Digital-Script database starts in the virtual space automatically when the system starts. actors

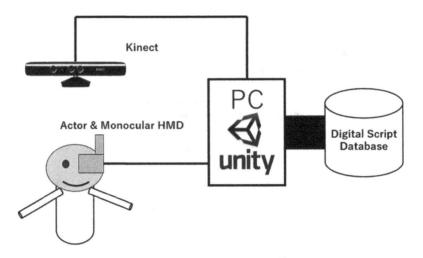

Fig. 2. System configuration

Fig. 3. Screen displayed on monocular HMD

start performance such as move or change head direction along with the play progresses in the virtual space. While actors are performing, the system detects their movement constantly. If user do different performance from the production in the Digital-Script, for example the user should move to right edge of the stage but he moves to center of the stage, then the theater progression in the virtual space stops automatically. When user did wrong performance the time progression stops and then user can recognize that he did wrong performance and then the system gives coaching about user's standing position or head direction. User acquire performance along with the production in Digital-Script database

Fig. 4. View image from user view point

by modifying their performance through being coach by the system. Theater progression restarts if the user can satisfy the production in the Digital-Script database. Thus, the user practice and correct their performance repeatedly, he acquires performance skill that satisfies the production.

Coaching by the Theatrical Practice System. Standing position and head direction are coached by the system. Standing position is detected constantly by using Kinect, and detected position is compared with the value in the Digital-Script database. If the difference between detected position and the position in the database exceeds 25 cm, the system coaches the user on the monocular HMD. Figure 5 shows how the system gives coaching to the user about standing position. The yellow marker shown in Fig. 5 is the correct standing position of the user. The user can acquire correct position by moving to the marker in the real space. After user moves to the position indicated by the maker, coaching ends and the yellow marker disappears. Head direction is detected constantly by monocular HMD and compared with the value in the Digital-Script database. If the difference between detected head direction and the direction in the database exceeds 10degrees, the system coaches user on the monocular HMD. Figure 5 shows how the system gives coaching to actors about head direction. The user is coached about his head direction by four patterns "Loot to the Right", "Look to the Left", "Look Up" and "Look Under". User correct his head direction in accordance with the coaching by the system. While user is looking wrong direction, the coaching is shown. If user can look right direction, the coaching that is about head direction shown on the screen disappears. Thus, user correct his head direction and acquire right performance with awareness of production. The user can correct their performance when he did wrong performance and acquire right performance in the body.

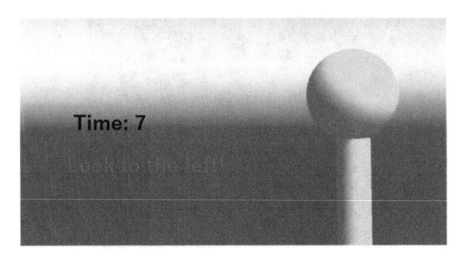

Fig. 5. Displayed Screen when user need coaching

5   Evaluation and Discussion

We evaluate efficacy of theatrical practice system by measuring the accuracy of actor's performance after practice in the situation that an actor and a director are absence.

5.1   Description

Six students participated this experiment. Subjects are divided into two groups, A and B. Each groups practice using theatrical practice system or visualization system. Two scripts used in this experiment is about one minute long. Two people, a subject and a experimenter participate in each practice and it is assumed that the experimenter can perform perfectly. We evaluate accuracy of subjects' performance by measuring the error about standing position and head direction by comparing their performance with the data in the Digital-Script database. We prepared two scripts for this evaluation. Each script is about one minute long and contains six instructions, three instructions about standing position and three instructions about head direction. Table 2 show two subject group and conditions of practice.

Table 2. Subject Group and Practice Condition

	Fisrt	Second
Group A	Practice System Script A	Visualization Script B
Group B	Visualization Script A	Practice System Script B

Comparison Item. In this experiment, subjects practice in two environments. Two environments are as follows.

- *Using theatrical practice system(system-method)*: Subjects practice performance by using Theatrical Practice System. Only subject equips monocular HMD.
- *Using application that visualizes Digital-Script(visualization-method)*: Subject uses application that visualizes Digital-Script. Figure 6 shows application screen that visualizes Digital-Script. Standing position, head direction and elapsed time are shown on the application screen. Virtual theater progresses on the simple virtual stage along with production in the Digital-Script. User's speeches are colored and the its color matches the virtual actor model's body color, so user can distinguish whose speech that is. User's head direction is represented by virtual actor model's nose direction. The subject practices by using this application freely. The subject can control the application with start, stop and reset functions.

 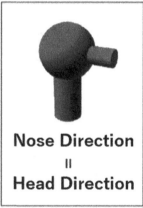

Fig. 6. Visualization application display

Procedure. Each subject practices twice on two conditions shown in Table 2. Experimental procedure is as follows.

1. Subject practice for ten minutes with experimenter. At this time, experimenter performs perfectly but does not coach subject.
2. After practice, the subject and the experimenter demonstrate. While this demonstration, subject equips monocular HMD to detect head direction but does not show anything on the screen. We use the data detected in this flow to measure accuracy of subject's performance.
3. The subject does a same procedure described above on another condition.

5.2   Evaluation Item

We evaluated about two points as follows.

– Accuracy of subjects' standing position
  We measured the differences between detected subject's standing position and the standing position value in the Digital-Script database.
– Accuracy of subjects' head direction
  We measured the differences between detected subject's head directin and the value in the Digital-Script database.

5.3   Results and Discussion

Results are obtained by calculating average about three instructions contained in each script. Result of each script (Tables 3 and 4) and total result (Table 5) is below.

Table 3. ScriptA result

	Head Direction(degree)	Standing Position(cm)
System-Method	19.3	25.0
Visualization	37.4	64.2

Table 4. ScriptB result

	Head Direction(degree)	Standing Position(cm)
System-Method	11.9	36.8
Visualization	33.4	87.6

Table 5. Total result

	Head Direction(degree)	Standing Position(cm)
System-Method	15.6	30.9
Visualization	35.4	75.9

It can be seen from Tables 3 and 4 that the errors of the subjects who used visualization-method is larger than that of subjects who used system-method in both A and B scripts. It can be thought from this result that subjects' error who used system-method is smaller than that of subjects' who used visualization-method about other scripts. It can be seen from Tables 3 and 4 that the errors of the subjects who used visualization-method is larger than that of subjects who used system-method about head direction. It can be thought that it is difficult for the subjects to acquire correct head direction by using visualized script. In addition, if it is possible for users to check rough direction, they could not correct details because they could not see absent actor. It can be seen from Tables 3 and 4 that the errors of the subjects who used system-method is smaller than that of subjects who used visualization-method about head direction. It can be thought that the subjects who used system-method could correct details about head direction because they could see virtual actor who performs instead of absent actor. In addition, subjects who used system-method could be coached by the system and they could correct their performance at the time they did wrong performance. It can be seen from Tables 3 and 4 that the errors of the subjects who used visualization-method is larger than that of subjects who used system-method about standing position. It can be thought that it is difficult for the subjects to acquire correct standing position in the real space by using visualized script. If it is possible for users to check rough position, they could not correct details because they could not see absent actor. Also, it can be thought that they could not perceive correct standing position in real space from visualized script. It can be seen from Tables 3 and 4 that the errors of the subjects who used system-method is smaller than that of subjects who used visualization-method about standing position. It can be thought that the subjects who used system-method could perceive distance sense with absent actor because they could see virtual actor from first-person viewpoint. In addition, subjects who used system-method could be coached by the system and they could correct their performance at the time they did wrong performance.

6 Conclusion

Theater organizations create theater through practice repeatedly for long term. All actors gather same place and make a practice based on the coaching of director to acquire performance with awareness of production and other actors. However, the amount of practice time that a director and all actors gather same place is limited. In this study, we built Digital-Script and Theater Practice System. Theater Practice System focuses on the roles of an actor and a director who is absence from practice. The system shows virtual actor in monocular HMD and gives coaching to a user. It is possible for actors to practice with awareness of standing position and head direction by using the system. We evaluated our system by measuring accuracy of subjects' standing position and head direction. We confirmed that users who practice with our system tend to acquire performance along with the production in Digital-Script.

References

1. Tsumura, T., Tsubochi, E.: Theater Creation Manual, Japan Foundation for Regional Art-Activities (2006). (in Japanese)
2. Agency for Cultural Architecture: Survey of Development and Use of Human Resources about Demonstration Artists (2009). (in Japanese)
3. Singh, V., Latulipe, C., Carroll, E., Lottridge, D.: The choreographer's notebook: a video annotation system for dancers and choreographers. In: C&C 2011, pp. 197–206 (2011)
4. Oshita, M., Yamanaka, R., Iwatsuki, M., Nakatsuka, Y., Seki, T.: Development of easy-to-use authoring system for noh (japanese traditional) dance animation. In: 2012 International Conference on Cyberworlds (CW), pp. 45–52 (2012)
5. Gandy, M., MacIntyre, B., Presti, P., Dow, S., Bolter, J.D., Yarbrough, B., O'Rear, N.: AR karaoke: acting in your favorite scenes. In: INISMAR, pp. 114–117 (2005)
6. Steptoe, W., Normand, J.M., Oyekoya, O., Pece, F., Giannopoulos, E., Tecchia, F., Slater, M.: Acting rehearsal in collaborative multimodal mixed reality environments. Presence **21**(4), 406–422 (2012)
7. Jacobson, J., Hwang, Z.: Unreal tournament for immersive interactive theater. Commum. ACM **45**(1), 39–42 (2002)
8. Cavazza, M., Lurgin, J., Pizzi, D., Charles, F.: Madame bovary on the holodeck: Immersive interactive storytelling. In: Proceedings of the 15th International Conference on Multimedia, MULTIMEDIA 2007, pp. 651–660. ACM, New York, NY, USE (2007)
9. Rijsselbergen, V.D., Van De Keer, B., Verwaest, M., Mannens, E., Van de Walle, R.: Movie script markup language. In: Proceedings of the 9th ACM Symposium on Document Engineering, pp. 161–170. ACM, September 2009
10. Zhang, L.: Contextual and active learning-based affect-sensing from virtual drama improvisation. ACM Trans. Speech Lang. Process. **9**(4), 8:1–8:25 (2013)
11. Szilas, N., Barles, J., Kavakli, M.: An Implementatoin of real-time 3d interactive drama. Comput. Entertain **5**(1), 35–42 (2007)
12. Hong, Z., Chin, K., Lin, J.: Developing embodied agent-based use interface by using interactive drama markup language. In: Proceedings of the 3rd International Conference on Digital Interactive Media in Entertainment and Arts, DIMEA 2008, pp. 427–434. ACM, New York, NY, USA (2008)
13. Horiuchi, Y., Inoue, T., Okada, K.-I.: Virtual stage linked with a physical miniature stage to support multiple users in planning theatrical productions. In: IUI 2012, pp. 109–118 (2012)
14. Shimada, M., Fujishige, S., Okada, K.-I.: Supporting actor's voluntary training considering the direction of drama. IPSJ Trans. Digit. Content **4**(1), 1–9 (2016). (in Japanese)
15. Yamazaki, G., Fujishige, S., Okada, K.-I.: Theatrical practice support system considering actor's position and gaze. In: IPSJ Workshop on Digital Content Creation, 2014-DCC-7, 17, pp. 1–7, 2014–05-07. (in Japanese)
16. Goan, M.: System dynamics on the creation of drama-making processes. Jpn. Cogn. Sci. Soc. Cogn. Sci. **14**(4), 509–531 (2007). (In Japanese)

A Video Chat System with Depth Information to Express 3-D Movement Between Remote Spaces

Hiroki Hamaue$^{(\boxtimes)}$ and Takashi Yoshino

Graduate School of System Engineering, Wakayama University,
Sakaedani 930, Wakayama-city, Japan
hamaue.hiroki@g.wakayama-u.jp, yoshino@sys.wakayama-u.ac.jp
http://www.wakayama-u.ac.jp/en/

Abstract. In recent years, the spread of tools with free video chat, such as Skype, has facilitated the use of video chat. We think that video chat can be used in informal communication. However, a problem with conventional video chat is that you feel a sense of distance to a dialogue partner compared to the face-to-face environment. In order to improve the problem, we have developed a partial overlay-type video chat system "DOACOM-Z." DOACOM-Z can connect between remote places virtually through the frame that exists in an actual space. The system can express three-dimensional movement in the remote space using a depth sensor in both places. The system can give both expression's "hiding in the remote space" and "pointing in the remote space." In order examine the usefulness of the expression of three-dimensional movement in the remote space, we carried out a verification experiment of a feeling of intrusion and a verification experiment of a feeling of being intruded. From the results of the verification experiments, we found that the expression of three-dimensional movement can improve the feeling of intrusion compared to the expression of two-dimensional movement. In addition, a feeling of intrusion was obtained with both methods. We found that there are no significant differences between expressions. Regardless of the method, the image pointing object in its own space can provide a feeling of being intruded.

Keywords: Video chat · Partial overlay display-type · Remote spaces · Sense of distance · Feeling of intrusion · Feeling of being intrusion

1 Introduction

In recent years, the spread of tools with free video chat, such as Skype, has facilitated the use of video chat [1]. We accept that video chat can be used in informal communication. However, a problem with conventional video chat is that you feel a sense of distance to a dialogue partner compared to the face-to-face environment. In order to improve the problem, many researchers tried to make remote spaces look like the face-to-face environment by utilizing media space. One researcher

© Springer Science+Business Media Singapore 2016
T. Yoshino et al. (Eds.): CollabTech 2016, CCIS 647, pp. 31–44, 2016.
DOI: 10.1007/978-981-10-2618-8_3

displayed the partner in the remote space life-size on the big screen [2]. Another researcher made it possible to make eye contact using the system utilizing the half mirror [3]. It turns out that the presence of the partner who is present in a remote place is increased by these methods.

Other researchers attempted a method that avoids making remote spaces look similar to a face-to-face environment. It was found that the feeling which is present in the same room as a dialog partner increases by the image of a partner reflected in the mirror [4].

However, there exists a major difference between the face-to-face environment and the remote chat environment even with these methods. As a result, we have developed a partial overlay-type video chat system "DOACOM-Z." DOACOM-Z can connect between remote places virtually through the frame that exists in an actual space. The system can express three-dimensional movement in the remote space using a depth sensor at both places. DOACOM-Z is using an interface in the form of a door in the same way as DOACOM [5] that Fujita has developed. A partial overlay-type video chat system is displayed over the original video. Users can talk about looking at the same image. DOACOM, developed by Fujita, was able to express the two-dimensional movement in the remote space; on the other hand, DOACOM-Z could express the three-dimensional movement in the remote space. We use a depth sensor as well as a webcam to express the three-dimensional movement in the remote space. In past research, researchers have expressed the positional relationship of the users in remote communication. We found it is possible to improve the feeling of presence and feeling of being in the same room of the dialogue partner. Unlike previous works, our system can express movement using the image, which is the novelty of this work.

2   Related Work

The problem with conventional video chat is that you feel a sense of distance with a dialogue partner as compared to a face-to-face environment. In order to address the problem, many researchers have attempted to render virtual presence. This section describes the two types of this research.

The first is a method that resembles face-to-face environment. A researcher displayed the partner in the remote space life-size on the big screen [2]. Another researcher made it possible to make eye contact using the system utilizing the half mirror [3]. Misawa et al. developed LiveMask [6], which uses a three-dimensional shape display to display the face of the dialogue partner. It turns out that the presence of the partner who is present in a remote place is increased by these method.

The second type is a method that does not resemble face-to-face environment. Morikawa et al. developed Hyper-Mirror [4] which is an overlay-type video chat system. This system reflects the video including the other party and the local party in the mirror together. In this research, it was found that presence is also raised in an impossible situation.

As for our system, we use an overlay-type video chat system. Both systems are WISIWYS (What I See Is What You See). Hyper-Mirror does not use any objects to interface, whereas our system uses a real object as an interface. Hyper-Mirror makes the video, including the other party, reflect in the mirror together with the local party; our system, on the other hand, connects remote places virtually through the frame which exists in an actual space.

In remote communication, a user's spatial relationship is an important element.

Hirata et al. developed t-Room [7], which can make the remote space feel like real room. This system aims to improve the feeling of being in the same room.

Tanaka et al. developed a system that moves the display physically [8]. They synchronized a dialog partner's movement and the movement of a display, thereby emphasizing the dialog partner's movement. It turns out that the feeling of a dialog partner's movement is increased by this method. However, the problem with this method is that it needs a moveable display, which is not the general environment for video chat. The emphasis of movement resembles our system, and the manner of emphasizing movement also resembles our system.

This system emphasizes movement by the physical movement of a display, but our system emphasizes movement by image.

Nakanishi et al. studied the method of strengthening telepresence by motion parallax [9]. They developed a system which can move the camera in sync with a dialogue partner's movement in the remote space. The result of an experiment shows that the presence of the partner in a remote place is increased by motion parallax.

3 DOACOM-Z

3.1 Conventional Problems

DOACOM that Fujita et al. [5] developed is a partial overlay-type video chat system. DOACOM can connect between remote places virtually through the frame which exists in an actual space. Moreover, this system makes gestures possible by using the door. For example, the user can extend a hand from a door. As a result, the feeling of existing in the same room increases and the effect of pointing is increased by this system. However, the feeling and effect are not enough. The main problem is increasing the feeling of being connected to the remote space. DOACOM was able to express only the two-dimensional movement in the remote space. The image of the user who is operating the door is always displayed as before. Even if user who is operating the door moves forward or backward, the image does not reflect this movement back. This may have influence on the feeling of being connected between remote places.

Moreover, there is a problem with pointing. A user who is operating the door can obtain the feeling of pointing in remote space. However, a user who is not operating the door is not able to fully realize the feeling of pointing in remote space; this is a problem that needs to be addressed.

3.2   Design Policy

In order to address these problems, we have developed a partial overlay-type video chat system "DOACOM-Z." If it is truly connected with a remote space, the order of relations arise on an image. For example, the door can be displayed behind something. The hand from a door is displayed before other objects. This suggests that the consideration of depth in the display is important. Therefore, the proposed system displays the superimposed image based on the actual spatial relationship. DOACOM-Z can express three-dimensional movement in the remote space.

3.3   System Configuration

Figure 1 illustrates the system configuration. DOACOM-Z communicates between the space of the user who is operating the door (Fig. 1(a)) and the space of the user who is not operating the door (Fig. 1(b)). Figure 2 shows a display image of DOACOM-Z. DOACOM-Z uses the door for going into the other's room as a metaphor. The user who is extending the hand with the door is user who is operating the door in Fig. 2. The user with the map is the user who is not operating the door in Fig. 2.

A user who is operating the door holds and opens the door. The user looks in at a door and talks.

The same image is displayed on both the screens. The image of the room of the user who is not operating the door and the image of inside the door in the remote space are overlapped and displayed on the screen. By using this method, it creates the illusion that the remote spaces are connected. We use Kinect as a depth camera. This system uses color image, depth image, and bone index obtained by Kinect.

(A) **Side without a door**

Figure 1(a) shows an example of the system configuration of a side without a door. This side uses a Kinect and a PC. This system collects user data using Kinect. This data includes color image and depth image. This data is processed to create the data for transmission. The data for transmission is sent to the PC of the side with a door. The PC of the side without a door receives the data from the PC of the side with a door. It composes these color images. The composed image is then displayed on a PC's display.

(B) **Side with a door**

Figure 1(b) shows an example of a system configuration of a side with a door. This side uses a door, a Kinect and a PC. This system collects a user's data using Kinect. This data includes color image, depth image and bone index. This data is processed to create the data for transmission. The data for transmission is sent to the PC of the side without a door. The PC of the side with a door receives the data from the PC of the side without a door. It composes these color images. This image that was composed is displayed on a PC's display.

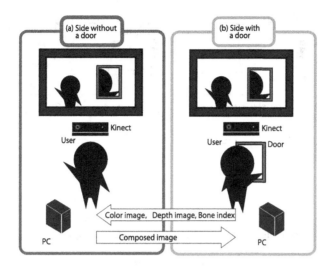

Fig. 1. System configuration. (Color figure online)

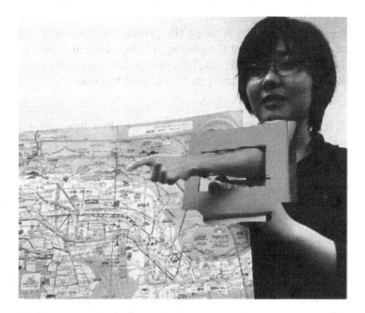

Fig. 2. Display image of DOACOM-Z. (Color figure online)

3.4 Expression of 3-D Movement Between Remote Spaces

We propose the mechanism of the overlay display that takes into account the positional relation. We use depth sense and a webcam to express the three-dimensional movement in the remote space. Our system recognizes a user's movement using the depth information obtained from Kinect. Therefore, it can

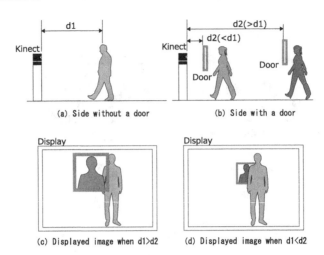

(a) Side without a door   (b) Side with a door

(c) Displayed image when d1>d2   (d) Displayed image when d1<d2

Fig. 3. Mechanism of the overlay display that takes into account the positional relation.

show an image that takes into account the positional relation. Figure 3 shows an example of this mechanism of the overlay display that takes into account the positional relation. The Fig. 3 (d1) is the distance between Kinect and the user. The Fig. 3 (d2) is the distance between Kinect and the door.

(1) **d1 > d2**

When d2 (the distance from the Kinect to the door in a side with a door) is nearer than d1 (the distance from the Kinect to a user in a side without a door), the image inside a door is displayed before the image of a user and an object (Fig. 3(c)).

(2) **d1 < d2**

When d1 (the distance from the Kinect to a user in a side without a door) is nearer than d2 (the distance from the Kinect to a door in a side with a door), the image of the user and an object is displayed before the image inside a door (Fig. 3(d)).

In the conventional system, the image inside the door was always displayed on the front. Therefore, the expression of "Hiding in the remote space" or "Pointing to the remote space" was not attained in the conventional method; however, those expressions are attained by the proposal method. Figure 4 shows an expression of "Hiding in the remote space." If the door exists in the area between a wall and the woman, the image makes it appear as if the door is hiding. Figure 5 shows an expression of "Pointing to the remote space." The depth of the user's hand was smaller than the depth of the door. The user can point at the inside of door.

The door is hidden back.

Fig. 4. Expression of "Hide in the remote space."

The User pointing to the inseide door.

Fig. 5. Expression of "Pointing to the remote space."

4 Verification Experiment of a Feeling of Intrusion

4.1 Outline of the Experiment

We conducted an evaluation experiment of the proposed method. We compared the feeling of intrusion of the proposed method with the feeling of intrusion of the conventional method.

4.2 Procedure of the Experiment

This experiment was conducted using depth images and color images obtained by Kinect in another room as before. There were 10 participants for the experiments, who were all university students. The tasks of this experiment are actions that produce different results obtain from an experiment using the proposal method and an experiment using the conventional method. The procedure of the experiment is as follows.

1. The experiment cooperator stands in front of the Kinect system with a door in a side with a door.
2. The experiment cooperator crosses the Kinect front.
3. The experiment cooperator crosses the Kinect front in the opposite direction.

Figure 6 shows an image of the verification experiment, wherein the user experiences a feeling of intrusion. In the conventional method, the image of a door is always displayed above the image in the remote space. In the proposed method, it can show the image that takes into account the positional relation. We divided the experiment cooperators into two groups based on the order effect. Two groups participated in the experiment by replacing an order of a method. We conducted a questionnaire survey after this experiment.

4.3 Results of the Experimental

Table 1 shows the results of the questionnaire-based survey at the end of the experiment. We used a five-point Likert scale for the evaluation: 1: strongly disagree, 2: disagree, 3: neutral, 4: agree, and 5: strongly agree. Table 1(1) shows

Table 1. The results of the questionnaire (5-point Likert scale).

	Question items	Method	Distribution of the evaluations					Median	Mode	Significant probability
			1	2	3	4	5			
(1)	I think that I had felt intrusion into the space in which a partner is present	Conventional method	1	6	3	0	0	2	2	0.00195*
		Proposal method	0	0	1	8	1	4	4	
(2)	I think that I just look image	Conventional method	0	0	1	7	2	4	4	0.00195*
		Proposal method	1	5	3	1	0	2	2	
(3)	Do you like expression of the proposal method or expression of the conventional method?	Both	0	0	0	2	8	5	5	

- (1), (2) Evaluation criteria (1: strongly disagree, 2: disagree, 3: neutral, 4: agree, and 5: strongly agree).
- (3) Evaluation criteria (1: conventional method, 2: rather conventional method, 3: neutral, 4: rather proposal method, 5: proposal method).
- *: There is a significant difference. $p < 0.05$.
- Significant probability is calculated by Wilcoxon signed-rank test.
- Significant probability is a difference of evaluation of the conventional method and the proposal method.

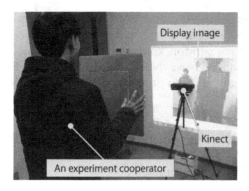

Fig. 6. Photograph of a verification experiment of a feeling of intrusion.

that for the question: "I think that I had felt intrusion into the space in which a partner is present." We found a significant difference between the conventional method and the proposal method. The result "Disagree" was obtained by the conventional method, whereas the result "Agree" was obtained by the proposal method. It turned out that the proposed method can give a feeling of intrusion in contrast to the conventional method. The experiment cooperator who answered "agree" commented as regards to the conventional method: "It seemed that the picture had merely overlapped. I did not feel a feeling of intrusion." It is thought that this cause is a superficial expression of the conventional method. The experiment cooperator who answered "disagrees" commented as regards to the proposed method: "I have grasped in which position of remote space I exist by the overlap of the image of a door," and: "It appeared that I exist before a partner." It is thought that experiment cooperators have grasped the position of the door in remote space by the image that considers depth.

Table 1(2) shows that for the question: "I think that I just look image." The conventional method and the proposal method had a significant difference. The result "Agree" was obtained by the conventional method. The result "Disagree" was obtained by the proposal method. The experiment cooperator who answered it agrees commented in regards to the conventional method: "Action which I did was not reflected." Whereas, in regards the proposal method, the experiment cooperator who answered it disagrees commented: "It is able to play.", "It is able to do any interaction, such as hiding" and: "I think that I have influenced to image." It turned out that the proposed method can give an impression that the user was influenced as opposed to the conventional method.

Table 1(3) shows that for the question: "Do you like expression of the proposed method or expression of the conventional method." The results showed that the expression of the proposed method is liked more than the expression of the conventional method. The experiment cooperators commented as regards to the conventional method: "I was able to feel depth", "I was able to hide in the partner's back." and: "There was no sense of incongruity in depth perception."

It is thought that experiment cooperators like the expression of the proposal method by the image based on actual spatial relationship.

Other experiment cooperators commented: "I think that this system can be hidden and played," and: "I was pleasant for me to have felt virtual space in the image." It is thought that the proposed method has usage different from the conventional method.

5   Verification Experiment of a Feeling of Being Intruded

5.1   Outline of the Experiment

We conducted an experiment to evaluate the applicability of the proposed method. We compared the "feeling of intrusion" of the proposed method with the "feeling of being intruded" of the conventional method.

5.2   Experimental Procedure

This experiment was conducted by dividing the users of a side with a door and the user of side without a door in two group. The two groups were stationed in different rooms. There were 10 participants for the experiment, who were all university students. Tasks of this experiment were actions, which produce different results by experiment of the proposed method and experiment of the conventional method. For example, they are "movement in remote space" and "pointing on map." The situation of an experiment is a conversation using a map. The procedure of the experiment is as follows.

1. An experiment cooperator sits in front of a Kinect with a map on the side without a door.
2. An experiment cooperator listens to an explanation about the map.
3. The subject in the side with a door explains about the map using a system. At this time, the subject points at an explanation part on the map.
4. The subject checks whether the experiment cooperator understands the point at any time.

Figure 7 shows a photograph of the verification experiment of the feeling of being intruded. Figure 8 shows a display image of a verification experiment of the feeling of being intruded.

Figure 8(A) is a display image of the conventional method. Figure 8(B) is a display image of the proposed method.

In the conventional method, the image of door is always displayed above the image of the remote space. In the proposed method, it can be seen that the image takes into account the positional relation between the user with door and the user without door. We divided 10 experiment cooperators into two groups in consideration of the order effect. Experiment cooperators were experimented upon by replacing the order of the method. We conducted the questionnaire survey after the experiments. We recorded the results of the experiment.

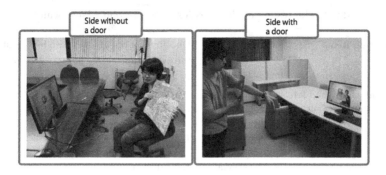

Fig. 7. Photograph of a verification experiment of a feeling of being intruded.

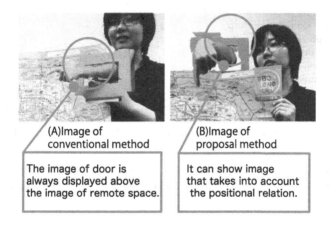

Fig. 8. Display image of a verification experiment of a feeling of being intruded.

5.3 Results of the Experimental

Table 2 shows the results of the questionnaire-based survey at the end of the experiment. We used a five-point Likert scale for the evaluation: 1: strongly disagree, 2: disagree, 3: neutral, 4: agree, and 5: strongly agree. Table 2(1) shows that for the question: "I think that I had felt intrusion into my own space." The experiment cooperators felt high feeling of being intruded by both of the methods. The conventional method and the proposal method did not have a significant difference. An experiment cooperator commented: "Because the finger extended from the door was pointing," and: "Because the finger was pointing to the map." It is thought that the image which a thing is pointed in own space gives a feeling of being intruded regardless of a method.

Some experiment cooperators commented by the proposal method: "I thought that the partner had invaded behind me." It turned out that some experiment cooperators feel a feeling of being intrusion by the proposal method than the conventional method.

Table 2. The results of the questionnaire (5-point Likert scale).

	Question items	Method	Distribution of the evaluations					Median	Mode	Significant probability
			1	2	3	4	5			
(1)	I think that I had felt being intrusion into the own space	Conventional method	1	0	1	4	4	4	4, 5	0.344
		Proposal method	1	0	1	4	4	4	4, 5	
(2)	I think that I just look image	Conventional method	1	5	0	4	0	2	2	0.500
		Proposal method	1	6	1	2	0	2	2	
(3)	Do you like expression of the proposal method or expression of the conventional method?	Both	1	0	2	5	2	4	4	

- (1), (2) Evaluation criteria (1: strongly disagree, 2: disagree, 3: neutral, 4: agree, and 5: strongly agree).
- (3) Evaluation criteria (1: conventional method, 2: rather conventional method, 3: neutral, 4: rather proposal method, 5: proposal method).
- *: There is a significant difference. $p < 0.05$.
- Significant probability is calculated by Wilcoxon signed-rank test.
- Significant probability is a difference of evaluation of the conventional method and the proposal method.

Table 2(2) shows that for the question: "I think that I just look image." The conventional method and the proposal method did not have a significant difference. An experiment cooperator commented in regards to the conventional method: "Because the arm had come out," and: "I had felt a feeling of being intrusion." An experiment cooperator commented in regards to the proposal method: "Because the arm had come out," and: "I had felt a feeling of being intrusion more than the conventional method. I also felt a little fear."

It is thought that experiment cooperators felt a feeling of being intruded by the arm that had come out.

Experiment cooperators who answered that they disagree commented: "I was not able to move spontaneously." It is thought that since experiment cooperators had a map, they were not able to move spontaneously.

Table 2(3) shows that for the question: "Do you like expression of the proposed method or expression of the conventional method." It turned out that the expression of the proposal method is liked more than expression of the conventional method. The experiment cooperators commented by the conventional method: "The image which has a door back was like reality." It is thought that experiment cooperators like expression of the proposal method by the image based on actual spatial relationship. The experiment cooperator commented by the proposal method: "This method can understand explanation." It is thought that image of the door did not hide in the map. There were some experiment cooperators who did not find a significant difference between both the methods. There was no significant difference in the image of the proposal method and the image of the conventional method.

6   Conclusion

In this study, we developed a partial overlay-type video chat system "DOACOM-Z." DOACOM-Z can connect between remote places virtually through a frame that exists in an actual space. The system can express three-dimensional movement in the remote space using a depth sensor in both places. Based on the results of the verification experiment, we reached the following conclusions.

1. From the results of the verification experiment of a feeling of intrusion, we found that the expression of three-dimensional movement can improve the feeling of intrusion as compared to the expression of the two-dimensional movement.
2. From the results of the verification experiment of a feeling of being intruded, a feeling of intrusion was obtained with both methods.

We found that there are no significant differences between the expressions. Regardless of the method, the image pointing at an object in its own space can provide a feeling of being intruded. We showed the possibility that the problem of feeling a sense of distance to a dialogue partner would be improved by the use of DOACOM-Z. In our future work, we will investigate the change of a user's action by use of DOACOM-Z.

Acknowledgment. This work was supported by JSPS KAKENHI Grant Number 15K12085.

References

1. Blogs, S.: The number of simultaneous connected users of Skype attains 40 million people. http://blogs.skype.com/2012/04/13/skype4000/. (in Japanese)
2. Mantel, M.M., Baecker, R.M., Sellen, A.J., et al.: Experiences in the use of a media space. In: CHI '99, pp. 203–208 (1991)
3. Bondareva, Y., Bouwhuis, D.: Determinants of social presence in videoconferencing. In: AVI 2004 Workshop on Environments for Personalized Information Access, pp. 1–9 (2004)
4. Morikawa, O.: HyperMirror: toward pleasant-to-use video mediated communication system. Trans. IPS Jpn. **41**(3), 815–822 (2000). (in Japanese)
5. Fujita, S., Yoshino, T.: Effect of movement in three dimensions and existence of frame in overlay-type video chat system. In: IPSJ, Interaction 2012 Proceedings, pp. 813–818 (2012). (in Japanese)

6. Misawa, K., Ishiguro, Y., Rekimoto, J.: LiveMask: a telepresence surrogate system with a face-shaped screen forsupporting nonverbal communication. In: IPSJ, Interaction 2012 Proceedings, pp. 41–48 (2012). (in Japanese)
7. Hirata, K., Harada, Y., Ohno, T., et al.: t-Room: telecollaborative room for everyday interaction. In: Proceedings of the 66th National Convention of IPSJ, 4B-3, pp. 4.97–4.98 (2004). (in Japanese)
8. Tanaka, K., Kato, K., Nakanishi, H., Ishiguro, H.: Representation of human movement: enhancing social telepresence by zoom cameras and movable displays. IPSJ J. **53**(4), 1393–1400 (2012). (in Japanese)
9. Nakanishi, H., Murakami, Y., Kato, K.: Movable cameras enhancesocial telepresence in media spaces. In: Proceedings of CHI 2009, pp. 433–442 (2009). (in Japanese)

Efficient Generation of Conductor Avatars for the Concert by Multiple Virtual Conductors

Naoki Katayama[1]([✉]), Ryosuke Takatsu[1], Tomoo Inoue[2], Hiroshi Shigeno[3], and Ken-ichi Okada[3]

[1] Graduate School of Science and Technology,
Keio University Kanagawa, Yokohama, Japan
{katayama,takatsu}@mos.ics.keio.ac.jp
[2] Faculty of Library, Information and Media Science,
University of Tsukuba Ibaraki, Tsukuba, Japan
inoue@slis.tsukuba.ac.jp
[3] Faculty of Science and Technology, Keio University Kanagawa, Yokohama, Japan
{shigeno,okada}@mos.ics.keio.ac.jp

Abstract. In orchestra performance, a single conductor directs all the players in the real world. However no restriction is applied when designing a virtual conductor in the virtual world. Thus a virtual conductor system that employed multiple virtual conductors has been proposed. The system assigns each virtual conductor to each musical instrument part, making players' performance better and more easier. Generation of the multiple conductor avatars is, however, still an issue of the system. It needs much time and work. In this paper, we propose a efficient virtual-conductor-avatar generation system. The time needed is surprisingly reduced while keeping the quality of the virtual-conductor avatars.

Keywords: Supporting musical performance · Virtual conductor · Individualize · Generating animation

1 Introduction

Sometimes people play music alone, but orchestras usually involve a group, often a big group of players. They use many kinds of instruments and play their parts according to the role or instruments. If they play music as they like, their performance will become execrable. To tune each part, players need to hear others' performances while performing their part, but it is difficult for unskilled players. Players also need to match their volume and timing with others to perform good music in a group. However, the note each player hears is different by position and players must tune their performances to those of the others. Thus performing music in a group requires a conductor who listens to the performance of all parts and instructs each part to control sound volume and timings of put on and off the notes for each part. A conductor has the essential role and is the leader of a performing group [1].

© Springer Science+Business Media Singapore 2016
T. Yoshino et al. (Eds.): CollabTech 2016, CCIS 647, pp. 45–57, 2016.
DOI: 10.1007/978-981-10-2618-8_4

An orchestra is a typical example of a large performing group requiring a conductor to perform. It has many parts and many kinds of instruments. The more parts and instruments players combine, the more difficult to play a good performance harmonized with the note of each parts. In a large group like an orchestra, the role of the conductor is essential, but a single conductor has a limited capability to conduct so many players. He can gives cues to a maximum of two players at the same time and cannot give new cues until he finishes cueing because he has only two hands. He must choose the most important instruction at that time, and only provides this to one or two players. When a conductor cues more than two players simultaneously, some players have to perform without instructions given by conductor. It is true that conduct is not necessarily essential to play their part. The Orpheus Chamber Orchestra has no conductors, but still performs impeccably. However, the high-level skills of such players make perfect performance possible without a conductor, a task that is all but impossible for unskilled players. Thus, players in a large group need a system supporting their performance.

2   Rerated Work

2.1   Supporting Orchestra

There are many studies supporting the players of an orchestra [2]. One such study is the immersive orchestra rehearsal simulator system [3]. In this system, a conductor can use this simulator to coach players remotely by transmitting records of practice. However, it can teach only one player, so the conductor cannot manage multiple players at once. To conduct for visually disabled people, Asakawa uses pre-vibration to give them feedback [4]. However, it only provides simple tempo and rhythm. These studies can give players too little information to support their performances. There are also studies using an electronic music score as another way to support players. An electronic music score system can automatically turn over sheets of music and display musical scores more easily. Iijima made a system that can reduce the page turning load by synchronizing the score of each player to that of the conductor [5] and Housley enlarged images on the display for visually impaired musicians [6]. These systems reduce the work of players and allow players to concentrate on their performance, but the conductor needs to turn over sheets and there is no change for the conductor.

2.2   Virtual System

Single Virtual Conductor. There are also studies supporting performance without a human conductor. In that situation, it is essential to provide players content about tempo, beat, and sound volume. Research has been conducted on a system using virtual conductors to show this information. For example, one study focuses on a string quartet without a conductor [7]. In this study, cues of tempo, beat, and sound volume are expressed by moving a sphere on a tablet display. This work changes the color of the sphere to express sound volume, while the movement of the sphere represents changes in tempo and rhythm. There is also a system using a humanoid virtual conductor created with computer graphics [8]. It is based on MIDI data and can display information about tempo, beat, and sound volume in the same way as human conductors, so they can clearly represent how to perform for all players. However, these studies can only present cues about tempo and sound volume for all players simultaneously. Human conductors can conduct specific instructions for each player using eye contact with the player they want to instruct [9], but a virtual conductor is shown on a plain display, so players cannot recognize the direction, which can cause confusion for players trying to understand the targets of cues.

Multiple Virtual Conductors. To perform music harmonically in a group, someone must cue the most suitable timing about tempo, beat, and timings of changes in the performance to help players perform each part. However, a single human or virtual conductor cannot always conduct for each part simultaneously. Thus, a system displaying the instructions for each role only is necessary for players in a large group. There is a multiple virtual conductors system in which players are individually conducted [10]. In a virtual world, there is no limit to the number of conductors. This study prepared as many virtual conductors as players and they conducted each role simultaneously on tablet displays set for each player. Each conductor conducts at the same tempo for all players, but information about sound volume and the timings of playing and suspending the notes are unique for each player. Players can perform harmonically by following their own conductors because these conductors show the content required for performing every moment. This system can conduct players without problems when conductors give each player cues for every role.

3   Issue and Proposal for the Multiple Virtual Conductors System

3.1   Issue

We identified the problem that the multiple virtual conductors system requires the preparation of as many virtual conductors as players. General purpose software was used to create the computer graphics to generate humanoid virtual conductors because there is no dedicated software for this purpose. We programmed a computer graphic model of a human body to pose according to every conducted element, but it is difficult to make them move naturally. This work was repeated until conductors were prepared for all roles, so the task of creating virtual conductors requires extensive time and effort. Moreover, it is necessary for the creator of the conductors to have knowledge of the conduct and some experience creating computer graphics. Players must secure personnel resources for creating virtual conductors to actually implement this proposal, but it is difficult because the field of music and the field of computer graphics are quite distinct and there are few people with the required knowledge and experience.

3.2 Efficient Generation of Conductor Avatars

To solve these issues, we proposed a system to generate virtual-conductor avatars more efficiently. In this system, virtual conductors for each role are generated automatically. The system selects the motion segment of the conductor according to the musical score and connects the segments selected in each timing to generate avatars. We use a paper score because many orchestras manage paper scores and often use them when players perform actually and a paper score has the information required to perform except for the information express artistic quality. All that is required to use this system is to push some buttons and wait until the system has created all the virtual conductors, so it requires less work, no knowledge of conducting players, and no experience creating computer graphics. For these reasons, this system saves much work and time for preparing avatars and enables players to perform with multiple virtual conductors even if a musical piece has many parts.

4 Implementation

A system was created for automatic animation of multiple virtual conductors based on the paper score to prepare multiple virtual conductors and we don't consider how these conductors are used actually in this paper. This system then connects the short movie segments and creates virtual conductors' movies for a piece of music. This section describes the implementation of this system that make virtual conductors' movies.

4.1 Outline of the System

Figure 1 is the image of the system. First, KAWAI's scoremaker 10st, that is software to compose a music and part of this system, read the paper score and divide into each part. After that, the scores for each part are converted into MIDI data. It extracts information needed for performing (e.g. the tempo, rhythm, sound volume, and the time to play and suspend the notes) from MIDI data and uses the timing of the paper score to connect short movie segments to create the conductor for a piece of music.

4.2 MIDI Data Analysis

MIDI is a common standard for transferring digital data between devices. MIDI data has information showing each note, including when the notes are played, when they are suspended, how loud they should be, how long they should be, and so on. This MIDI format was chosen because it has all the information for players to perform without artistic interpretation. MIDI data is composed of an array

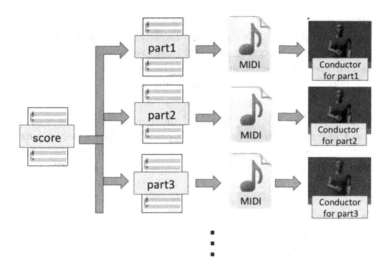

Fig. 1. Image of the system

of two character hexadecimal numbers as shown in Fig. 2. Each hexadecimal number is comprised of two digits except first some numbers has information of one note, from which this system analyzes these numbers and extracts the necessary information.

Address	00 01 02 03 04 05 06 07 08 09 0A 0B 0C 0D 0E 0F
00000000	40 54 68 64 00 00 00 06 00 01 00 02 01 E0 40 54
00000010	72 6B 00 00 00 18 00 FF 03 00 00 FF 58 04 04 02
00000020	18 08 81 70 FF 51 03 07 A1 20 00 FF 2F 00 40 54
00000030	90 30 64 83 60 80 30 00 00 90 32 64 83 60 80 32
00000040	72 6B 00 00 00 90 34 28 00 FF 03 80 34 64 83 00
00000050	00 81 18 72 00 00 90 64 87 00 FF 2F 00

Fig. 2. MIDI data

4.3 Short Movie Segments

Our virtual conductors can conduct cues of tempo, beat, sound volume, and the timing for playing and suspending notes. Expressing these contents with one hand made the process of creating conductors too complicated and time consuming. As such, the system expresses the contents with both hands and enables avatars to simultaneously indicate two instructions. As a result, the system was designed to display short segment movies of the right hand and left hand. The virtual conductor movies were created using e-frontier's Poser 10. This software has humanoid computer graphics models, whose joints throughout the body can be modulated to create detailed poses resembling human conductors. Movements can also be created by setting the poses for each frame and then playing back the animation at a constant frame speed.

The Right Hand. The minimal length of short segment movies is the length of one beat and these movies were created at a rate of 60 beats per minute (BPM). In creating the conducting cues for tempo, beat, and sound volume, we referenced a textbook of conducting methods [11]. To express the sound volume, six levels of avatar's dynamics from pianissimo (pp) to fortissimo (ff) were prepared and movies were made as shown in Fig. 3. The conductor's subsequent movement of these levels changed according to the levels for each rhythm. For example, if the rhythm was binary time, twelve segment movie segments ($2\,beat \times 6\,levels = 12\,movies$) were prepared.

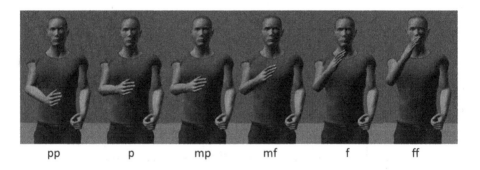

Fig. 3. six levels of dynamics expressing sound volume

The Left Hand. The avatars provide instructions to keep making no sound, to performing a long tone, and the timing of suspending the notes with their left hands. There are two kinds of movies: one showing gestured instructions and one is a motionless state holding a gestured pose. The system connects gestures and poses to make movies of any length. This study includes prepared movies of 1 s and 0.1 s in length. When the conductor instructs the player to keep performing a tone for 3.5 s, the system connect movies of a gesture for 1 s and a pose for 2.5 s. The movie of pose for 2.5 s is composed of two segment movies of 1 s each and five 0.1 s segments.

4.4   Selecting Segments

The system selects the short segment movies based on information extracted from MIDI data. The algorithms to select the movies are different between the right-hand and left-hand sides.

Right-Hand Algorithm. The piece of music is divided into beats and the system applies each beat according to the algorithm.

The way to determine the sound volume: First, the system checks the number of the current beat in the music, checks the number of the current beat is in the measure, and checks the sound volume to select the movie segments. When a player makes no sound, the system deals with the selection as if the sound volume was pianissimo because players can't grasp where players perform now without the conductor's action. To instruct players in the correct timing, the conductor conducts one beat before the timing to conduct. Thus, for example, the system stocks information of the sound volume at third beat and uses this stock information when selecting the fourth beat movie.

The way to determine the timing of playing the notes: We define a conductor's rest if the conductor instructs nothing for two beats and the timing of playing the notes is the first note after the rest of conductor, which it extracts from the MIDI data. When the conductor instructs players to play a note, the system checks the length from the current note to the time the player should suspend the note to determine whether it is longer than two beats. The avatars throw their hand up and down a beat before the note should be suspended.

The way to determine the tempo: According to the tempo of the score, the system change the segment movie's frames per second (FPS). The prepared movie segments are 60 BPM and 30 PFS, so their FPS is changed according to this numerical expression.

$$fps = 30 \times (60 \div The\,tempo\,of\,music) \tag{1}$$

Left-Hand Algorithm. In the left-hand algorithm, the system is managed in time. Time in MIDI data is expressed by a unit called a "tick". The following is the numerical expression to convert the "tick" to a "mili second".

$$time[msec] = All\,ticks \div tick\,per\,beat \times 60 \div The\,tempo \tag{2}$$

Using this numerical expression allows us to know the time from the beginning of the music to the timing of the cue. When the time from playing the note to suspending the note is longer than the length of the left-hand gesture, the conductor instructs the player to perform a long tone. If, after a long tone, the time between suspending the note and playing the next note is longer than the time of two beats, the conductor always cues the timing of suspending the note.

4.5   Connecting Segments

The short movie segments in this system were connected with OpenCV. The system deconstructed movie segments into still picture files and arranged these files to create the conductor animations. This process was repeated for each part to prepare the conductor movie segments.

5   Experiments

This section describes the evaluation of the system generating virtual-conductor avatars automatically. To evaluate, we compared two virtual-conductor avatars: one generated automatically by the system and one created manually(Creating manually means that we programmed a virtual-conductor avatar to pose according to the music with Poser 10.) At first, we tested how long the system saved time to create virtual conductors, comparing the time required to create automatically (by the system) and manually.

5.1   Required Time for Avatar Generation

To investigate how long it took time to create virtual conductors made both manually and automatically, this study measured the time required to create conductors for a musical piece of one minute in length and five parts. It proved too difficult to manually create a virtual conductor using Poser 10, so we estimated the amount of time required to create a conductor for this music from the work hours required to make a conductor for the first twenty seconds of the music. On the other hand, we measured the amount of time required to create conductors automatically with the system. The result shown in Table 1 proves the system remarkably reduced the number of required work hours.

Table 1. Required Time for Avatar Generation

	Automatically	Manually
20 s work		About 1 h
1 part(about 1 min) work	9 min and 14 s	About 3 hours and half
All parts (5 parts) work	46 min and 5 s	About 18 h

5.2   The Quality of the Avatar

Second, we evaluated the quality of two virtual-conductor avatars to confirm that the automatically created virtual conductor was as easy to understand as one created manually.

Participants. This study included 96 participants with experience performing in an orchestra, playing instruments like violin, trumpet, clarinet, horn or piano, and so on. The participants demonstrated a wide range of experience from 2 to 32 years.

Questionnaire. Participants completed a web-based questionnaire after watching two videos in which two virtual conductors cued performance instructions. In this questionnaire, participants evaluated the following questions on a scale of one to five (one is low and five is high)

- Was the tempo correct?
- Was the volume easy to understand from the dynamics?
- Was the timing of playing the notes easy to perform?
- Was the timing of suspending the notes easy to perform?
- Did the conductor move naturally?
- Was your comprehensive evaluation of conductor good?

The participants were also asked to give reasons for evaluating the conductor's movements and to provide a comprehensive evaluation.

Fig. 4. The image in the experience

Procedure. The music used in this experiment was Eugene Bozza's "Variations Sur Un Theme Libre: Quintette a Vent." This experiment used the first two minutes and only the flute part of this music. Participants were shown two virtual conductors, each of which presented the music based on MIDI data. Participants evaluated short movie segments of both conductors, then completed a web-based questionnaire. Figure 4 shows the image used in the experiment.

6 Result

6.1 Questionnaire Result

The participants' responses to each item on the questionnaire were averaged and the results of the experiment are shown in Fig. 5. These results demonstrate that players gave average ratings for both virtual conductors, with values around 3. The results are likely lower because the conductor only conducted the flute part, not fully demonstrating the advantages of the system. The comparison of each average shows significant differences between the virtual conductors about the volumes ($P(t) = 1.5 \times 10^{-9} < 0.05$), the timing for playing the notes ($P(t) = 0.041 < 0.05$), the natural movement ($P(t) = 4.6 \times 10^{-6} < 0.05$) and the comprehensive evaluation ($P(t) = 2.1 \times 10^{-4} < 0.05$), but no significant difference related to the tempo ($P(t) = 0.93 > 0.05$) and the timing for suspending the notes ($P(t) = 0.24 > 0.05$). These results shows that the automatically-created virtual conductor received a lower evaluation than the manually-created virtual conductor regarding the dynamics, the timing for playing the notes, natural movement, and comprehensive evaluation, but both conductors were equally good at conducting the tempo and the timing for suspending the notes.

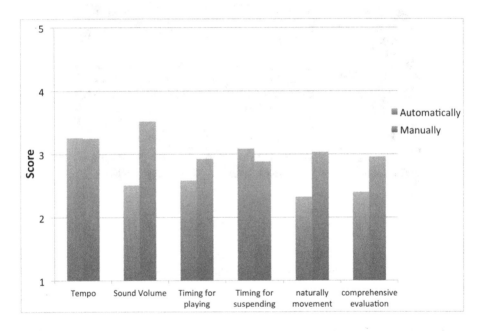

Fig. 5. Scores of the question items

The following is the reason why participants evaluate about the movement and the comprehensive evaluation.

– Automatically generation(by the system)
  - it use both hands for conducting and its movement is natural.
  - It beats with regularity
  - It feels good for the timing of put off the notes
  - It has only two scales of the dynamics.
  - It feels mechanical.

- Its conduct is monotonous and doesn't have musical fine expression.
- It is void of facial expression.
- Its instruction is too short period of time to answer.
- It can't conduct with fine movement of fingers and shoulder

- Manually generation
    - It looks livelier than the other.
    - Its hands move smoothly.
    - Its movement is smoother than the other because of use of its shoulder.
    - I feel it is easy to understand when I should put on the notes because of explicit instructions.
    - It is easy to understand about the dynamics.
    - It use almost only right-hand and can't beat the rhythm during gesture to perform long tone.
    - After instruct to put off the notes, it rapidly conduct to put on the notes.
    - It doesn't conduct using the whole arm.

6.2 Discussion

The automatically-generated virtual conductor was divided into two parts, with each part conducting different content so that it can simultaneously indicate two instructions. One participant said that the automatic conductor "use[s] both hands for conducting and its movement is natural." About the manual conductor, another participant said "It [almost exclusively] use[s] [the] right-hand and can't beat the rhythm during gesture[s] to perform long tone[s]." So the evaluation about the automatically-generated virtual conductor using both hands was good. Using these comments as a reference, the researchers considered why the evaluations of the automatically-generated virtual conductor was lower than the manually-created virtual conductor with regard to the dynamics, the timing for playing the notes, the natural movement, and comprehensive evaluation.

The Dynamics. One participant said, "it has only two scales of the dynamics." This comment implies that the automatically-generated virtual conductor cannot finely express the sound volume to participants. When the system converts the score to MIDI data, the dynamics are expressed in a numeric value of "the velocity" and it is necessary to change the movement expressing the dynamics to change the value of the velocity, which is not smaller than a fixed value. If the velocity changes within the numerical range of a fixed value, there are no changes to the conductor. This is likely the reason that participants didn't feel the dynamics. As a solution for this problem, the fixed value of the velocity need to change the conductor must be decreased and further divided into the levels of the dynamics.

The Timing of Playing the Notes. Automatically-generated virtual conductors instructed players to play the notes by moving their right-hand up and down. As previously noted, the algorithms selecting the movies is dependent on the side. In the algorithm of the right-hand side, the minimal length of short movie segments was one beat. The system can't finely adjust the timing any shorter than the length of one beat. For example, if the timing for playing the notes is on the first beat and a half, the system instructs on the first beat. As a solution to this problem, the conductors should instruct with their left-hand. In the algorithm of the left-hand side, the system can adjust the timing in 0.1 s increments. In this case, new left-hand gestures are required to easily express instructions for playing the notes.

The Natural Movement. Participants reported that the virtual conductor "feels mechanical" and that "its conduct is monotonous and doesn't have fine musical expression." Virtual conductors consist of short movie segments, so the instructions depend on the quality of these movies. The researchers don't have detailed professional knowledge of conducting, so preparing high quality movies of conductor was a challenge. Clearly, these movies can be improved by asking people with more professional knowledge and experience to help or supervise them.

Further changes will improve the automatically-generated virtual conductors and eliminate the difference between automatically and manually generated conductors.

7   Future Work

We developed the system which create the virtual-conductor avatars with less effort and time. However, to completely establish the multiple virtual conductors system, we need to implement synchronization of these avatars and suppose how these conductors are used. it is essential to synchronize avatars and show each conductor to each player. In future work, we should implement the synchronization function and improve the quality of generating conductors.

8   Coclusions

Usually, orchestras and bands perform as a group of several people, each of whom individually play the parts assigned to them. In this case, it is difficult for players to tune their performance themselves, so performing music in a group requires a conductor who listens to performance of all parts and instructs each part to control sound volume and the timing of notes. There are some studies to support performing with a virtual conductor. However, these studies demonstrate that a virtual conductor cannot give separate cues to each player because it is impossible for the players to recognize who the conductor is conducting. A human conductor is also unable to conduct each part simultaneously. Thus, this study proposed a new conducting environment in which players are individually conducted using multiple virtual conductors. This proposal enables virtual conductors to conduct specific instructions for each player. However, this requires preparing as many virtual conductors as players, which requires extensive time and effort. To solve this problem, we proposed a system to efficiently generate virtual conductors. The system automatically generates virtual conductors by connecting the motion segments selected according to the score, which saves much time and effort, and enables players in a large group such as an orchestra to perform with multiple virtual conductors. The experiment evaluated whether an automatically-generated virtual conductor was as easy to understand as one created manually, and results confirmed that the automatically-generated virtual conductor had some as good points as a manually-created virtual conductor and showed promise that it is possible to eliminate the remaining differences.

References

1. Wendy, K.M., Anastasia, K.: The role of the conductor's goal orientation and use of shared performance cues on collegiate instrumentalists' motivational beliefs and performance in large musical ensembles. Psychol. Music **2013**(41), 630–646 (2013)
2. Dennis, R., Mustafa, R., Anton, N.: Mediated interactions and musical expression-a survey. In: Digital Da Vinci, Computers in Music, pp. 79–98 (2014)
3. Adriana, O., Nicolas, B., Trevor, K., Nordhal, M., Jeremy, R.C.: A high-fidelity orchestra simulator for individual musicians' practice. Comput. Music J. **36**(2), 55–73 (2012)
4. Takashi, A., Noriyuki, K.: An electric music baton system using a haptic interface for visually disabled persons. In: SICE Annual Conference 2012, Akita University, Akita, Japan
5. Yasue, I., Susumu, K., Yositomo, F.: Design and production of an electronic musical score system to reduce the load of page turning for wind orchestra. In: 2014 IEEE 13th International Conference on Cognitive Informatics and Cognitive Computing (ICCI*CC 2014), London, pp. 242–246 (2014)
6. Laura, H.T, Rajiv, L., Peter, R., Rogers, F.: Implementation considerations in enabling visually impaired musicians to read sheet music using a tablet. In: 2013 IEEE 37th Annual Computer Software and Applications Conference, Kyoto, pp. 678–683
7. Baez, R., Barbancho, A.M., Rosa-Pujazón, A., Barbancho, I., Tardón, L.J.: Virtual conductor for string quartet practice. Proc. Sound Music Comput. Conf. **2013**, 292–298 (2013)
8. Anton, N., Dnennis, R., Rob, E., Mark, T.M.: The virtual conductor: learning and teaching about music, performing, and conducting. In: Eighth IEEE International Conference Advanced Learning Technologies. (ICALT 2008), pp. 897–899 (2008)
9. Harold, F.: The Art of Conducting Technique: A New Perspective. Alfred Music (1997)
10. Ryosuke, T., Yusaku, M., Tomoo, I., Ken-ichi, O., Hiroshi, S.: Multiple virtual conductors allow amateur orchestra players to perform better and more easily. In: 2016 IEEE 20th International Conference on Computer Supported Cooperative Work in Design(CSCWD), Nanchang, China (2016)
11. Basic Music Course - Conducting Course. The Church of Jesus Christ of Latter-day Saints (1992)

Comparison of Input Methods for Remote Audiences of Live Music Performances

Yuya Morino, Kei Miyazaki, Hiroyuki Tarumi[(✉)], and Junko Ichino

Kagawa University, Takamatsu, Japan
tarumi@eng.kagawa-u.ac.jp

Abstract. With the spread of the Internet broadcasting services, live music performances on the streaming service are getting popular. However, real time communication between performers and remote audiences is insufficient. We have developed a system using animation that supports communication between performers and remote audiences. With the system, remote audiences can show three types of their body actions to the performers. We have implemented three input methods – mouse devices, keyboards, and smart phones – and evaluated them. According to our evaluation, subjects who have experiences in listening to live music preferred smartphones, but some subjects liked keyboard input.

1 Introduction

Live streaming on the Internet is getting more and more popular. It enables many people, including musicians who only have tight budget, to have their own channel that reaches everyone on the net. In case of musicians, they often make use of the streaming channel to show their live music performances.

However, one of the problems in those cases is that the communication channel is basically one-way. In case of live music performances, especially in cases of rock or popular music, audiences take actions responding to the played music. Responses from the audiences are considered as important elements of the successful live performances. Live streaming on the net lacks upstream communication functions that let the musicians perceive remote audiences' responses.

Of course, live streaming tools have limited functions of communication from the audiences to the musicians: text chat. Ustream [1] and Niconico Live [2] provide text chatting interfaces to the audiences. In case of Niconico Live, especially, it has a very unique user interface that displays chatted texts overlaid on the main video contents. Nicofare [3] is a live concert hall in Roppongi, Tokyo, which has walls where text comments from remote audiences are displayed. However, they do not satisfy our requirements. We need non-verbal communication channels from the audiences to the musicians.

Yoshida and Miyashita tried to display audiences' body actions overlaid onto the video contents [4]. However, it was developed for stored video contents, not for real time live performances. Several projects are found that try to enhance communication between musicians and audiences at the live venue (e.g., [5–7]). But they are using local

© Springer Science+Business Media Singapore 2016
T. Yoshino et al. (Eds.): CollabTech 2016, CCIS 647, pp. 58–64, 2016.
DOI: 10.1007/978-981-10-2618-8_5

communication technologies like WiFi or ultra sound (in case of [5]), which cannot be applied to remote audiences.

Our research is focusing on these problems: how to support remote audiences to give their responsive actions and how to let musicians perceive audiences' responses. It is an important key to have successful collaboration between the music players and remote audiences.

We limit the problem domain to only rock and popular music, because audiences' responses differ depending on the music genre. We also exclude "big" artists' cases, because huge budgets completely change the problem conditions. We know many young fledgling musicians want to give their music to as many audiences as possible, with limited money. They are our target users.

In this paper, we focus on the input methods for remote audiences. We have implemented three methods to input their responsive actions and compared them from the viewpoint of remote audiences. Other aspects, such as evaluations from the players' side, are not described in this paper.

2   Experimental System

2.1   Actions

According to our experiences, we have selected five typical responsive actions by audiences for rock and popular music performances [8]. They are: *sing*, *wave* (wide movement of one hand), *push-up*, *joggle* (rhythmical shakes of one hand), and *hand-clap* (Fig. 1). These actions are usually taken by audiences all together, during particular parts of songs or especially encouraged by musicians. Of course, they do not cover all kinds of actions observed at live venues. However, these five actions are common to many musicians' cases and we consider they are enough to support typical cases.

Currently, we have implemented three of them: *wave*, *push-up*, and *joggle*.

Fig. 1. Five typical responsive actions

2.2   System Configuration

Figure 2 shows the system configuration. Remote audiences watching the live streaming video can input three types of responsive actions by one of the three methods: *moving mouse pointers*, *typing keyboard*, or *using smartphones*. The information of actions is sent back to the computer at the live venue. The format of action information is very simple. It does not show analog values of each motion (e.g., amplitude, acceleration, time, and speed), but shows only the type of actions taken by each audience.

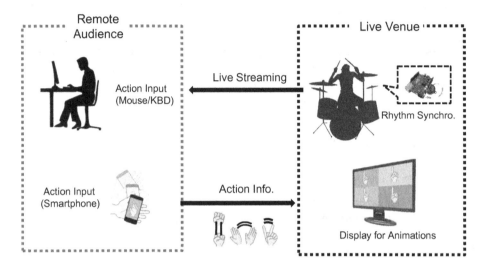

Fig. 2. System configuration

The actions taken by each audience are displayed to the musicians during their play, by animations. The animation is represented by avatars by illustrations of hands. The motions of animations are synchronized with the music played at the live venue, by detecting the drum beats with a vibration sensor. The synchronization technique is still under research to pursue a better solution, but we support a very simple synchronization technique for the current prototype.

2.3   Input Methods

We have implemented three input methods for remote audiences, to compare and evaluate them.

Keyboards. Audiences can simply type "b" key for push-up actions, "n" key for joggling actions, and "m" key for waving actions.

Mouse Devices. In this case, we have defined a "mouse event area" overlaid on the motion video (Fig. 3). It is needed to detect mouse motions. Audiences can move the mouse pointer horizontally within the "mouse event area" to input the waving actions.

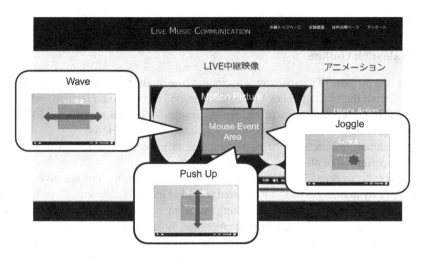

Fig. 3. Input method for a mouse

They can move it vertically to input the push-up actions. In order to input the joggling actions, they need to click the mouse within the "mouse event area."

Smartphones. In this case, each audience needs an additional device, a smartphone, other than the computer to watch the live streaming. We used the acceleration sensors (x, y) and a gyro sensor (z) to detect the hand motions. Figure 4 illustrates how we have defined the movements of smartphones corresponding to the audiences' actions. The current implementation is tuned for ASUS ZenFone2.

Fig. 4. Motion sensing with smartphones

3   Evaluation

3.1   Evaluation Outline

This time, the purpose of experiment is to evaluate the input methods and acquire general comments from the test audiences. Hence we recruited test users and let them experience the system in the environment of remote audiences. After the experience with three different input methods, we gave them questionnaire and interviews.

From January to February, 2016, we had nine test users. All of them were students and had experiences of attending real live concerts.

To make the evaluation setting simple, stable, and even, we did not give real live performance by human players, but adopted recorded live performance of a professional rock band. Figure 5 is a picture of testing scene in case of the input method with a keyboard. The test user was watching the recorded music performance on the left LCD. He was giving his responsive actions using the keyboard. His action was confirmed by the animation of hand motion at the left LCD. The right LCD was showing a virtual display that should have been shown to the musicians at the live venue. The test user's action was shown at the upper-leftmost sub-window. Other seven sub-windows were dummies, representing other audiences. The reason we set the right LCD was to let the test user know the total system concept.

Fig. 5.   Testing environment

The process of experiment was as follows. First, we gave explanations of the research background and the system concept. Next, we gave instructions of the system operation to test users, for all input methods. The users had some test practices. After the practices, all users experienced all input methods, each of which took four minutes. After the experience, test users answered the questionnaire on the web. We also gave interviews with them.

3.2   Results

Comparison of the Three Input Methods.   Table 1 shows the results of questionnaire comparing the three input methods.

We had supposed that smartphone should be the best input method because it was most similar to the body actions given at the real concert. However, the result was a little different. From the viewpoint of concentration on the music, keyboards seemed to be the best solution. However, smartphones were best preferred totally and they had the feeling of attending the concert better than other devices. Mouse devices did not have any advantage.

Table 1. Comparison of three input methods.

Question	Device	Strongly agree	Slightly agree	Neutral	Slightly disagree	Strongly disagree
I was able to concentrate my attention on the music	Mouse	1	2	0	4	2
	Keyboard	3	5	1	0	0
	Smartphone	1	4	0	2	2
I felt like I really attended the concert	Mouse	0	4	1	3	1
	Keyboard	1	2	2	3	1
	Smartphone	2	6	0	1	0
		Yes				
I like to use this device (Multiple selections are allowed)	Mouse	2				
	Keyboard	3				
	Smartphone	6				

We have given more consideration based on the comments from the test users given in the interviews. The merit of keyboard was that it was physically easy and the input was stable. In case of smartphones, weight of the device was a physical burden. We also had a problem that the gesture recognition was not always perfect, which might be a psychological burden for the users.

It was interesting that some users who did not like keyboard commented that it was like a "task" to hit keys, but some users who liked keyboard commented that they felt like playing action games when hitting keys with the music.

Other Comments.   One test user requested us to introduce virtual penlights for the responsive actions. He said that some live venues inhibited audiences from using penlights due to the safety reasons, but remote audiences did not have safety problems with other audiences.

This comment is important. We have two approaches to such kind of remote systems. One is to make the remote environment as similar to the local environment as possible, and to give remote users same kind of experiences with local users. The other approach is to determine the difference between the remote and local environments and exploit the difference to give advantages to remote users. Hitting keys instead of waving or joggling by their own hands is an example of the latter approach.

If it is a business system, practical advantages (e.g., efficiency) would be almost always accepted. However, it is a community support system. We should consider psychological and social issues. The question is, how the music players or local audiences think about it.

4   Conclusion

We are developing a system to support remote audiences to give their responsive actions during the live music performance to the players at the live venue. In this paper, we compared three input methods for the remote users: mouse devices, keyboards, and smartphones. We have conducted experiments with test users and found that smartphones are the best device to give users experiences feeling like attending the real concerts. However, keyboards were also preferred by some users, because of the low physical burden and a different kind of fun like gaming.

For the future work, we will evaluate the system totally with music players, local audiences and also remote audiences. Evaluations that should be done with musicians will include, for example, animation representation, animation synchronization mechanism, etc.

As stated in the last section, it is an important problem how the remote environment should be designed. Should the remote audiences have experiences similar to the local audiences? Or would it be accepted that they take advantage of the remote environment? We will still consider this problem with evaluating other aspects of this system.

Acknowledgments.   This research is partially supported by KAKENHI (15K00274).

References

1. Ustream. http://www.ustream.tv/
2. Niconico live. http://live.nicodivdeo.jp/
3. Nicofare. http://nicofare.jp/
4. Yoshida, A., Miyashita, H.: Video sharing system that overlays body movements for the sense of unity. In: Proceedings of Interaction 2012 (IPSJ), pp. 187–188 (2012). (in Japanese)
5. Hirabayashi, M., Eshima, K.: Sense of space: the audience participation music performance with high-frequency sound ID. In: Proceedings of the International Conference on New Interfaces for Musical Expression (NIME2015), pp. 58–60 (2015)
6. Lightwave. http://www.lightwave.io/
7. FreFlow. http://freflow.com/
8. Tarumi, H., Akazawa, K., Ono, M., Kagawa, E., Hayashi, T., Yaegashi, R.: Awareness support for remote music performance. In: Nijholt, A., Romao, T., Reidsma, D. (eds.) ACE 2012. LNCS, vol. 7624, pp. 573–576. Springer, Heidelberg (2012)

Civic Social Network: A Challenge for Co-production of Contents About Common Urban Entities

Alessio Antonini[✉], Guido Boella, Lucia Lupi, and Claudio Schifanella

Department of Computer Science, University of Turin, Turin, Italy
{antonini,boella,lupi,schifanella}@di.unito.it

Abstract. Developing a civic social network requires to consider users meeting in real life, collaborating on digital entries related to real urban entities. This makes necessary to think about collaboration tools in a new perspective: ensuring the participation of users with different levels and forms of legitimacy to represent complex relations among entities, and ensuring the accountability of each contributor. We present a set of technical solutions allowing the collaboration on complex entities, keeping interactions simple, and representing multiple perspectives about shared entities.

1 Introduction

The fragmentation of information is one of the outcomes of the multiplication of web sources. A new type of social media is starting to address this issue by establishing a framework to gather multiple levels of contributors and to evaluate the relevance of information in relation to their sources. Civic social networks (CSN) [2, 4, 10] or rather social networks based on citizenship and public engagement at local and urban level, belong to this new model of social media.

Design and developing a CSN is not an easy task, because user legitimacy and responsibility over contents are already complex problems to address, but they becomes blocking in a digital environment where users and entities are referred to a confined physical space and digital conflicts can break through real life and vice versa. The main approaches about collaboration on digital platforms do not deal with the chance of users interacting in real life and with concurrent perspectives and goals.

In particular, we focus our attention on users with different and maybe irreconcilable positions interacting on the same digital entities corresponding to real places, events, and so on such as a square or monument description. Indeed, at urban and neighborhood level, real life entities are involved in very complex dynamics generating many different perspectives on the same entity that potentially can be expressed in a digital space.

In our opinion, a CSN cannot force a simplification of such entities without embracing very strong positions in favor of one of many parties. Moreover, a CSN aimed to represent urban and local reality avoiding the fragmentation of information should

A part of the research leading to these results has received funding from the European Union's Horizon 2020 research and innovation programme under grant agreement n° 693514.

© Springer Science+Business Media Singapore 2016
T. Yoshino et al. (Eds.): CollabTech 2016, CCIS 647, pp. 65–73, 2016.
DOI: 10.1007/978-981-10-2618-8_6

not host multiple parallel unconnected definitions of entities, but rebuilding the context integrating different contributions. Allowing the mere multiplication of viewpoints will engage users in a battle of popularity for the right above entities representing the reality as how users may want it to be (simple), instead of representing the reality as it is with its facets and issues.

Since there is not one legitimate position and there is not a single local actor having the right about what is common, a CSN has to provide the means to build a common platform for concurrent positions without exacerbate conflicts but promoting collaboration in real life. About the cooperation on common entities on a digital platform, we see three main issues:

1. Given different forms and levels of legitimacy of local players, how to let various sources coexist without forcing a common position or an unilateral perspectives?
2. How to share the responsibility among proactive contributors on the platform preserving the different perspectives and goals of real life involving a close relationship with urban entities?
3. How to build the complex identity of shared urban entities?

During a participatory design process involving 600 people in 50 meetings and workshops, we engaged potential users in evaluating the main approaches about collaboration on digital platforms in their context. Considering their inputs, we designed and developed a set of solutions oriented to the following goals:

1. Providing a mechanism to contribute to contents regardless their initiators,
2. Providing a mechanism to share the responsibility of moderation,
3. Ensuring a clear accountability of users even in case of multiple contributors.

We wish to avoid taking a side, preserving the richness of the context and letting users make their own interpretation and choices according to their own goals. The result is a system capable of representing a network of digital entities corresponding to real urban and local things, each one of them enriched with second order entities decoupled from the entity authorship. Moreover, we defined a mechanism to share the responsibility about contents related to each entity among the contributors, releasing the first author (initiator) from the burden of moderating a growing entity.

In this paper, we are going to present a brief analysis about the main approaches used by the most successful digital platforms based on users' collaboration for the content production. In Sect. 3, we describe the main issues behind the technical solutions we implemented, which are illustrated in Sect. 4. Lastly, we synthesize our conclusions and the future developments of our CSN.

2   State of the Art

Nowadays, social networks are the most commonplace where to find different perspectives about almost anything. Pages and groups about real entities are widespread, but even in a virtual spaces conflicts rise about how an entity should be described, who holds the right to say something about it, etc. When this happens about common urban entities, or in other words about places lived by multiple actors and actions made by more than one of them in the same shared space, many players may hold a vital piece of information, a perspective that can help others in their tasks, and consequently a point of view that need to be represented and integrated with others preventing or solving virtual conflicts. Existing digital platforms implement different strategies to mediate among users according to the platform goal and the type of information they handle.

We are focused on finding a solution that may work with real users in a real application. For this reason, we focused our attention on the standard approaches from major web players rather than searching among theoretical analysis of the problems mentioned above.

In order to make a comparison, we introduce an emblematic example we found during our workshops with potential users.

We need to map a school in the neighborhood. Who is legitimate to describe the school? The dean, the school board, school employees, teachers, students' parents, former or current students? The school board and the dean can describe the school in term of educational vision and methods, or syllabus and training paths; employees are qualified to write about the public services offered by the school; students and parents can share their experience lived in the school environment.

What if the school is hosted in an historical building? What is more prominent? The historical or the educational aspects? Therefore, who is legitimate to describe the historical aspects? Historians, architects, local experts, students, neighborhood inhabitants, cultural heritage authorities, or local administrations? The local administration can motivate the change of destination of a monumental place to a public facility in order to revitalize the local area. Historians can describe the significance of that building in the city history. Architects and local experts can describe stylistic and technical characteristics and why the building is worth to be preserved. The cultural heritage authority can place the building into the local cultural assets. For the inhabitants is a focal point in the neighborhood over the time.

The example can become even more complex. What if the school gym is used by sport organizations for their activities? What if the school is managed by a religious organization?

The school is a complex urban entity that lends itself to be represented by a multiplicity of descriptions, all fitting a specific aspect of the reality, with different forms and levels of legitimacy.

In our opinion, there are two main approaches to collaboration in content production on digital platform: *common goals* and *ownership*. Considering these two approaches, in reference to the example 1, we highlight: the ability to represent the complexity of the example, the quantity and quality of required interactions among users and the social acceptability of the output.

When the platform purposes are clear and self explanatory is it possible to assume the collaboration of users toward a common goal, which may be the definition of an encyclopedia page about the school or a parents group. This first approach moves the problem of plurality to the goal of collaboration: users work to build something specific. Potential conflicts about attribution and legitimacy are solved addressing the compliance of each contribution to the common goal, done by editors in the case of Wikipedia [1], group owners in Facebook or moderators in forums.

Considering Wikipedia for the example 1, the result will be two interlinked pages addressing the school and the historical building. Homogenous groups of experts, with the supervision on Wikipedia editors [6], will develop each one of them [5]. Personal experience will not be allowed and contingent activities will not be documented.

Considering Facebook groups [9], the result will be a parents group about sharing personal experiences as students' parents or former students. The dean or other authorities will not be included in this kind of group or they may participate as individuals and not as in charge of institutional authority.

The premise of choosing one common goal follows the choosing of one perspective; therefore, this approach fails to represent the complexity of reality we intend to reach. This methodology requires strong and strictly regulated interactions among users and an overall guide to obtain homogenous and sharable results. It is acceptable since it implies collaboration only among willing contributors sharing the common goal.

When expressing the identity is more prominent than other goals, the legitimacy issue is solves in an ownership assessment. In other words, if the goal is to represent an entity in an official way the problem is to identify who has the right on this entity. Collaboration on defining the entity can be done, but under the owner's supervision and permission. In some cases, owners may allows contrasting opinions if the drawback of censuring is bigger than the contrast itself, but contributors have no rights to demand a fair acknowledgement of their positions. This is the approach of Facebook and Google + pages, of Google maps about places and of websites integrating social media features. The collaboration mechanisms are meant to mediate the asymmetric relation between one owner and many contributors with no rights.

Considering Facebook applied to the example 1, the dean will open an official Facebook page [8] of the school giving the responsibility of managing contents to an employee that will publish only general information and official announcements. If the dean wants, the page can collect comments, which will be moderated by the same employee, or simply ignored. It will result in parents and students opening their own groups about specific topics or even fake or unofficial pages about the school in order to express other positions than the official one.

Considering Wikipedia, a contrast of opinions will be resolved asking for sources such as the official school website or the school board documents. The hierarchy of sources leads to the users' hierarchy.

Anyone can add information on Google maps, but in order to claim the ownership of a place [7], a postal card is sent to the declared address in order to verify the owner identity. But then, once a place is mapped, also anonymous users can indiscriminately post comments, ratings and pictures which the owner has to keep in check in order to avoid attacks from rivals.

In each case, the perspective is one and limited by the tool. The result is the multiplication of entry points, which is not a problem for Google and Facebook but it is for users that must know where to search information. In these systems, interactions among users are simple and clear but mostly left to the good will of the owner, which has actually no obligations toward others. The acceptability is very low for the excluded users that are the large majority.

Can a virtual space host multiple representations of reality avoiding forced interactions and difficult collaborations? In our opinion, this issue is specifically tied to the CSN context, rather than to other platforms managed by the major web players considered before even if they are collaborative platform. Indeed, a CSN is aimed to support real interactions of users and their actions in a physical world, and therefore it is mandatory to provide ways of coexistence helping users to negotiate in mutual respect of their roles and to integrate their perspective because in reality it is not possible to avoid who is physically close to you.

Summarizing, we need a way to manage the complexity of example 1 keeping interactions simple and avoiding uproars in the neighborhood.

3   Open Issues

There are different forms and levels of legitimacy, but is it something a CSN should mettle on? In our opinion, users should make their own evaluation about the relevance of each contribution considering their context and contents of interest. About sources, we consider only real users: single citizens or collective bodies if regularly registered at local level. The evaluation of the different level of legitimacy among single citizens, institutions or local organizations is left to users case by case. Moreover, users may have different legitimacy according to the type of content they are providing: a citizen may not be entitled to provide an official representation of an urban entity, but a personal experience can be more valuable coming from a single citizen than from a public office for other users. Following the example 1, the experience expressed by former students may be much more relevant than a dean statement about how the school experience will be for your children.

In order to ensure plurality and cooperation, the responsibility should be shared among the interested parties. Who are the interested parties? We cannot enter in each dynamic, but what we can do is to identify the proactive contributors investing enough energy to be recognized worth of responsibility. Being proactive is not related to the production of digital contents in general, but to documenting real actions having an effect at local level using the platform functionalities to enhance processes and outcomes. On the contrary, sharing opinions does not mean be proactive, because not necessarily an opinion is related to what is happening in real life.

How to share the responsibility among contributors preserving their different perspectives? Private goals are legitimate in real life, but in digital platforms are not so evident and this is one of the reasons leading conflicts in entity representation and experience sharing. On the other hand, providing means to express explicitly a perspective can help solving and avoiding misunderstanding making the contents much more "semantically accessible" to users.

How to build complex entities preserving their identities? In our opinion, the identity is preserved only if an entity has a single evident entry point. The multiple facets of an entity should be solved with an internal and external structure rather then multiplying the entity. Structuring entities can still grant the chance of having different responsible groups for different purposes.

Summarizing, the desiderata are: structured single entry point for entities, shared responsibility instead than ownership, public visibility of all point of views and user accountability, and content driven solutions.

4   Technical Solutions

In order to build a common ground for many points of views, we separate the creation of a new entity on the platform from its descriptions, or in other words, we make a distinction between entity properties and description properties.

Technically speaking, we have first order entities working as shared entry points and second order entities. We defined a shared set of primary properties belonging to the entity and defined in the creation process[1]: title, valid time interval, categories, tags, external URL, coordinates (latitude and longitude). Each primary entity may have specific primary properties, for instance: events have door time, duration, organizer, attendees and performer[2]. Primary properties should be more or less objective in order to avoid the proliferation of proliferation of homonymous entities. Following the example 1, we want to avoid many parallel entries about the same school letting the first one defining a "place" school without having the concern of making a general or official description.

Then we defined a set of second order entities to describe a primary entity. The second order entities are available for any primary order entity as its complement and to any user, except into groups where the content creation is reserved only to the group members. The second order entities are meant to be fast to create. As today, we implemented: descriptions requiring a title and a text, comments requiring just text and images (Fig. 1).

Fig. 1.   On the left a place containing an event, on the center the editor for descriptions, on the right the first place with a description made by a different user.

---

[1] A sandbox can be found at http://test.firstlife.di.unito.it.

[2] The entity properties are mostly implementation of http://schema.org specifications.

The result of combining light weighted primary entities with structured fields made of secondary order properties is having a sharable entry point collecting different perspective with a clear attributions related to each second order entity.

Managing typed single entry points is not enough to catch the complexity of real life entities. In general, we consider part of relations among entities of the same type:

1. A place can contain sub-places, such as office rooms
2. An event can be composed by several sub events
3. Articles can have sub-topics
4. Groups can be spliced in operative or thematic sub-groups.

There are other relations cross type we introduced:

1. "location", from an event to a place
2. "news of" from news to an entity that is not a news
3. "group of" from a group toward an entity
4. "group from" an entity to a group

Adding relations among entities results in giving the possibility to build complex structures from a single entry point from different users' contributions (Fig. 2).

For instance, following example 1, the "place" school can hosts events, organized in many sub-events, and groups, structured around a class or a type of activity. An events organized by a sport organization can be independent from the school context, but it can be hosted in the school and the same for the news related to this event (registration, updates, etc.).

Fig. 2. Left, a place containing two other places and an event. On the right, a map view.

An entry point is the result of one user initiative but one user, even if legitimate, cannot cover all the point of views about an urban entity. Moreover, one user should not have the monopoly of an entity for many reasons.

1. Lack of perspective, as we just stated he/she cannot pretend to express everything can be said about an entity;
2. Dynamic reality, things change and so users commitment toward taking care of a piece of information;
3. Excess of responsibility: the burden is too heavy from the user perspective and the risk of missing an important and vital piece of the puzzle is too high from the community perspective.

4. Coproduction of social reality, nothing social is made by one person but everything requires others and so their representation.

We do not recognize the role of owner, but the greatest importance is referred to contributors. Each primary level entity has one initiator (the first contributor) and contributors. From an entry point, in parallel with the graph of entities, we defined a network of collaborations replacing the standard friendship/following-relations of social networks. Users are connected through contents and so they share the responsibility of taking care of contents acting at content level.

The initiators still play an important role in the beginning, but on the contrary of other web 2.0 and social network mechanisms, the burden is released as the entities becomes more complex relying on collective moderation. Contributors are engaged in self moderating themself, being notified about activities and comments added to the entity they contribute to create, and they can comment, report abuses or eventually delete a contribution.

A user can always be identified playing the contributor or the moderator role resulting in exposing yourself and your own reputation. Contributor and moderators conduct must be compliant with the guidelines included in the ethical code of the platform. Moreover, they can always report abuses to the platform administrators.

5 Conclusions

This contribution addressed the concept of civic social network as collector of urban information and cooperation environment for public actors and citizens. The design process of 50 workshops and meetings involving local actors highlighted three main issues related to collaboration in representing real entities:

1. The coexistence of contributions from different perspective;
2. The distribution of responsibility among users;
3. The complexity of the identity of real life entities.

Following, we developed an alternative approach to the mainstream in order to tackle the users' demands enabling multiple perspectives and contributions, shared moderation, content-based networks.

Currently, we are in an advanced testing phase engaging users in representing real scenarios. An English version is available for the project WeGovNow![3].

References

1. Ray, A.: Reviewing the author-function in the age of Wikipedia. In: Ray, A., Graeff, E., (eds.) Originality, Imitation, and Plagiarism: Teaching Writing in the Digital Age, p. 39 (2008)
2. Kaplan, A.M., Haenlein, M.: Users of the world, unite! the challenges and opportunities of social media. Bus. Horiz. **53**(1), 59–68 (2010)

---

[3] WeGovNow! is H2020 project about developing a we-government platform at European level. The demo is available at http://wegovnow.firstlife.di.unito.it.

3. Kietzmann, J.H., et al.: Social media? Get serious! understanding the functional building blocks of social media. Bus. Horiz. **54**(3), 241–251 (2011)

4. Gordon, E., Mihailidis, P.: Civic Media: Technology, Design, Practice. MIT Press, Cambridge (2016)

5. https://en.wikipedia.org/wiki/Wikipedia:Reviewing

6. https://en.wikipedia.org/wiki/Wikipedia:Editorial_oversight_and_control

7. https://support.google.com/business/#topic=4539639

8. https://www.facebook.com/page_guidelines.php

9. https://www.facebook.com/help/162866443847527/

10. Pasek, J., More, E., Romer, D.: Realizing the social internet? Online social networking meets offline civic engagement. J. Inf. Technol. Politics **6**(3-4), 197–215 (2009)

Key-Typing on Teleconference: Collaborative Effort on Cross-Cultural Discussion

Hiromi Hanawa[1(✉)], Xiaoyu Song[1], and Tomoo Inoue[2]

[1] Graduate School of Library, Information and Media Studies,
University of Tsukuba, 1-2, Kasuga, Tsukuba, Ibaraki 305-8550, Japan
{hanawa,songxy}@slis.tsukuba.ac.jp
[2] Faculty of Library, Information and Media Science, University of Tsukuba,
1-2, Kasuga, Tsukuba, Ibaraki 305-8550, Japan
inoue@slis.tsukuba.ac.jp

Abstract. It often causes difficulty to participate in teleconference for foreign language learners due to language and cultural barrier. In this paper we proposed Key-Typing method to investigate its effects on a conversation. This method successfully enhanced mutual understanding in point of presence of Evidence in Grounding, and promoting retention of shared-knowledge in real-time interactive telecommunication as a consequence. Most of the experiment participants assessed overall conversation quality enhancement and highly evaluated the proposed method in subjective evaluation surveys, also mentioned its potency for further cross-cultural communication.

Keywords: Cross-cultural communication · Discussion · Teleconference · Common ground · Keyword · Character input

1 Introduction

The number of foreign people visiting Japan has been increasing on a daily bases. Especially in Trans Asia-Pacific Area it's frequent for them to contact and collaborate with Japanese. Communication with local people requires learning language and culture, which still includes high barriers to entry for those purposes. International people from other countries in Japan need Japanese proficiency and learn Japanese as a second language because those non-native Japanese speaker and native Japanese speakers as local residents communicate and collaborate in Japanese at the work places or at school for business, education, and so forth.

Related researches using multiple languages and cultures have also increased its number in Cross-culture Computer-Mediated Communication field. There are consecutive researches and observation through technology to report its effects and features in different language and culture for a variety of conversational themes and modes of communication. Since international conversation consists of people from different languages and cultures, they are mutually incapable of understanding each other in conversation. Moreover those of other language face difficulty to keep up with the conversation in real time and miss chance and information, or drop their task performance to achieve their objectives. This prevents them from performing effective communication

© Springer Science+Business Media Singapore 2016
T. Yoshino et al. (Eds.): CollabTech 2016, CCIS 647, pp. 74–88, 2016.
DOI: 10.1007/978-981-10-2618-8_7

and contributing to the conversation. Such communication deficit demands supporting tool that enables to share the content accurately with people of limited language proficiency. In this paper, dyad of non-native speaker (NNS) and native Japanese speaker (NS) exercises the computer mediated communication to enhance comprehension of the conversation and it is observed its effects on a conversation and also reported participants' evaluation of the method through the experiments.

2 Related Work

2.1 Cross Cultural Communication

Novinger [1] shows cases of cross-cultural communication in the US, Mexico and Japan from the aspect of international business. Through those cases it refers to people of different cultures embrace communication obstacles, which delivers misunderstanding and ineffectual communication in business and social situations. It is also pointed that language is an important factor in communication and is certainly responsible for many obstacles, and contact with international people has rapidly increased along with the development of communication technologies. It occurs verbal and non-verbal communication gaps and different perceptions based on different cultural backgrounds. Analyses of these interactions were concluded that some prescriptions towards intercultural communication, that stated necessity of adoptability referring to every kinds of communication includes minor cultural gaps in-between.

Fujita [2] emphasizes an importance of travel agency business in Japan for domestic economic development, and its integrity in cross-cultural communication become imperative need. Some examples show communication behavior gaps and misunderstanding between foreign tourists and local businesses in Japan, which is not rare to lead to troubles and complaints. It argues a conversation as an interactive activity using the communication model and explains a communication noise of cultural differences regarding an information transmittance. Hence it is stated cross-cultural communication issues are an urgent task among the tour industry, and the government officials and colleges of tourism are to improve communicative competency and foreign language proficiency as for the tourism host country.

2.2 Automatic Speech Recognition and Machine Translation

Computer mediated communication specialists have developed a variety of support and technique over the decades. Audio conference supporting systems have worked on collaboration in a distance call and multiparty conferences. Pan et al. [3] append real-time transcript on TV news programs and audio using an automatic speech recognition (ASR) system and found NNS comprehension significantly improved for both audio and audio with video conditions when real-time transcription is provided. Pan [4] also finds ASR creates imperfect transcripts including errors, which impairs NNS comprehension compared to the perfect transcripts.

Gao et al. [5] investigates effects of public and automated transcript with ASR between native and non-native English speakers in a story telling task conversation among triad. It states publicly shared transcripts enhanced the quality of group communication and clarify NS speech by contrast with limited transcript locked up NNS's recognition. Gao et al. [6] utilizes the keyword highlighting on machine translation (MT) in multilingual collaboration in brain storming tasks. It indicates the highlighting essential portion enhances intelligibleness and quality of collaboration with subjective impressions by all means.

Yamashita [7] compares regular communication to MT mediated communication with referring behavior that assists MT quality in multilingual tangram task conversation. This research reveals difficulties in establishing common ground via MT with referring communication despite using English as a common language realizes more accurate communication between a follower and guiders in tangram matching tasks. Miyabe [8] investigates the cost of back translation repair on MT to show the extent of imprecision of MT. This research refers to improvements over six times could be required through the trials although its repair cost is dependent on the original sentences' accuracy and cross-culture collaboration accuracy. In sum showing perfect transcript in real time still have been developing technology in bidirectional natural language conversation.

2.3 Audio and Text Communication

As its reported in ASR and MT researches, provision of literal information significantly improves NNS comprehension. Hirai [9] shows strong correlation between second language learners' optimal listening rate and reading rate in comparison to similarity of the first language optimal listening rates and reading rates among college students. Takagi [10] refers to the process of note taking for a medical purpose in interviewing and counseling. Such conversation shares hand writing characters on a paper between a doctor and a patient. Okamoto [11] develops the system to visualize some pictures along with cultural proper nouns to support dyadic intercultural communication. System enhances direct face to face (FTF) communication and comprehension with verbal and visual clues.

Clark [12] declares producing an utterance has a cost that varies from medium to medium. Speaking or gesture is the quickest that takes the least effort, typing on a computer keyboard is slower that takes more effort, and writing by hand is slowest and takes the most effort.

Echenique et al. [13] investigates comparison of video and audio with transcript for NNS comprehension in tangram matching triad conversation in English. ASR substitutes NS typing on a computer keyboard as real time transcripts. Consequently both of NS and NNS establish common ground and enhance comprehension in audio with NS typed transcript that shows essential portion.

Chapanis [14] compares some modes of communication in problem-solving tasks such as FTF, Televoice and Teletype, and the experiments discoveres voice with typing are much more likely to share and exchange information than communicators in FTF or voice only communication. It shows details the interaction and communicators in modes of Communication Rich, Voice, Handwriting, Typewriting by experienced typists and Typewriting by Inexperienced typists, which discoveres counterintuitive results that typing skill of communicators is not significantly affect accuracy and duration of time to solve decision-making problem in a conversation. Accurately typed material is not important for interactive communicators in a task-oriented conversation.

2.4 Successful Intercultural Communication with Common Ground

Yamashita [7] argues effectual and accurate intercultural communication referring Common Ground Theory. According to Clark [12] Common Ground is so basic to communicate of two people working together both the coordination of content and process. Shared information, knowledge, beliefs and assumptions are coordination content of a collective activity between a speaker and a listener moment by moment. Contribution to a conversation presents evidence of understanding utterance in shape of forming initiating the answer and accepting information.

2.5 Purpose and Hypotheses

Previous studies show cross-cultural communication often cause misunderstanding and ineffectual communication. Thus it is important not only to establish conversational sequence but also to accomplish mutual understanding. Since intercultural conversation consists of people from different languages and culture, they are mutually incapable of understanding each other and those of other language face difficulty to keep up with the conversation in real time. This ineffectual communication demands assistance on a conversation that contributes to share the content accurately with people of limited language proficiency to accomplish higher task performance. In this paper we proposes a method to pursue comprehension and contribution on dyadic collaboration and achieve interactive and natural human communication in cross-cultural transaction. Purpose of study is to investigate effects of the proposed method that NS typing the essential portion of a conversation on a computer keyboard to support NNS comprehension of the content. Intercultural dyadic teleconference presents provision of textual essence of words/phrases (Keyword) so that it works as an integral function of the textual reference and voice in teleconference. To examine its effects on a conversation we hypothesize below and test their validation through the quantitative and qualitative data analyses. According to Gao et al. [23], accurate comprehension of NS message accelerates NNS own communication. Therefore *H1* is hypothesized when experiment participants utilize the method and increase modality of conversation. *H2* is derived from a research that is about group communication enhancement using technology [5, 24]. Previous studies show that collaborative tasks and group performance are influenced by technologies, information cues from partners and impression of work context, and those cues convey different collaborative task performance and perception of participants. Hence *H2* is hypothesized to investigate the influence of the proposed method on NS and also dyadic conversation as a whole.

H1: NNS apprehends a conversation and improves own communication when NS utilizes the method.

H2: The method also works for NS when a conversation becomes easily comprehensible.

3   Method

The method is that NS types the keywords (Key-Typing) of a conversation on a computer keyboard to support NNS comprehension of the content. Keyword is an essential portion of the speech or words/phrases that suppose to be hard to apprehend for NNS. The method targets NNS to pursue not only comprehension but also communication enhancement simultaneously. Typed letters along with NS voice provide a function of self-reference of literal information and natural human support in teleconference. The method increases modality of a conversation, that is a simple task of NS becomes a useful assistance for NNS. Reasons and advantages of the method are described as follows;

Spontaneity. NS spontaneously key-types with talking by self-motivation and it doesn't deteriorate natural human communication as well as assisting NNS communication.

Validity. NS pays attention and considers reasonably what to type depends on the context. NNS refers to the key-typed characters only if NS remarks are unclear and keep an eye on somewhere incomprehensible. The method effectively utilizes human resource on computer-mediated communication.

Versatility. Simplicity of the method allows flexible, adoptable and user-friendly system for everybody. ASR and MT are exclusive for someone affordable and also produces higher rate of word errors than NS Key-Typing. Those technological malfunctions of presentation compound NNS comprehension and overload NNS cognition such as thinking, correcting, reading, listening and talking during a conversation.

4   Experiment

4.1   Overview

Using all experimental process on a computer, conversation experiments were executed under two different conditions. One was NS Key-Typing condition that NS types an essential portion of speech on a computer keyboard, and the other was the control condition that was a conversation that nobody types on a computer keyboard *Ceteris Paribus*. Experimental design was a single factor two-level and between subjects. NS and NNS were randomly distributed to organize dyads and 16 pairs participated in both conditions. The conversation tasks and its order were also balanced between subjects, and every single pair participated in both of conditions within a day.

4.2   Participants

The experiment participants were 16 people of Native Japanese speakers and the same number of non-native speakers. The native speakers were all Japanese who were born and grew up in Japan. Non-native speakers were international students from China whose Japanese Language Proficiency Test N1 average score were 118.9, and they had studied Japanese for 4 years on average. The JLPT N1 requires competency to understand Japanese. Can-Do Self-Evaluation Survey of JLPT [15] refers less than 50 % of N1 successful examinees' bottom one-third near the passing line thinks they can express their opinions in discussion. Demographic survey asking Japanese competency of international students rated average 3.5 out of 7 by self-evaluation. Differences in Japanese competency were randomly spread over the conditions and were arbitrary organized according with participants' schedule and availability. Gender distribution was 17 male and 15 female, and their average age was 25.3. Native speakers' average age was 26.6, 12 graduate students, 2 undergraduate students, and 2 were faculty members. Chinese students' average age was 24, 6 graduate students and 10 undergraduate students. The participants were randomly distributed into pairs throughout between-subject conditions.

4.3   Materials

Laboratory Environment. The pair seated at the PC tables back to back (BTB) in the laboratory, which was a simulation environment to keep deploying audible space and remove mechanical noise and distortion of teleconference. In front of each participant there was a 39 inch monitor, a mouse, a keyboard and a microphone extended from a 15 inch laptop (PC) to allow experimenters to operate with sitting behind the large monitor and participant to use extended materials. Single video camera captured the entire laboratory space including experimenters' figures. Another two cameras tracked each participant's upper body from the side, which captured action of PC usage as well as their conversation. Desktop screen and conversation voice were synchronously captured by computer software (Fig. 1).

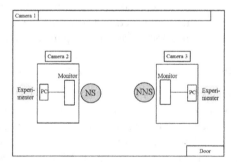

Fig. 1. Laboratory environment.

Software and Equipment. Each PC with turned off speaker, and microphone was simply used for voice recording. PC connected to the intramural LAN network and was synchronized with the other PC on Skype. Skype's Share-screen feature was enabled to show only a Key-Typing window for experiment. NS typed keywords were synchronously shared on NNS PC monitor through the network. Monitor showed two MS Word 2013 windows, the left was for Key-Typing and the right was for task-oriented information that included supplemental reading materials provided and revised beforehand. Allocating two different windows separately on 39-inch monitor side by

Fig. 2. Software and equipment.

side, the PC setup simplified and reduced the participants' physical load. Typed data of MS Word were saved after a conversation for analyses (Fig. 2).

Procedure. Conversational tasks were to debate the pros. and cons. of nuclear electric power generation and capital punishment system. Debate was one of an interactive activity that the pairs expressed agreement or disagreement in a logical manner, and these were well-known and commonly used debate topics. To adopt contentious and divisive problems for both of pros. and cons., each participant chose own role at the beginning of the experiment. There was no judge who determined a winning side of a debate because all participants did not have a debate training for an educational practice, participants thereby conducted it as a sort of a conversation. Supplemental reading materials were distributed to both sides of agreement and disagreement that provided definition of terminologies, major issues and representative opinions as a common sense for a self-guide. Participants then composed and modified the reading material on PC according to own opinion and did not see also the opponent's role material. The given time was 7 min for each round, which was a predetermined period according to our preliminary. The combination of topics and conditions were balanced between subjects.

1. *Preparation.* Participants sat at the PC tables back to back (BTB) in the laboratory, and experimenters were seated behind the large monitor to ask participant to use a PC following the instruction. Participants filled out the consent forms and demographic surveys that asked age, nationality, gender and so on, and then left personal belongings including smartphones on a table. Written Experimental Procedures were handed and experimenters orally explained operations. International students also received instruction in Chinese unless s/he understood instruction in Japanese. All participants confirmed there were two debate problems in different situation and post experimental surveys that asked some memory of conversation in advance.

2. *Instruction.* Experimenter asked participants to wear a microphone and checks its located upright position, also instructed that Key-Type condition took a little time for practice when the PC left-side screen was synchronized with interlocutors PC. NS types keywords during talking and keywords were not an entire message as a whole but a part of an important point.

3. *Tasks and Surveys.* Two rounds of 7 min debate were videotaped, screen captured, and voice recorded. 3 kinds of post-experimental surveys were conducted.

5 Measures

To investigate effects of NS Key-Typing on a conversation between NS and NNS of Japanese, the experiment was videotaped. The proposed method was that NS types the essential portion of a conversation on a computer keyboard to support NNS comprehension of the content. We tested the hypotheses utilizing analyses both of quantitative and qualitative data collection.

5.1 Observation

Coding of Evidence in Grounding. We coded a conversation line by line based on Clark's Common Ground Theory, Evidence in Grounding [12]. The Coding scheme shows three different types of conversational sequences during discussion, which ensures dyads present process of grounding in shape of forming initiating the answer and accepting information.

Shared-knowledge Retention. Participants consented in advance that there were two debate topics in two different situations, and each round had the post-experimental survey that asked some memory about the conversation content. This survey was to explore comprehension and retention of the conversation content from memory of both of NS and NNS.

5.2 Survey

Workload. NASA-TLX [16] is a subjective workload assessment tool consists of 6 descriptive rating scales. Paper version NASA-TLX rating sheet evaluates each factor from 0 (low)-100 (high). Simple usage of testing only calculates an average score ratings [17]. Experimenters interviewed detailed comments about the ratings thereafter.

Questionnaire Survey. Questionnaire survey assesses participants' perception via 23 scales of 5 major attributions such as interlocutor's communication, own communication, collaboration, mood and technology. Every single scales are retrieved from previous works and modified for the current study. [18–22, 24].

Table 1. NASA Task Load Index.

Title	Descriptions
Mental Demand	How mentally demanding was the task?
Physical Demand	How physically demanding was the task?
Temporal Demand	How hurried or rushed was the pace of the task?
Performance	How successful were you in accomplishing what you were asked to do?
Effort	How hard did you have to work to accomplish your level of performance?
Frustration	How insecure, discouraged, irritated, stressed, and annoyed were you?

Interview. Detailed description about the experiment was also asked to obtain credible proof of N/NS assessment. Interview items were prepared beforehand based on our preliminary study. Bilingual students were interviewed in dominant language either Japanese or Chinese.

6   Result

6.1   Evidence in Grounding

Conversation was transcribed for the purpose of coding based on Evidence in Grounding [12]. In accordance with Common Ground Theory, Evidence in Grounding Coding Manual on Table 2 along with the context of discussion was founded as a standard of a conversational sequence presenting evidence of understanding utterance in shape of forming initiating the answer and accepting information. Obvious forms of Positive Evidence presents three most common schema as Acknowledgement, Relevant Next Turn, and Continued Attention. Current computer-mediated communication hardly seeks Continued Attention through Eye gaze that is *Ad Infinitum*, we thereby did not count it (Table 2).

Table 2. Evidence in Grounding Coding Manual.

Category	Definition	Example	Example of current study
Acknowl-edgement	Much of back-channel responses	B: Um well I ha((d't)) done any English at *all,* A: *((1 syll))* B: You know, since O-level. A: Yea. B: And I went to some second year seminars, where there are only about half a dozen people, A: *m* B: *and* they discussted what ((a)) word was. A: **m** B: **and-** what's a sentence. That's *ev* en more difficult. A: *yeah* yeah - (and so on)	NNS:m- murd(.)Murderer NS:Yes NNS:m-Um criminal, criminals take someone's, life, that,this, not this, NS:Yes NNS:Not only this, his family,al(.)all,very,m-a-sad(.)was sad[that NS:Yes] NNS:and, m(.)m- m- I agree with the death penal-ty because, that, terrible, m-(.)cruel, terribly, m-for bad people(.)m-and. this(.)m-social safety,rest of,for safe community,m-that, danger, to society(.) NS:Yes NNS:Natio,um,for people, NS:Yes NNS:I think extremly(.)dangerous NS:Yes NNS:For safe,community,that,this,that, dangerous,m-th,m-this,m-crime(.)case, NS:Yes NNS:m(.)I think crime prevention,um,that is very (.)that,is required. NS:Yes(.)uh(.)I understand.
Relevant Next Turn	Adjacency Pairs	A: Did you know mother had been drinking - B: I don't think, mother had been drinking at ali .	NNS:Well,what kind of punishment(.) is there, for example? NS:In Japan, (.) there is life imprisonment
	Repetition with an Acknowl-edgement	A: F. six two B: F six two A: Yes B: Thanks very much	NNS:g(.)some,(1)what(.)execution, is difficult, I think. (.) NS:Execution is, difficult ? NNS:Yes(.) NS:m-,I see :
Continued Attention	Attention through Eye gaze	X	X

Two experimenters worked independently for coding, one was Japanese and the other was Japanese-Chinese bilingual speaker. Inter-coder agreement was good (85 %) for the first time, and both data sets showed the significant difference between conditions[$p = .016$, $Z = -2.413$]. Afterword coders discussed and found one's coding scheme was a little different from the Coding Manual, thus justified and improved inter-coder agreement higher (90 %). Key-Typing had significantly larger number of Evidence in Grounding [$p = .001$, $SE = 3.09$, $t(15) = 4.04$], and showed large effect size (Cohen's $d = 1.00$). Figure 3 showed average numbers (times/pair) of Evidence in Grounding.

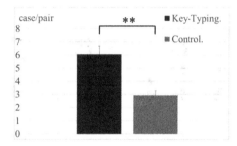

Fig. 3. Evidence in Grounding Coding result. (N=16; P<0.05:**)

6.2 Shared-Knowledge Retention

Participants composed their own writings on PC without any references but only by recalling their memory that they assumed to share information and knowledge with an interlocutor by words, phrases, or sentences on a conversation as much as they can individually. We double-checked them through the video and count the number of common information that are the same with the interlocutor's writing to compare them between conditions. The average value on Key-Typing condition produced significantly larger number of shared-knowledge retention [$p = .000$, $SE = 1.15$, $t(15) = 8.89$]. The average value is shown on Fig. 4.

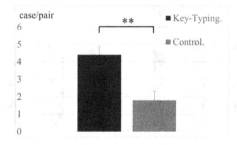

Fig. 4. Shared-Knowledge retention. (N=16; P<0.05:**)

6.3 Workload

It shows a score average and the significant difference by factors between conditions in Fig. 5. Scores were not weighted averaged but simply averaged throughout each factor [17]. NNS significantly decreased Frustration in Key-Typing condition [p = .01, Z = −2.566], we therefore asked for description in the interview. NS on the other hand significantly increased Physical demand [p = .038, Z = −2.079], Effort [p = .022, t(15) = 2.54], and Frustration[p= .049, Z= −1.968].

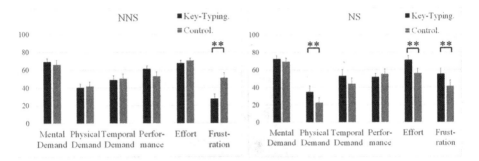

Fig. 5. Workload. (N=16; P<0.05:**)

6.4 Survey

Questionnaire survey assesses participants' perception via 23 scales of 5 major attributions such as interlocutor's communication, own communication, conversation, mood and technology. Every single scale was retrieved from the previous works and slightly modified for the current study. Scales were served in random order to cancel out the order effect on participants, and they responded questions on a scale of 1 (strongly disagree) to 7 (strongly agree). In Fig. 6. scores were averaged for 5 attributions

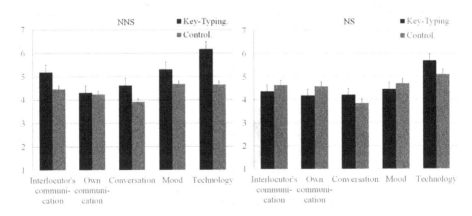

Fig. 6. Questionnaire survey result. (N=16; P<0.05:**)

throughout 23 scales such as "It was easy to understand what an opponent said." and so on. The questions formed a reliable scale of Interlocutors communication [Cronbach's α = .75], Own communication [α =.71], Conversation [α = .77], Mood [α = .77] and Techonology [α = .78]. NNS rated higher in Key-Typing condition for factors of Interlocutor's communication, Own communication, and Conversation. NS highly rated Conversation and Technology of Key-Typing.

6.5   Interview

At the end of the experiment, we interviewed each participant about Frustration factor of Workload. Most of NNS testified the Key-Typing method eased anxiety caused by much of terminologies in debate, and promoted comprehension of NS utterances. On the contrary some of NS remarked it was hard to type during talking.

7   Discussion

7.1   Evidence in Grounding

Conversation with Key-Typing method has significantly large number of Evidence in Grounding compared to control condition, and shows large effect size. The method solves problem of understanding and difficulty on a conversation, and also have interlocutors realized mutual understanding. Utterances found a sequence presenting evidence of understanding in shape of initiating the answer and accepting information, Key-Typing method hence naturally promoted discourse comprehension with courteous consideration utilizing human resource initiating textuality. We tested significance and it was supported *H1*:NNS apprehends a conversation and improves own communication when NS utilizes the method. NNS utterance was not supported in the current study although it was assessed NNS own communication was highly rated in Key-Typing condition. Ongoing process of analyses may describe it in respect of timing and utterance in chronological order.

7.2   Shared-Knowledge Retention

The average value of Key-Typing condition produces larger number of shared-knowledge retention on Fig. 5. This indicates Key-Typing conversation presents accurate information transaction and it is kept in their mind. Conversation is interactive activity and it is beneficial for both sides when information is accurately shared and commonly retained, which exists in-between participants. Hence it is supported *H2*:The method also works for NS regarding a conversation become easily comprehensible.

8 Limitations and Future Works

Comparing to computer researches that have developed ASR and MT, Key-Typing method requires human resource to input. Key-Typing method takes sometime to type on a keyboard, which may cause Production cost [12] that is typing is slower than speaking or gesture even though Key-Typing conversation mediates simultaneous media. Such cost would have to be minimized when further analyses suggest an effective methodology of typing in respect of timing and content. It also may be applicable not only for NS and NNS but also every kinds of communication in every natural languages and occasions across the world, as Novinger said every communication includes minor cultural gaps and language plays an important role [1]. Since the previous study has examined how audio with transcript influences NNS comprehension in triad conversation using English and show that NNS comprehension is improved [13], NS typing on a computer keyboard would be possible to apply to other natural languages. We would like to keep working on analysis to expand research range of spectrum of the method so that it would be universally exercised in interactive dialogue where is unaffordable of expensive technologies.

9 Conclusion

In this paper we proposed a method to pursue comprehension and contribution on dyadic collaboration and achieve interactive and natural human communication in cross-cultural transaction. Purpose of study was to investigate effect of the proposed method that NS types the essential portion of a conversation on a computer keyboard to support NNS comprehension of the content. The Key-Typing method enhanced mutual understanding in point of presence of Evidence in Grounding and promoting retention of shared-knowledge. Overall cost of NS keyword-typing resulted in benefit of improving mutual understanding and increasing shared knowledge. By all means questionnaire survey showed higher ratings on factor of participants' perception of conversation and technology through the experiment, and the interview assessment obtained much of reviews that Key-Typing method would be going to perform effectively on a conversation including daily occasion of potential cross-cultural communication.

Acknowledgements. This research was partially supported by the JSPS Grants-in-Aid for Scientific Research No. 26330218.

References

1. Novinger, T.: Intercultural Communication: A Practical Guide. University of Texas Press, Austin (2001). ISBN 0292755716
2. Fujita, R.: Yokoso japan!: the significance of intercultural communication competence. J. Commun. Stud. **30**, 3–14 (2009)

3. Pan, Y., Jiang, D., Picheny, M., Qin, Y.: Effects of real-time transcription on non-native speaker's comprehension in computer-mediated communications. In: Proceeding CHI 2009 Proceedings of the SIGCHI Conference on Human Factors in Computing Systems, pp. 2353–2356 (2009)

4. Pan, Y., Jiang, D., Yao, L., Picheny, M., Qin, Y.: Effects of automated transcription quality on non-native speakers' comprehension in real-time computer-mediated communication. In: CHI 2010 Proceedings of the SIGCHI Conference on Human Factors in Computing Systems, pp. 1725–1734 (2010)

5. Gao, G., Yamashita, N., Hautasaari, A., Echenique, A., Fussell, S.R.: Effects of public vs. private automated transcripts on multiparty communication between native and non-native english speakers. In: CHI 2014 Proceedings of the SIGCHI Conference on Human Factors in Computing Systems, pp. 843–852 (2014)

6. Gao, G., Wang, H., Cosley, D., Fussell, S.R.: Same Translation but different experience: the effects of highlighting on machine-translated conversation. In: CHI 2013 Proceedings of the SIGCHI Conference on Human Factors in Computing Systems pp. 449–458 (2013)

7. Yamashita, N., Inaba, R., Kuzuoka, H., Ishida, T.: Difficulties in establishing common ground in multiparty groups using machine translation. In: CHI 2009, April 4–9, Boston, MA, USA, p. 680 (2009)

8. Miyabe, M., Yoshino, T., Shigenobu, T.: Effects of undertaking translation repair using back translation. The IEICE Trans. Inf. Syst. (Japanese edetion), J90-D(12), 3141–3150, 2007

9. Hirai, A.: The relationship between listening and reading rates of Japanese EFL learners. Modern Lang. J. **83**(3), 367–384 (1999)

10. Nishizaka, A., Takagi, T., Kawashima, M.: Conversation analysis of woman's medicine, studies of technosociety. Bunka-shobo Hakubun-sha. [in Japanese] (2008) 6. ISBN 4830111283

11. Okamoto, K., Yoshino, T.: development and evaluation of face-to-face intercultural communication support system using related information of nouns in conversation. J. Inf. Process. Soc. Jpn. **52**(3), 1213–1223 (2011). [in Japanese] p. 1219

12. Clark, H.H., Brennan, S.E.: Grounding in communication. In: Resnick, L.B., Levine, J.M., Teasley, J.S.D. (eds.) Perspectives on Socially Shared Cognition, American Psychological Association, ISBN 1-55798-376-3 (1991)

13. Echenique, A., Yamashita, N., Kuzuoka, H., Hautasaari, A.: Effects of video and text support on grounding in multilingual multiparty audio conferencing. In: CABS 2014, August 20–22, Kyoto, Japan (2014)

14. Chapanis, A.: Human Factors in Teleconferencing Systems. Final Report, John Hopkins University, Baltimore, Maryland. Department of Psychology, p. 53, 30 November 1976

15. Japanese Language Proficiency Test. http://www.jlpt.jp/e/about/levelsummary.html

16. NASA-TLX: Task Load Index. http://humansystems.arc.nasa.gov/groups/tlx/

17. Tokunaga, R., Hagiwara, T., Kagaya, S., Onodera, Y.: Effects of talking through cellular telephone on driving behavior. Infrastruct. Plann. Rev. **17**, 995–1000 (2000)

18. Liu, R., Inoue, T.: Application of An Anthropomorphic Dining Agent to Idea Generation UBICOMP 2014 ADJUNCT, SEPTEMBER 13–17, SEATTLE, WA, USA p. 610 (2014)

19. Inoue, T.: Naturalistic control of conversation by meal: induction of attentive listening attitude through uneven meal distribution in Co-dining. In: UBICOMP 2014 ADJUNCT, SEPTEMBER 13–17, SEATTLE, WA, USA, p. 605 (2014)

20. Nishimura, R., Kitaoka, N., Nakagawa, S.: Response timing and prosody change modeling in conversations and their application to a spoken dialog system. In: Proceeding of the 48th SIG-SLUD of the Japanese Society for Artificial Intelligence, 37–42, 2006-11-16, SIG-SLUD-A602-07, pp. 37–42

21. Takahashi, T., Hamazaki, M., Takeda, H.: Web community system mediated by avatar-like agents. In: Proceedings of the 15th Annual Conference of JSAI, 2001, JSAI01, p. 80 (2011)
22. Okazaki, K., Kanda, T.: The effects of conversational fillers by virtual agents. In: The 76th National Convention of Information Processing Society of Japan, 1, 237–238 (2014)
23. Gao, G., Xu, B., Hau, D., Yao, Z., Cosley, D., Fussell, S.R.: Two is better than one: improving multilingual collaboration by giving two machine translation outputs. In: Proceedings of the 18th ACM Conference on Computer Supported Cooperative Work and Social Computing, pp. 852–863
24. Diamant, E.I., Fussell, S.R., Lo, F.: Where did we turn wrong?: unpacking the effect of culture and technology on attributions of team performance. In: Proceedings of 2008 ACM Conference on Computer Supported Cooperative Work, pp. 383–392 (2008)

How Non-native Speakers Perceive Listening Comprehension Problems: Implications for Adaptive Support Technologies

Xun Cao[1,2(✉)], Naomi Yamashita[2], and Toru Ishida[1]

[1] Kyoto University, Kyoto, Japan
`xun@ai.soc.i.kyoto-u.ac.jp, ishida@i.kyoto-u.ac.jp`
[2] NTT Communication Science Laboratories, Kyoto, Japan
`naomiy@acm.org`

Abstract. Previous studies have suggested many technologies to support non-native speaker comprehension in real-time communication. However, such technologies may impose an extra burden on non-native speakers (NNSs) if they do not match their current needs. To design a system that adapts to the changing needs of NNSs, we need to understand the types of problems NNSs face and how these problems are perceived by them. To explore such issues, we conducted a laboratory experiment with 40 NNSs (and 20 native speakers as a control group) who engaged in a listening task. During the task, the participants pressed a button whenever they encountered a comprehension problem. Next they explained each problem, the point at which they recognized the problem, and for how long it persisted. Our analysis identified twelve types of listening comprehension problems, which we further classified into three patterns based on their persistence and the time taken to perceive them. Our findings have implications for designing adaptive technologies to support listening comprehension of NNSs in real-time communication.

Keywords: Non-native speakers · Listening comprehension problems · Adaptive support

1 Introduction

More and more global organizations are forming multinational teams so that people from different language backgrounds can work together to generate new ideas, solve problems, and make decisions. Even though multinational teams offer potential for gathering various creative ideas from different cultural perspectives, they also run the risk of suffering from various barriers [3]. One such barrier is caused by language [19]. To communicate and collaborate, multinational teams often adopt a common language [4]. However, a common language does not necessarily ensure effective communication [17].

Non-native speakers (NNSs) often face comprehension difficulties when listening to native speakers' (NSs') speech [2, 30]. Due to the need to process continuous streams of speech during listening, even when NNSs encounter a comprehension problem, they

© Springer Science+Business Media Singapore 2016
T. Yoshino et al. (Eds.): CollabTech 2016, CCIS 647, pp. 89–104, 2016.
DOI: 10.1007/978-981-10-2618-8_8

cannot dedicate the time and resources to resolve such problems [22, 25]. As a result, NNSs often miss parts of the speech, and cannot comprehend the full meaning of what was said.

Previous works have proposed many technologies for supporting NNS comprehension in real-time communication, such as providing a speech translation system that translates NSs' spoken language into NNSs' language [18, 29], providing NNSs with real-time automatic speech recognition (ASR) transcripts as supplemental information for their comprehension [6, 21, 32], and adding artificial delays between NSs to provide more processing time for NNSs [31]. Some researchers even suggested providing NNSs with multiple supports, for example, automated transcripts and bilingual dictionaries, so that they can choose whichever support they wish to use that matches their needs [7]. However, providing multiple supports to a user and allowing him/her to make a choice is not necessarily the best solution – while it allows a user to deal with various kinds of problems, it often imposes extra burden to the user. Particularly in the case of a non-native user, choosing a support when encountering a listening comprehension problem could be burdensome because he/she is already overwhelmed by processing large amounts of speech information in a limited time (e.g., when listening to a lecture or in a meeting with many NSs) [25].

Our goal is to design an adaptive system, which automatically changes the type of support based on the NNSs' changing needs so that it does not impose additional burden on them. According to previous studies [5, 12], to design such a problem adaptive system, we first need to understand the types of real-time comprehension problems faced by NNSs and how these problems are perceived by them. In other words, (1) what types of listening comprehension problems emerge when NNSs are listening to native speech? (2) when do NNSs notice each problem and how long do such problems persist? In this paper, we particularly focus on NNSs' listening comprehension problems that occur during their cognitive processing of speech input. We decided to focus on the cognitive aspect of their listening comprehension problems because the accumulation of these problems leads to cognitive overload, which is the most common and fundamental problem faced by any NNS [1, 2, 9].

To answer the research questions stated above, we conducted a laboratory experiment with 40 NNSs (and 20 NSs as a control group) who engaged in a listening task followed by in-depth interviews. During the task, the participants pressed a button whenever they encountered anything about which they were unclear or did not understand: comprehension problems. In the interviews, they explained what kind of problems they faced, at what point during the listening task they recognized the problems, and for how long these problems persisted. Through an exploratory analysis of the interview data, we identified twelve types of listening comprehension problems, which we further classified into three patterns based on their persistence and the time taken to perceive them.

In the remainder of this paper, we first review previous studies and discuss how our study extends them. We then describe our study that identified the comprehension problems faced by NNSs during a listening comprehension task. We conclude with a discussion of the implications of our findings for supporting/facilitating NNS comprehension during real-time listening.

2 Background

In this section, we first review technologies that support NNS comprehension in real-time communication; we then introduce previous works that examined the listening comprehension problems of NNSs.

2.1 Technologies Supporting NNS Comprehension in Real-Time Communication

Compared to asynchronous communication, NNSs face more difficulties in real-time communication. Although in asynchronous communication NNSs have more time to resolve their problems by accessing various language resources or services and considering the context [13, 22], in real-time communication they often cannot dedicate enough time and resources to resolving their problems because they are overwhelmed by processing continuous streams of speech [25].

Previous studies, which suggested technologies to support NNS comprehension in real-time communication, mainly concentrated on speech-to-speech translation and automatic speech recognition (ASR). The most direct way to support NNS comprehension is providing a speech translation system, which transcribes NSs' speech to text, translates the text into the NNSs' language, and outputs speech synthesized from the translated text [18, 29]. However, such technology remains far from satisfactory, and the combination of recognition and translation errors often disrupts comprehension.

Another widely investigated line of support uses ASR technologies. Pan et al. showed that real-time transcripts generated by ASR technologies can improve NNS comprehension when their accuracy and delay fall within a reasonable range [21]. While Pan et al. investigated the benefits of showing ASR transcripts to NNSs in a non-interactive setting (i.e., using pre-recorded speech), Gao et al. moved a step further and showed the benefits of providing ASR transcripts in an interactive setting (i.e., real-time multiparty communication) [6]. However, despite the positive effects of introducing ASR transcripts, research has also reported that NNSs are often overwhelmed when they simultaneously listen to speeches and read transcripts with errors and delays [6, 32].

Yamashita et al. provided a different perspective for supporting NNSs in real-time communication. They investigated the benefits of providing NNSs with additional processing time by adding artificial delays in NSs' speech. They found that short silent gaps produced by such delays improved the comprehension of NNSs, but more attention and effort were required to follow the speech [31].

Overall, the proposed technologies do seem to help NNSs improve their listening comprehension. However, most had some negative effects, such as placing an additional cognitive load on NNSs. We suspect that the cognitive load could be lightened if NNSs were provided with appropriate support at more propitious timing. Indeed, researchers found that NNSs themselves developed their own strategies for effectively utilizing ASR transcripts; some reviewed the transcripts only when they were not sure if they had heard a word/phrase correctly or when they had missed some words. In most parts, they ignored the transcripts because they found it difficult to simultaneously focus on two modalities (audio and ASR transcripts) [6, 11]. This strategy implies that ASR transcripts could be useful for resolving some types of problems, but they may only impose more burdens during other parts of listening.

2.2 Listening Comprehension Problems of NNSs

To design a problem adaptive support for NNSs, we need a better understanding of the types of real-time listening comprehension problems and how NNSs perceive them.

In the second language learning field, much listening comprehension research has examined listeners' difficulties/problems while they are listening to a non-native language. Rubin conducted an extensive review of second language listening comprehension research and attributed the factors that affect listening comprehension to five characteristics: text characteristics (e.g., speech rate), interlocutor characteristics, task characteristics (e.g., task type), listener characteristics (e.g., language proficiency level, memory), and process characteristics (e.g., listening strategies) [24]. Goh offered a cognitive perspective on understanding NNSs' listening comprehension problems [9]. She used the weekly diaries of 40 students as her main data source and identified ten listening comprehension problems (Table 1).

Table 1. Listening comprehension problems identified in Goh's work [9]

Problems
1. Do not recognize words they know
2. Unable to form a mental representation from words heard
3. Cannot chunk streams of speech
4. Neglect the next part when thinking about meaning
5. Do not understand subsequent parts of input because of earlier problems
6. Concentrate too hard or unable to concentrate
7. Understand words but not the intended message
8. Confused about the key ideas in the message
9. Miss the beginning of texts
10. Quickly forget what is heard

Overall, these research studies aim for improving second language learning. The findings are used for designing effective training programs or materials to improve NNSs' listening skills [9, 28, 30]. Even though these findings are also useful for our research, we still need to extend them so that they provide more detailed understanding of how each problem is perceived by NNSs (e.g., when each problem is perceived and how long it persists). We believe such detailed understanding of each comprehension problem will provide insight for designing adaptive technologies to support NNSs in real-time listening comprehension.

To gain a detailed understanding of each comprehension problem, we decided to take an approach/method that is different from previous studies. While researchers have chosen such methods as diaries [8, 9], interviews [8, 9], questionnaires [16], and think-aloud [10] to reveal the comprehension problems faced by NNSs, they may not be suitable for our case for the following reasons: since diaries, interviews, and question-naires are based on retrospection, we are skeptical whether they can capture the detailed process of each comprehension problem (e.g., the timing when that problem is perceived by NNSs). Furthermore, transient problems, which were tentatively confusing while listening, might not be remembered at the time of retrospection if the problem was eventually resolved. As for the think-aloud approach, even though this approach might provide a deeper understanding about some comprehension problems, participants' listening experiences during the think-aloud process could be completely different from regular listening, since the think-aloud approach requires participants to explain what they were thinking while they were listening. In our study, we use a method that allows us to record the comprehension problems faced by NNSs in real time, while keeping the listening experience as close to regular listening as possible. Using the method, we uncover the types of comprehension problems faced by NNSs and how these problems are perceived during real-time listening.

3   Current Study

In this paper, we set two research questions. First, we investigate the types of compre-hension problems NNSs encounter in real-time listening. Our work builds on Goh's work, which has also focused on the cognitive aspects of NNSs' listening comprehension problems. Note that our study covers transient problems, which tentatively confused the NNSs but were eventually resolved or quickly forgotten.

RQ1 (types of real-time listening comprehension problems): What types of listening comprehension problems are identified in real-time listening?

In addition, we reveal the process of how NNSs perceive each listening comprehen-sion problem and are burdened by them. Specifically, we posed the following question:

RQ2 (persistence and identification time of each problem): When do NNSs notice each listening comprehension problem and how long do such problems persist? Do the patterns of persistence and identification time differ among different types of problems?

This information is important when designing a problem adaptive system because providing support with inappropriate/inaccurate timing might impose an extra burden on NNSs. For example, a previous study showed that delayed transcription reduced the benefits and increased the listening effort [34].

4   Method

4.1   Overview

To explore the above research questions, we used a method that allows us (i) to record NNSs' comprehension problems in real time and (ii) to scrutinize each problem by allowing the NNSs to explain each one (iii) while keeping the listening experience close to regular listening experiences.

We developed a software tool that logs participants' listening comprehension prob-lems in real time. During the listening task, participants pressed a button to indicate when they heard confusing language or they did not understand something: comprehension problems. Pressing the button marked specific places in the lecture transcripts, which were visited later to explain the details of the problems. We chose this "pressing a button" method because it has low-overhead, as suggested by previous work [15]. In addition, this method guarantees that we can record the problems NNSs faced in real time and simultaneously keep the task close to the actual listening experience.

4.2 Participants

We recruited 40 non-native English speakers (22 females, 18 males) as participants. 20 were native Japanese speakers and 20 were native Chinese speakers. Their mean age was 30.4 (SD = 9.97). Their English proficiency varied from intermediate to advanced, indicated by their Test of English for International Communication (TOEIC) scores, which ranged from 650 to 960 (M = 828, SD = 95.18). They did not identify themselves as fully proficient (M = 4.36, SD = 0.86, on a 7-point Likert scale; 1 = not proficient at all, 7 = very proficient). Their average overseas experience in English speaking countries was 0.3 years (SD = 0.54).

As a control group, we also recruited 20 native English speakers (13 males, 7 females) as participants whose mean age was 37.9 (SD = 11.98). Among these NSs, 14 were from the United States, three from Canada, two from New Zealand, and one from the United Kingdom.

4.3 Materials

Five audio clips from the Test of English as a Foreign Language (TOEFL) test were chosen as task materials. Two clips were conversations, and the other three were lectures. The length of the clips varied from two to five minutes. We chose such task materials to maintain consistency with Goh's setting, whose materials were collected from a second language listening course. The tasks were randomly assigned to each participant.

4.4 Procedure

Step 1 (real-time listening). The participants listened to the audio clip and pressed a button whenever they encountered anything about which they were unclear (i.e., comprehension problems). When the participants pressed a button, the software logged a timestamp.

Step 2 (retrospective listening). The participants listened to the same audio clip again. While listening, the computer automatically stopped at the place where they pressed the button during Step 1, using the timestamps logged by the software. At this point, the participants briefly explained what kind of problem they faced, at what point they recognized the problem, and for how long it persisted. This step helped participants re-experience the first step and recall their comprehension problems.

Step 3 (interviews). The participants were handed complete transcripts of the audio clip with markings that indicated their listening comprehension problems. Based on the marked-up transcripts, they further explained the problems they faced during the listening task. This step was designed to get more detailed information about the comprehension problems mentioned in Step 2. Interviews were conducted in each participant's native language.

4.5 Data Analysis

To identify each type of listening comprehension problem faced by the participants during the listening task, we first transcribed the interview data and removed any problems that were not directly related to their cognitive processing of speech input (e.g., lack of vocabulary). Then we classified the problems into ten categories based on Goh's work. We created a new problem category if a problem did not belong to any of the ten categories. All the interview data were coded independently by two coders, and discrepancies were discussed until an agreement was reached.

5 Findings

The results are presented as follows. First, we report all the types of listening comprehension problems that were identified in our experiment. We separately present the problems faced by non-native and native participants. Then we describe in further detail the two types of listening comprehension problems that were newly discovered in our study. Finally, we group the listening comprehension problems into three patterns based on the persistence and identification time of each problem.

5.1 Types of Listening Comprehension Problems

NNSs. RQ1 asked what types of listening comprehension problems emerged in real-time listening. To identify all the listening comprehension problems faced by non-native participants, we counted the number of times problems occurred based on the markups (times they pressed the button). In a few cases when participants described two problems for one markup, the occurrences of problems were counted as two. 513 problem occurrences were initially identified by the non-native participants. Among them, 366 problem occurrences were "cognitive problems," 144 were due to "language skills" (e.g., lack of vocabulary), and the rest were due to "situational factors" (e.g., not being able to distinguish different speakers). The average number of problem occurrences identified by each non-native participant was 2.2 times per minute.

Tables 2 and 3 provide an overview of all the problems faced by non-native participants. Table 2 shows the real-time listening comprehension problems shared by Goh's work, and Table 3 shows two newly identified problems: "confused about unexpected word appearance" and "unsure about the meaning of words." The tables show the sample excerpts extracted from our interviews and the percentage of the occurrences of each problem (i.e., number of times each problem occurred/total number of occurrences).

Table 2. Example and percentage of each listening comprehension problem faced by non-native participants: problems shared by Goh's work

Problem	Example interview excerpt	Percentage
1. Do not recognize words they know	Since I misheard "slides" as "flive," I couldn't understand it. If I had read it, I would've understood it. (NNS 2)	27%
2. Unable to form a mental representation from words heard	I didn't really understand "bubble gas." Although I caught both words, I couldn't form a picture of them. (NNS 6)	20%
3. Cannot chunk streams of speech	I couldn't catch "cause you loved them too much." I couldn't divide that chunk into separate words. (NNS 9)	15%
4. Neglect the next part when thinking about meaning	While I was wondering what "bubble gas" meant, I missed the subsequent words. They just drifted away, so I gave up. (NNS 10)	5%
5. Do not understand subsequent parts of input because of earlier problems	I couldn't understand this part: "scientist decided that the best place to see a whole root system would be to grow it, where." Maybe the lecturer is asking a question, but since I couldn't get that part, I also couldn't understand the answer to it. (NNS 13)	5%
6. Concentrate too hard or unable to concentrate	I couldn't concentrate. I was almost panicking. (NNS 19)	5%
7. Understand words but not the intended message	I could understand the meaning. But I couldn't understand why he repeated the words. It seems that I didn't get the point.... (NNS 32)	4%
8. Confused about the key ideas in the message	Until now, the lecturer has been talking about "growing stuff in water," "bubble gas through water," and "growing plants in soil." Now, she's saying that giving too much water will kill a plant... I don't understand. What on earth did they want to say? (NNS 19)	4%
9. Miss the beginning of texts	I wasn't quite ready and missed the beginning of the lecture. (NNS 10)	2%
10. Quickly forget what is heard	When I heard "bubble gas," I thought I understood. But when the lecturer continued to the next sentence, I suddenly forgot what it was. I got confused whether it was gas or gassed water. (NNS 16)	1%

Table 3. Example and percentage of newly identified listening comprehension problems faced by non-native participants: transient problems

Problem	Example interview excerpt	Percentage
11. Confused about unexpected word appearance	"Commercially" came out of the blue. I got confused when I heard it because I thought they were talking about stuff happening in a lab. (NNS 1)	7%
12. Unsure about the meaning of words	When I heard "root system," I wasn't sure what it meant. I came up with many possibilities. It could be the roots of plants, but when combined with "system," I got confused. I thought it might have something to do with a Linux file system or something related to a chart in linguistics. (NNS 10)	5%

NSs. We did the same count and categorization for the listening comprehension problems faced by native participants. Only twelve problem occurrences were identified. Among them, ten were "cognitive problems," and the other two were due to "situational factors." The average number of problem occurrences identified by each native participant was 0.27 times per minute.

Out of 20 native participants, eleven reported that the listening material was quite clear to them and they did not encounter any comprehension problem. Nine participants reported confusion, but most solved their confusion quickly and fairly easily during the listening tasks. For example, one participant mentioned:

The first time the lecturer said, "bubble water," I was like "huh?" But then she explained it (self-corrected it), I was like "ah." (NS7).

Difference between NNSs and NSs. Overall, although the NSs did encounter slight minor and infrequent listening comprehension problems, they resolved them fairly easily.

In contrast, the NNSs in our study faced many problems during the listening tasks. From the interviews with them, a snowball effect of listening comprehension problems seemed to occur during their listening, meaning that one problem triggered another problem. For example, one non-native participant reported that due to his uncertainty about the correct meaning of "root system," he couldn't understand the subsequent parts of the lecture well. Others reported that, when thinking about the meaning of particular words, they missed subsequent speech. Some also mentioned that failing to catch some parts of the speech created concentration lapses. Such snowball effects of listening comprehension problems were only found in the NNS listening.

5.2 Transient Problems Identified by NNSs

As shown in Table 3, since 12 % of the problems did not fit into Goh's categorization, we created two new categories, each of which we describe in further details below.

Confused about unexpected word appearance. Previous research has indicated that people generally use information from a prior discourse to rapidly predict specific upcoming words as the discourse unfolds [20, 23]. However, a failed prediction hinders the processing of an unexpected word or phrase [27]. While NSs can quickly resolve problems and catch up with the current speech, NNSs tend to have difficulties recovering from such problems [25].

In our experiment, participants reported that they got confused about the appearance of a word or phrase that seemed unrelated to the current context. For example, in one lecture, the lecturer introduced an experiment of "growing plants in water to observe the root systems" but then slipped into a tangent about "how hydroponics is popular commercially." However, many non-native participants had difficulty understanding the connection between the tangent and the main topic. Some non-native participants were confused by the term "commercially." One participant explained:

I know the word "commercially," but I couldn't understand why it appeared in this context. I wondered if it had another meaning related to plant systems (NNS 15).

The non-native participant lost confidence in his ability to understand the context when he heard the word "commercially." Although this participant regained his confidence (i.e., he could follow the speech again) when the tangent was over, such problem was problematic because it confused him and sapped his confidence.

Unsure about the meaning of words. Some participants in our study got confused about the correct meaning of words/phrases that carried multiple meanings. Especially when such words/phrases were keywords that appeared repeatedly in the speech, the problem bothered them until they determined the correct meaning. Most participants in our study gradually solved their doubts using context information. When the words/phrases that confused the participants appeared only once, they tended to be easily forgotten.

Participants also reported confusion when they encountered homonyms. For example, in one listening task, the lecturer mainly discussed how big root systems of plants can be. "Root system," as one of the keywords, appeared several times during the lecture. However, the keyword "root system" confused some of the non-native participants:

At first, I couldn't tell whether this "root" meant "the root of plants" or "the route" of something. I finally realized that it meant "the root of plants" somewhere about here when I heard "the best place to see" (NNS 3).

Although they had a guess or multiple candidates in mind, they were not sure if their guess was correct, or which candidate was correct. As a result, they had to think hard to resolve the problem by listening to subsequent speech, which burdened them and sometimes triggered other problems.

5.3   Persistence and Identification Time of Problems

RQ2 asked the following two questions: (a) When do NNSs notice each listening comprehension problem and how long do such problems persist? (b) Do the patterns of persistence and identification time differ among different types of problems?

To answer these questions, we calculated the duration of each problem (T(dur)) and the response time taken to press the button (T(res)) by counting the number of words spoken in each time period. In Fig. 1, for example, T(dur) is ten words and T(res) is three words.

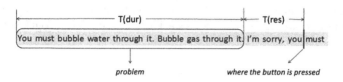

Fig. 1. Measuring "duration of each problem" (T(dur)) and "response time taken to press button" (T(res))

Figure 2 shows how T(dur) and T(res) differed among various types of problems. Each dot represents the average T(dur) and T(res) values of each problem. To determine whether the problems can be divided into different patterns, we carried out single-linkage hierarchical clustering [14]. Based on the optimal grouping of the problems, results showed that the problems can be classified into three clusters: "immediate listening comprehension problems" (74 % of all problem occurrences), "extant listening comprehension problems" (25 %), and "delayed listening comprehension problems" (1 %).

Pattern 1: "immediate" listening comprehension problems. The first pattern represented listening comprehension problems with short T(dur) and short T(res) values. In other words, the duration of these problems was short, and participants perceived them

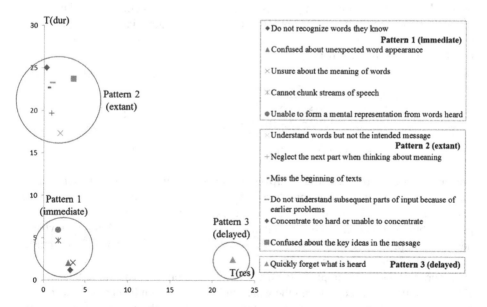

Fig. 2. Different patterns of listening comprehension problems faced by NNSs

relatively quickly. Five types of problems fell into this pattern: "do not recognize words they know," "confused about unexpected word appearance," "unsure about the meaning of words," "cannot chunk streams of speech," and "unable to form a mental representation from words heard."

Figure 3 shows an example of a listening comprehension problem (in this case, "do not recognize words they know") in this pattern. In this example, the participant had a problem with the word "fertilizer," which she knew but couldn't recognize it when she heard it.

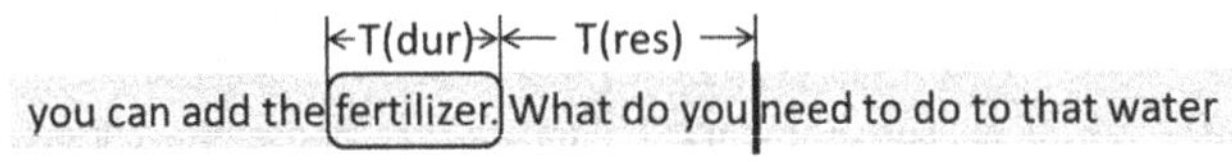

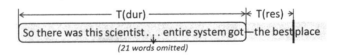

Fig. 3. Example of "immediate" listening comprehension problem

Pattern 2: "extant" listening comprehension problems. The second pattern represented listening comprehension problems with long T(dur) and short T(res) values. The duration of these problems tended to be long and they continued to burden the participants to the point at which they pressed the button. Six types of problems fell into this pattern: "understand words but not the intended message," "neglect the next part when thinking about meaning, "miss the beginning of texts," "do not understand subsequent parts of input because of earlier problems," "concentrate too hard or unable to concentrate," and "confused about the key ideas in the message."

Figure 4 shows an example of the listening comprehension problem in this pattern. Here, the participant lost concentration and missed the entire sentence ("So there was this scientist… entire system got"). As shown in this example, non-native participants facing an extant listening comprehension problem had difficulty with the whole sentence, rather than just words or phrases. Compared to immediate listening comprehension problems (pattern 1), NNSs seemed to feel much more burdened when they faced problems under this pattern.

```
|←————————— T(dur) —————————→|← T(res) →|
| So there was this scientist. . . entire system got|—the best|place
              (21 words omitted)
```

Fig. 4. Example of "extant" listening comprehension problem

Pattern 3: "delayed" listening comprehension problems. The third pattern represented listening comprehension problems with short T(dur) and long T(res) values. The duration of these problems was short, and it took participants a relatively long time to press the button. Only one type of problem fell into this pattern: "quickly forget what is heard." This problem emerged when the participants tried to recall words or phrases they had just heard a few seconds ago.

Figure 5 shows an example of the listening comprehension problem in this pattern. Here the participant tried to recall the word "bubble gas" when he heard the lecturer's self-correction, "I'm sorry, you must bubble gas through it." According to the participant, when he tried to recall the word to understand the speech, he realized that he had already forgotten it.

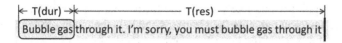

Fig. 5. Example of "delayed" listening comprehension problem

6 Discussion

In summary, we categorized twelve types of listening comprehension problems, two of which were newly identified in this study. We found that the problems can be classified into three patterns based on the persistence of each problem and the time taken to perceive it.

6.1 Interpretation of Findings

How a "pressing a button" method might have affected the results. In our experiment, participants pressed a button whenever they encountered a comprehension problem during listening tasks. Although "pressing a button" requires low over-head from the NNSs, it requires some sort of trigger or decision-making process (i.e., deciding when to press a button), which might have affected the results. For "immediate listening comprehension problems," such as "do not recognize words they know," pressing a button to indicate a problem may be easy. The word they cannot recognize would serve as a trigger to press the button. However, for such "extant listening comprehension problems" as "concentrate too hard or unable to concentrate," participants might have found it difficult to decide when to press the button. For example, one participant reported that *"While listening, I thought I needed to press the button, but I kept having problems, so I didn't know when to press it."* Similarly, for such "delayed listening comprehension problems" as "quickly forgot what was heard," deciding to press the button was also difficult. One participant mentioned that *"I was a little hesitant since I had a problem with the previous speech and I wonder if this was the good timing (for pressing it)."* These situations could be one reason for the unbalanced distribution of the problems identified in three patterns: "immediate listening comprehension problems" (74 % of all problem occurrences), "extant listening comprehension problems" (25 %), and "delayed listening comprehension problems" (1 %).

6.2 Design Implications

Providing different support for different patterns of problems. Our findings show three different patterns of problems. We suggest providing different types of support for each one.

Most of the immediate listening comprehension problems are related to words or phrases. Since NNSs instantly perceive the problems, it would be best to provide support that could immediately solve their problems. For example, bilingual dictionaries, machine translation, illustrations may be helpful [13].

For extant listening comprehension problems, NNSs are already overburdened. Inappropriate support would likely to impose further burdens on them. Therefore, the support should focus on reducing their burdens and help them quickly catch up with the speech. For example, showing them keywords extracted from previous speech [26] or providing them with a small amount of time to process speech [31] may be helpful.

For delayed listening comprehension problems, NNSs notice that they forgot some words or phrases earlier in the speech. Since a possible cause of such problems is the limited capacity of the NNSs' short-term memory [1, 9], support should focus on providing memory cues for them. For example, automatically providing text summarizations of previous speech [26] or showing images that can instantly remind them what the speech was about may be of help.

Using advanced sensing technologies, we may be able to associate each problem pattern with certain NNS behaviors. For example, previous research has suggested that pupil response can be used as an indication of effortful listening [33]. If such effortful listening continues for a while, it may indicate that the NNS encounters an "extant listening comprehension problem."

7   Conclusions and Future Directions

In this study, we explored how different types of listening comprehension problems are perceived by NNSs as speech unfolds in a one-way communication setting. Through exploratory analysis of the collected data from a laboratory experiment, we identified twelve types of listening comprehension problems, which we further classified into three patterns based on their persistence and the time taken to perceive them. We believe that our findings serve as a basis for designing adaptive systems to support NNSs in real-time listening comprehension. For future studies, we plan to develop such a system. In addition, we plan to investigate if NNSs with different listening abilities perceive comprehension problems differently. Finally, we will examine how our findings are compatible with an interactive multilingual communication setting.

Acknowledgments. This research was partially supported by a Grant-in-Aid for Scientific Research (S) (24220002, 2012-2016) from Japan Society for the Promotion of Science (JSPS).

References

1. Anderson, J.R.: Cognitive psychology and its implications, 4th edn. Freeman, New York (1995)
2. Bloomfield, A., Wayland, S.C., Rhoades, E., Blodgett, A., Linck, J., Ross, S.: What makes listening difficult? factors affecting second language listening comprehension. Technical report, DTIC Document (2010)
3. Cox, T.H., Blake, S.: Managing cultural diversity: Implications for organizational competitiveness. Executive **5**, 45–56 (1991)

4. Feely, A.J., Harzing, A.W.: Language management in multinational companies. Cross Cult. Manag. Int. J. **10**(2), 37–52 (2003)
5. Feigh, K.M., Dorneich, M.C., Hayes, C.C.: Toward a characterization of adaptive systems a framework for researchers and system designers. Hum. Factors: J. Hum. Factors Ergon. Soc. **54**(6), 1008–1024 (2012)
6. Gao, G., Yamashita, N., Hautasaari, A.M., Echenique, A., Fussell, S.R.: Effects of public vs. private automated transcripts on multiparty communication between native and non-native english speakers. In: Proceedings of the SIGCHI Conference on Human Factors in Computing Systems, pp. 843–852. ACM (2014)
7. Gao, G., Yamashita, N., Hautasaari, A.M., Fussell, S.R.: Improving multilingual collaboration by displaying how non-native speakers use automated transcripts and bilingual dictionaries. In: Proceedings of the 33rd Annual ACM Conference on Human Factors in Computing Systems, pp. 3463–3472. ACM (2015)
8. Goh, C.: How much do learners know about the factors that influence their listening comprehension? Hong Kong J. Appl. Linguist. **4**(1), 17–40 (1999)
9. Goh, C.C.: A cognitive perspective on language learners' listening comprehension problems. System **28**(1), 55–75 (2000)
10. Goh, C.C.: Exploring listening comprehension tactics and their interaction patterns. System **30**(2), 185–206 (2002)
11. Hautasaari, A., Yamashita, N.: Do automated transcripts help non-native speakers catch up on missed conversation in audio conferences? In: Proceedings of the 5th ACM International Conference on Collaboration Across Boundaries: Culture, Distance and Technology, pp. 65–72. ACM (2014)
12. Höök, K.: Steps to take before intelligent user interfaces become real. Interact. Comput. **12**(4), 409–426 (2000)
13. Ishida, T.: Language grid: An infrastructure for intercultural collaboration. In: International Symposium on Applications and the Internet, 2006. SAINT 2006, p. 5. IEEE (2006)
14. Johnson, S.C.: Hierarchical clustering schemes. Psychometrika **32**(3), 241–254 (1967)
15. Kalnikaitė, V., Ehlen, P., Whittaker, S.: Markup as you talk: establishing effective memory cues while still contributing to a meeting. In: Proceedings of the ACM 2012 Conference on Computer Supported Cooperative Work, pp. 349–358. ACM (2012)
16. Lotfi, G.: A questionnaire of beliefs on english language listening comprehension problems: Development and validation. World Appl. Sci. J. **16**(4), 508–515 (2012)
17. Marschan, R., Welch, D., Welch, L.: Language: The forgotten factor in multinational management. Eur. Manag. J. **15**(5), 591–598 (1997)
18. Nakamura, S., Markov, K., Nakaiwa, H., Kikui, G.I., Kawai, H., Jitsuhiro, T., Zhang, J.S., Yamamoto, H., Sumita, E., Yamamoto, S.: The ATR multilingual speech-to-speech translation system. IEEE Trans. Audio Speech Lang. Process. **14**(2), 365–376 (2006)
19. Neeley, T., Hinds, P.J., Cramton, C.D.: Walking through jelly: language proficiency, emotions, and disrupted collaboration in global work. Harvard Business School Organizational Behavior Unit Working Paper (09–138) (2009)
20. Otten, M., Van Berkum, J.J.: Does working memory capacity affect the ability to predict upcoming words in discourse? Brain Res. **1291**, 92–101 (2009)
21. Pan, Y., Jiang, D., Yao, L., Picheny, M., Qin, Y.: Effects of automated transcription quality on non-native speakers' comprehension in real-time computer-mediated communication. In: Proceedings of the SIGCHI Conference on Human Factors in Computing Systems, pp. 1725–1734. ACM (2010)
22. Pérez, L.C.: Foreign language productivity in synchronous versus asynchronous computer-mediated communication. CALICO J. **21**, 89–104 (2003)

23. Pickering, M.J., Garrod, S.: Do people use language production to make predictions during comprehension? Trends Cogn. Sci. **11**(3), 105–110 (2007)
24. Rubin, J.: A review of second language listening comprehension research. Mod. Lang. J. **78**(2), 199–221 (1994)
25. Takano, Y., Noda, A.: A temporary decline of thinking ability during foreign language processing. J. Cross-Cult. Psychol. **24**(4), 445–462 (1993)
26. Tucker, S., Kyprianou, N., Whittaker, S.: Time-compressing speech: asr transcripts are an effective way to support gist extraction. In: Popescu-Belis, A., Stiefelhagen, R. (eds.) MLMI 2008. LNCS, vol. 5237, pp. 226–235. Springer, Heidelberg (2008)
27. Van Petten, C., Luka, B.J.: Prediction during language comprehension: Benefits, costs, and ERP components. Int. J. Psychophysiol. **83**(2), 176–190 (2012)
28. Vandergrift, L.: Recent developments in second and foreign language listening comprehension research. Lang. Teach. **40**(03), 191–210 (2007)
29. Wahlster, W.: Verbmobil: Foundations of Speech-to-Speech Translation. Springer, Heidelberg (2013)
30. Yagang, F.: Listening: problems and solutions. Engl. Teach. Forum **31**, 16–19 (1993). Teacher Development, Making the Right Movies
31. Yamashita, N., Echenique, A., Ishida, T., Hautasaari, A.: Lost in transmittance: how transmission lag enhances and deteriorates multilingual collaboration. In: Proceedings of The 2013 Conference on Computer Supported Cooperative Work, pp. 923–934. ACM (2013)
32. Yao, L., Pan, Y.-x., Jiang, D.-n.: Effects of automated transcription delay on non-native speakers' comprehension in real-time computer-mediated communication. In: Campos, P., Graham, N., Jorge, J., Nunes, N., Palanque, P., Winckler, M. (eds.) INTERACT 2011, Part I. LNCS, vol. 6946, pp. 207–214. Springer, Heidelberg (2011)
33. Zekveld, A.A., Kramer, S.E., Festen, J.M.: Pupil response as an indication of effortful listening: The influence of sentence intelligibility. Ear Hear. **31**(4), 480–490 (2010)
34. Zekveld, A.A., Kramer, S.E., Kessens, J.M., Vlaming, M.S., Houtgast, T.: The influence of age, hearing, and working memory on the speech comprehension benefit derived from an automatic speech recognition system. Ear Hear. **30**(2), 262–272 (2009)

Floor Interaction with Wearable Projection Interface Using Hand and Toe

Fumihiro Sato, Tomu Tominaga, Yoshinori Hijikata, and Nobuchika Sakata[✉]

Division of Systems Science and Applied Informatics, Graduate School of Engineering Science,
Osaka University, 1-3 Machikaneyama, Toyonaka, Japan
{sato,tominaga,hijikata,sakata}@hlab.sys.es.osaka-u.ac.jp

Abstract. We conducted a user study to unveil the usability of a wearable input/output interface using hands and toes for operating applications such as telephone calls and e-mails. Specifically, subjects performed tasks in the states "hands-free," "having baggage in their dominant hands," and "having baggage in both hands" using the proposed system and a smartphone. Then, we evaluated the usability according to a questionnaire, an interview, and the task completion time. The results indicate that hand and toe input in the proposed system were accepted when performing simple button operations such as answering the phone. In addition, hand input in the proposed system was accepted when performing scroll operations such as reading an e-mail. However, when performing accurate button operations such as text entry tasks, hand and toe input in the proposed system were seldom accepted.

Keywords: Floor projection · Wearable computer · Augmented reality · Toe input · Wearable projection

1 Introduction

The widespread use of mobile terminals such as smartphones enables us to access information services both indoors and outdoors, even while walking. For example, we use information services to find a route, check e-mails, and update a social network service (SNS). These information services are used frequently and briefly. Furthermore, most of them can be used by a simple operation. However, such mobile terminals have several limitations. First, the mobile terminal cannot indicate information larger than the display size. Second, it is difficult for users to give attention to their surroundings due to watching the display screen in their hands. Third, the mobile terminal needs to be retrieved from a pocket or bag. Fourth, the user has to hold the device itself with at least one hand, even while only viewing. Therefore, it is difficult to use the mobile terminal when both hands are occupied.

Thus, we focus on a type of projection system that can compensate for these limitations and provide a more efficient way of viewing information [1, 2, 23]. We especially focus on a wearable projection system that enables the user to access information via a large screen without retrieving the device [3, 4]. Additionally, Matsuda proposed a wearable projection system composed of a mobile projector, depth sensor, and gyro

© Springer Science+Business Media Singapore 2016
T. Yoshino et al. (Eds.): CollabTech 2016, CCIS 647, pp. 105–116, 2016.
DOI: 10.1007/978-981-10-2618-8_9

sensor, which are equipped on the user's chest [5, 17]. This system allows the user to conduct "select" and "drag" operations by footing and fingertips controlling in the projected image on the floor (Fig. 1). In this paper, we evaluate the usability of hand and toe input in our system and propose applications for our system based on the results.

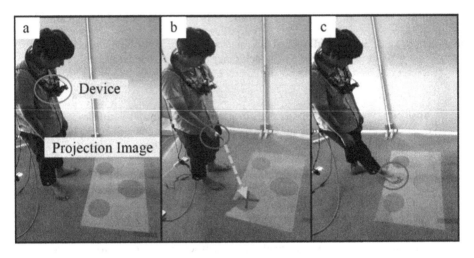

Fig. 1. System overview

2   Related Work

In this section, we discuss related work regarding the input interface to a graphical user interface (GUI) and the input method using the foot.

2.1   Input to GUI

Standard GUIs are operated using a pointer on the screen with pointing devices such as a mouse and trackball. However, the operability has worsened as the devices have been downsized for portability. Mobile terminals also restrict the use of one hand, and these devices need to be taken out of a pocket or bag. Related work has investigated hands-free input with wearable computing devices. For example, there are systems that accept finger-pointing input, such as a hand mouse [6], and input systems based on the line of sight [7]. These systems are accompanied by the burden of attaching and detaching required special devices. They also occupy the hands and eyes, which makes it difficult to conduct other tasks because these are the most frequently used parts of a user's body.

2.2   Accessing Information Using Projector

Accessing information via a projector has been studied for many years [8]. Technology that combines reality with wearable computers has been developed. The use of a projector instead of a head-mounted display (HMD) offers advantages such as mobility by accurately displaying images in a certain location. Studies on augmented reality have used projectors such as the tele-direction interface [20]. These studies have demonstrated the effectiveness of displaying annotations in the real world using a projector. T. Karitsuka superimposed a movie and annotated a real-world surface with graphics and characters [9]. However, the system required a marker on the projection surface, which made it difficult to project the image anywhere. Yamamoto projected information on a palm-top using a projector attached to the shoulder, which provided a stable display [10]. However, this system was not hands-free, and the display was not large enough to allow the user to access information. P. Mistry projected information onto a wall and real objects using a head-mounted or neck-strap-mounted projector, where inputs using finger gestures were recognized by an RGB camera [11]. However, this system required image processing because it often failed to recognize fingers with different ambient light and background colors. C. Harrison studied the "OmniTouch," which uses a depth sensor to detect finger input on many surfaces [12]. These studies show that using hands and fingers as input interfaces is an available and efficient approach for wearable projection systems. However, these studies required the users to raise their arms, which led to strain, and the system occupied both of the users' hands.

2.3 Foot-Based Input

There are studies that design input interfaces using the foot. Some deal with attaching sensors to the objects in the environment; others, to the user's body.

An example of a study that involved attaching sensors to the environment is Multitoe [13], designed by T. Augsten, which enables highly accurate user input using the floor. Users invoke menus and operate a keyboard with this system.

Studies involving systems that attach sensors to the user's body include the WARAJI [14] projects conducted by S. Barrera. Those sensors are attached to the user's legs and determine leg acceleration. This system is used to realize movement in virtual reality. However, this system demands the attachment of a device to the leg, and it does not consider the interaction between the foot and display. Another study investigated foot input based on a sensor in the user's pocket [15] to obtain the acceleration of the foot. Also, Daisuke [22] conduct research to detect user's posture based on a sensor in the user's pocket for investigating risk management. This study did not require the attachment of a device to the feet; however, it also failed to consider the information display. Other studies have recognized the toe using a camera on a mobile terminal device. One of these involved the input for a soccer game using the foot. The device was attached to one of the user's hands, and it did not consider the interaction between the toe and the floor. V. Paelke used a mobile device and a toe for inputting information [16], but that study did not consider the interaction between the toe and the floor. Simpson considered the interaction between the toe and the floor, but not with a mobile projector [21].

According to these works, it is effective to input to the floor projection by hands and toes, which is the principal point of our work.

3   System

We implemented the system as shown in Fig. 2. The system consists of a depth sensor, mobile projector, and gyro sensor. All the components are mounted on the user's chest. We used a seeser M1 (ESplus, Inc.) laser micro projector to project visual feedback onto the floor. Furthermore, we used an InertiaCube4 (InterSense, Inc.) to measure the orientation of the system and to fix the projected image on the floor. This prevented the projected image from moving due to the user's motion when stepping on the floor. We used a DS325 (SoftKinetic) as a depth sensor to detect the user's hands and toes. The DS325 is robust against changes in background color and ambient light. This depth sensor estimates the position and the motion of hands and toes. The physical burden is smaller and more socially acceptable than mounting at the user's head—the user wears only one device on the chest.

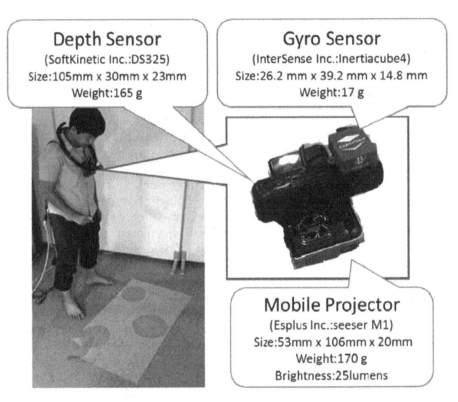

Fig. 2. System configuration

There are input motions to the floor projection by the hands. We focus on the pinch interface [18, 19] as shown in Fig. 3. The user can select contents from the floor projection by means of attaching the forefinger to the thumb. In addition, the hand position synchronizes with the pointing position. The hand position and select motion are detected by the depth sensor. The detection algorithm is similar to the algorithms of related works [21]. However, we do not utilize the direction of the user's hand as input. Figure 4a shows the raw image of the depth sensor. To separate the hands and feet, we set a threshold at the height of the hips empirically. The input position of the floor projection is evaluated by means of the position of the tip of the hand. The select motion is judged by means of a closed area of the hand as shown in Fig. 4b.

Not Select   Select

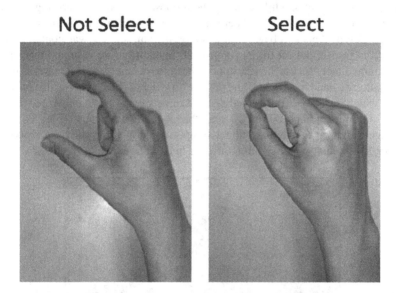

Fig. 3. Select motion of hand input.

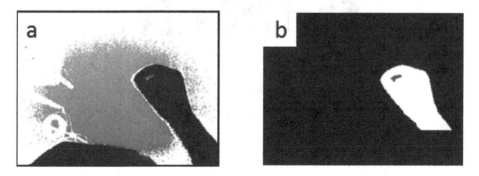

Fig. 4. Hand detection

In the preliminary experiment, we evaluated the accuracy of hand and toe input. Subjects (4 male) selected to the target 50 times. As a result, the average error of hand input was 4.5 cm, and the average error of toe input was 13.4 cm. The negative and positive false detection rate of hand input was 3.5 %, and that of toe input was 16.5 %. Considering this result and [17], we designed the icon size for this user study.

4   User Study

We evaluated the usability of hand and toe input of the proposed system by means of operating existing smartphone GUIs. We also evaluated the usability of input by a smartphone for comparison. The subjects performed tasks such as answering telephone calls and processing e-mail while wearing the proposed system and carrying the smartphone (Sony Ericsson Xperia arc). There are various places to contain the smartphone, such as clothing pockets and bags. In this study, the smartphone was contained in the subject's front trouser pocket for easy retrieval. In addition, we assumed that the user could not immediately access the smartphone because of hand restraints such as holding baggage, putting a hand in a pocket, and putting on gloves. Therefore, we also conducted a study in which the subject performed tasks in three situations: "hands-free" (Fig. 5a), "baggage in dominant hand" (Fig. 5b), and "baggage in both hands" (Fig. 5c). We set the baggage weight to 1.0 kg under the assumption that the user purchased food and a 500 ml bottle of water, which is often the case in daily lives.

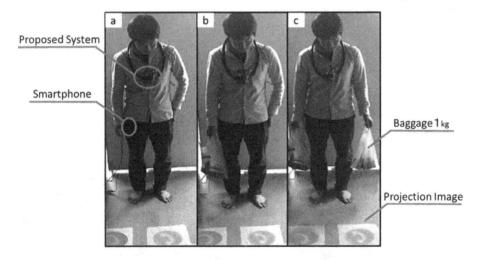

Fig. 5. Experimental apparatus

Before the tasks started, the subject was explained how to provide input and also the situation being addressed. The tasks started with attaching the proposed system to the subject and placing the smartphone in the subject's pocket for the Fig. 5 situations. A sound on the PC signaled the start of the task. Then, the task was displayed on the floor in the case of input by the proposed system, or on the smartphone's screen in the case of input by the smartphone. When the subject was performing the task, he/she was allowed to put down the baggage or to hold the baggage in the other hand. After input for task, the subject has to be the initial situation as the end condition.

The subjects performed three tasks. The first task was a one-button operation that did not require high accuracy. This operation is commonly used when answering a call and checking a short message. Specifically, the subject had to select the button once as shown in Fig. 6a. The second task was a scroll operation, which requires two-dimensional motion. This operation is commonly used when reading an e-mail and Web browsing. Specifically, the subject had to scroll to read text as shown in Fig. 6b. Then, the subject had to select the button to clear the end time. The text consisted of 150–200 Japanese characters, which can be read wholly by means of about five drag scrolls. The third task was an accurate button operation that required a lot of two-dimensional motion and high accuracy. This operation is commonly used during text entry such as replying to an e-mail and uploading articles to SNS. The preliminary experiment indicated that input using a QWERTY keyboard layout is quicker and more comfortable than the flick input in the proposed system. Moreover, the flick input is not used daily by all subjects. Therefore, we adopted input by QWERTY keyboard layout to perform the text entry task. Additionally, the toe input is considerably uncomfortable for this task and was therefore not conducted. The text entry task is shown in Fig. 6c. The subject inputs an English word of four characters.

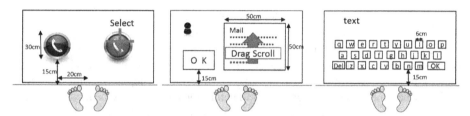

Fig. 6. Experimental task

There were 14 subjects (13 male, 1 female) aged 21 to 25 years, all of which were right-hand dominant. All tasks are conducted indoor situation. In addition, they performed each task five times to practice, and we take care of order of tasks to compensate order effects. We evaluated the usability according to a questionnaire, an interview, and the task completion time.

5   Result and Discussion

The task completion times are shown in Fig. 7. Whisker of box-and-whisker plot in Fig. 7 means standard variation. Also small "o" represent outlier. Input by the proposed system was quicker than input by the smartphone in the one-button operation task. Moreover, the toe input was the quickest when subjects had in both hands. In the scroll task, hand input by the proposed system and input by a smartphone were quicker than toe input. In the text-entry task, hand input by the proposed system was as quick as input by the smartphone when subjects had either no baggage, or baggage in both hands. However, hand input by the proposed system often took more time than input by the smartphone when subjects had baggage in their dominant hands because subjects frequently made mistakes due to input by their non-dominant hands.

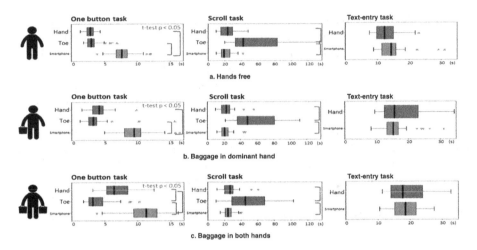

Fig. 7. Task Completion times

The results of the questionnaire are shown in Figs. 8, 9 and 10. In the one-button task, when subjects had either no baggage, or baggage in their dominant hands, the hand input by the proposed system was accepted, while the toe input was not accepted, whereas, when subjects had baggage in both hands, the toe input was the most accepted.

Most subjects cared for easy input, but a few subjects cared for certain input by the smartphone. In the scroll task, regardless of the situations of the subjects, they preferred hand input and input by smartphone, rather than toe input, because of the accuracy. Some subjects preferred the smartphone because it is more private than the projection image, which may be seen by people around them. In the accurate button task, regardless of the

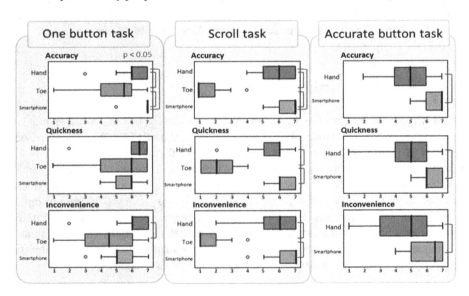

Fig. 8. Results of questionnaires in hands-free situation

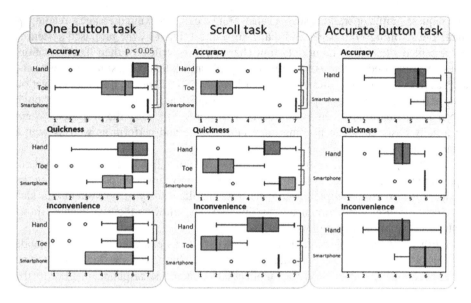

Fig. 9. Results of questionnaires with dominant hand occupied

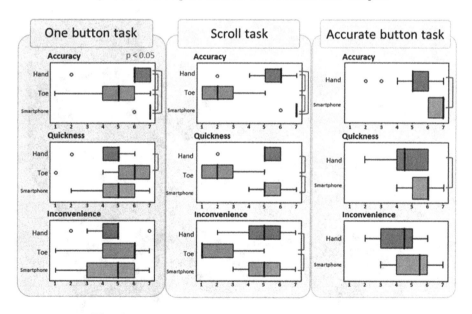

Fig. 10. Results of questionnaires with both hands occupied

situations of the subjects, they preferred to input by smartphone rather than the proposed system because of the input accuracy.

From these results, it was determined that toe input is accepted only for simple operations when both hands are occupied and that hand input is accepted for simple operations when both hands are free. Namely, the proposed system is fitting for applications that request simple operations such as answering a call, checking messages, reading e-mail, and scrolling Web pages and maps. In contrast, input by the proposed system is not accepted when users input only four characters, regardless of their hand situation. Thus, the proposed system is not suited for applications that request more operations, such as replying to e-mail and uploading articles to SNS. However, the task completion time of hand input by the proposed system was as quick as by smartphone, even though subjects use smartphones on a daily basis. Therefore, if they use the proposed system on a daily basis, they can become more comfortable and perform as well as with a smartphone.

Our future work will investigate applications and utilization of the proposed system. For example, the proposed system allows input not only from one person wearing the device but also from people around the user simultaneously. This system can also provide multi-user interaction using multiple devices, allowing the user to share information and communicate with other users.

Furthermore, the projection area can be utilized as an extended display for mobile devices as shown in Fig. 11. For example, in cases in which users should keep watching an application, they can drop the application from the smartphone display to the

Fig. 11. Extended display for mobile devices

projection area. The projection area allows users to improve the usability of a multitask application and to check notifications without the inconvenience of using mobile devices. In addition, in cases of simple operations, users can process information without retrieving their mobile devices.

6 Conclusion

In this work, we studied the usability of our proposed system when performing tasks such as answering phone calls and processing e-mails. From this study, we suggest that the proposed system is fit to be used for most information services that are used outdoors. The proposed system is convenient in a variety of situations, even when the user's hands are occupied. We believe that our system will be innovative in mobile computing.

References

1. Pinhanez, C.S.: The everywhere displays projector: a device to create ubiquitous graphical interfaces. In: Ubiquitous Computing 2001 (Ubicomp 2001), pp. 12–17 (2001)
2. Wilson, A.D.: PlayAnywhere: a compact interactive tabletop projection-vision system. In: Proceedings of the 18th Annual ACM Symposium on User Interface Software and Technology, UIST 2005 (2005)
3. Konishi, T., Tajimi, K., Sakata, N., Nishida, S.: Projection stabilizing method for palm-top display with wearable projector. In: 13th IEEE International Symposium on Wearable Computers, Advances in Wearable Computing 2009, pp. 13–20, September 2009
4. Tajimi, K., Uemura, K., Kajiwara, Y., Sakata, N., Nishida, S.: Stabilization method for floor projection with a hip-mounted projector. In: Proceedings of ICAT 2010, pp. 77–83, December 2010
5. Matsuda, D., Sakata, N., Nishida, S.: Wearable input/output interface for floor projection using hands and a toe. In: ICAT, pp. 122–128 (2013)
6. Kurata, T., Okuma, T., Kourogi, M., Sakaue, K.: The hand mouse: GMM hand color classification and mean shift tracking. In: Proceedings of the 2nd International Workshop on Recognition, Analysis and Tracking of Faces and Gestures in Realtime Systems, pp. 119–124 (2001)
7. Ono, T., Mukawa, N.: An eye tracking system based on eye ball model. Toward Realization of Gaze Controlled Input Device. Information Processing Research Report 2001-HI-93, pp. 47–54 (2001)
8. Wellner, P.: Interacting with paper on the DigitalDesk. Commun. ACM **36**(7), 87–96 (1993)
9. Karitsuka, T., Sato, K.: A wearable mixed reality with an on-board projector. In: ISMAR 2003 Proceedings of the 2nd IEEE/ACM International Symposium on Mixed and Augmented Reality (2003)
10. Yamamoto, G., Sato, K.: PALMbit: a PALM interface with projector-camera system. In: 9th International Conference on Ubiquitous Computing, UbiComp 2007 Adjunct Proceedings, Innsbruck, Austria, pp. 276–279 (2007)
11. Mistry, P., Maes, P., Chang, L.: Wuw - wear ur world - a wearable gestural interface. In: Proceedings of the 27th International Conference Extended Abstracts on Human Factors in Computing Systems, pp. 4111–4116 (2009)

12. Harrison, C., Benko, H., Wilson, A.D.: OmniTouch wearable multitouch interaction everywhere. In: Proceedings of the 24th Annual ACM Symposium on User Interface Software and Technology, UIST 2011 (2011)

13. Augsten, T., Kaefer, K., Meusel, R., Fetzer, C., Kanitz, D., Stoff, T., Becker, T., Holz, C., Baudisch, P.: Multitoe: high-precision interaction with back-projected floors based on high-resolution multi-touch input. In: UIST 2010: Proceedings of the 23nd Annual ACM Symposium on User Interface Software and Technology, pp. 209–218 (2010)

14. Barrera, S., Romanos, P., Saito, S.: WARAJI: foot-driven navigation interfaces for virtual reality applications. In: International Workshop on Advanced Image Technology 2005 (2005)

15. Scott, J., Dearman, D., Truong, K.: Sensing foot gestures from the pocket. In: UIST 2010, pp. 199–208 (2010)

16. Paelke, V., Reimann, C., Stichling, D.: Foot-based mobile interaction in mobile games. In: Proceedings of ACE 2004, Singapore, 3–5 July, pp. 321–324 (2004)

17. Matsuda, D., Uemura, K., Sakata, N., Nishida, S.: Toe Input using mobile projector and kinect sensor. In: 16th International Symposium on Wearable Computers (ISWC 2012), pp. 18–22 (2012)

18. Wilson, A.D.: Robust computer vision-based detection of pinching for one and two-handed gesture input. In: Proceedings of the 19th Annual ACM Symposium on User Interface Software and Technology, UIST 2006, pp. 255–258. ACM Press (2006)

19. Fukuchi, K., Sato, T., Mamiya, H., Koike, H.: Pac-pac: pinching gesture recognition for tabletop entertainment system. In: Proceedings of ACM AVI 2010, pp. 267–273 (2010)

20. Tojo, K., Hiura, S., Inokuchi, S.: 3-D tele-direction interface using video projector. Trans. Virtual Reality Soc. Jpn 7(2) (2002)

21. Simpson, Z.B.: Walk on Salmon. Interactive installation. http://www.mine-control.com/salmon.html

22. Honda, D., Sakata, N., Nishida, S.: Activity recognition for risk management with installed sensor in smart and cell phone. In: Jacko, J.A. (ed.) Human-Computer Interaction, Part III, HCII 2011. LNCS, vol. 6763, pp. 230–239. Springer, Heidelberg (2011)

23. Kurata, T., Sakata, N., Kourogi, M., Okuma, T., Ota, Y.: Interaction using nearby-and-far projection surfaces with a body-worn ProCam system. In: Proceedings of the Engineering of Reality of Virtual Reality, the 20th Annual IS & T/SPIE Symposium on Electronic Imaging (EI 2008), pp. 6804–6816 (2008)

Development of Body Conversion System with Motion Picture for Presenting Other's Bodily Sensations

Misato Imamura$^{(\boxtimes)}$ and Takashi Yoshino

Faculty of Systems Engineering, Wakayama University,
930 Sakaedani, Wakayama, Japan
imamura.misato@g.wakayama-u.jp, yoshino@sys.wakayama-u.ac.jp
http://www.wakayama-u.ac.jp/~yoshino/lab/

Abstract. There are several problems caused by differences in people's bodies in daily life. For example, tall people feel uncomfortable working at low desks, whereas short people cannot reach high places. However, it is not easy for other people to experience other people's bodily sensations. To experience the sensations of others, we believe that it is effective to link video of the body of another person to their own behavior, and thereby, experience the physical scales that are experienced by others. Therefore, we have developed the "Ima-mirror," which converts user movements into a model with the physical attributes of someone else, and presents the mirror image on a screen. The results of evaluation experiments produced the following findings: (1) Users are greatly interested in moving the body of others. (2) Users feel sensations matching their own senses when the system uses their own body model. (3) Users feel sensations that do not match their own senses when the system presents another person's body model.

Keywords: Understanding of people · Motion capture · Physical attribute · Mirror image

1 Introduction

There are several problems caused by differences in people's bodies in daily life. However, it is not easy for other people to understand another person's bodily sensations or orientations. For example, in a city, children are less visible from a car because of their short stature. Therefore, children have been taught to raise their hands when crossing the street to make themselves more visible.

It can be difficult for two people with height differences to cook together. In a house, there is different usability of the kitchen based on height. For the purpose of understanding the experiences of others, various studies have been carried out. Shibata et al. have developed a system to let users experience the view of others [1]. This produces a field-of-view model from the parameters of visual acuity, age, and height. The user perceives the world using a head-mounted display,

© Springer Science+Business Media Singapore 2016
T. Yoshino et al. (Eds.): CollabTech 2016, CCIS 647, pp. 117–129, 2016.
DOI: 10.1007/978-981-10-2618-8_10

and experiences a change of view. Nishida et al. developed "CHILDHOOD", which is a device to reproduce a child's perception system [2]. By converting the experience of the user's field of vision and hands to the child's perspective, the user feels like a child. Tamaki et. al. developed PossessedHand [3]. The device controls a user's fingers by applying electrical stimulus to the muscles around the forearm. They also developed a support system based on PossessedHand for playing koto. In these studies, the user uses a head-mounted display or wearable devices; thereby, the user can experience the physical sensations of others from a first-person viewpoint. However, in a first-person viewpoint system, the user cannot see their own shape. By showing the body of other people to the user, the user can easily understand their (converted) height and body shape. Furthermore, it is possible to present the identity attributes of others based on the characteristics of appearance such as clothing or hairstyle. This is considered to result in psychological changes to the user.

In this paper, we propose "Ima-mirror", which is a system that presents the physical sensations of others to the user. Ima-mirror uses a mirror display to present the body of another person to the user, the body model moves with the motion of the user. The term "body sensation", as used in this paper, refers to the feeling of interaction with the surrounding environment and others based on the size and shape of the physical body. In this paper, we describe an evaluation experiment and a method of realizing Ima-mirror. The name of this system is derived from "imaginary mirror." In Sect. 2, we describe related works to clarify the position of our study. In Sect. 3, we describe Ima-mirror. In Sect. 4, we describe the evaluation experiment. In Sect. 5, we discuss the results of the evaluation experiment. In Sect. 6, we conclude our study.

2   Related Works

We describe several studies to develop the context of our study.

Yoshida et al. developed a system that displays video of the body operation of several viewers [4]. Using this system, the viewer sees another place and time, feeling a sense of unity with people there. "Gokinjo silhouette" by Nakamori et al., Presents the user in silhouette [5]. This prompts an interest in familiar others, and supports gradual connections. "HyperMirror" by Morikawa is a video chat system that displays users in the same image [6]. Users are in remote locations, but they feel like they are sharing the same space. Several similar studies use a mirror for image display. Perttu Hämäläinen has conducted a study that trains users using video recording and mirrors [7]. In addition, Martin Tomitsch has developed a public display viewing articles [8]. The goal of the experiment was to target passers-by; public display prompted playful behavior in some users. These systems represent images using mirror images, the same method as in our study. These systems present a symbolic body representing the body or skeleton of a user on the screen. In this study, the body of the other person follows the behavior of a user. Okamoto et al. presented "Silhouettel", which projects people's shadows and their profile and interests on the screen, and thereby promotes conversations among users [9]. Mikhail Jacob et al. presented "Viewpoint AI", which projects particles with an artificial intelligence on the plane [10]. Particles become human shaped, and dance with the human. These studies present user shadows or particles derived from the user. These systems project on a large screen at a size that is close to life-sized. These features are the same as those in the present study. In this study, the actions of the user are reflected using the physical attributes of others.

3   Ima-mirror

We have developed a body conversion system, Ima-mirror, using the body shape of a real person. In this section, we describe a design policy and a method for realization of Ima-mirror.

3.1   Design Policy and Method

(1) Presenting a model of the entire body
To give the impression (and identifying characteristics) of another person to the user, the system provides a full-body model of the other person that is linked to the user's movement as mirrored on the screen. When the user faces the model on the screen, the model is their own model mirrored, so as to move in the same direction as the user.

(2) Displaying the image at close to life-size
For the user to be able to experience the system by moving their entire body while looking at the screen, the system displays the model at a size that is close to life-sized. Therefore, the system displays a screen on the projector and the screen.

(3) Using the body shape of a real person
To give the impression of the conversion of sensory and identifying characteristics for a specific other person to the user, the system presents the body shape of a real person. Using the body shape of a real person, it is possible to provide personality such as body type, dress, and attitude to the model.

3.2   Realization Method

Figure 1 shows the flow of the realization method. Ima-mirror performs the following four steps.

1. Obtain the body shape [Fig. 1 (1)],
2. Create a moveable model [Fig. 1 (2)],
3. Select the model from the height of the user [Fig. 1 (3)], and
4. Reflect the user's attitude to the model [Fig. 1 (4)]

Figure 2 shows the body shape of a real person as an implementation example of a movable model. The following section describes the details of each procedure.

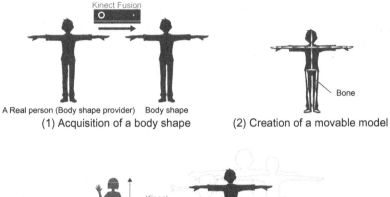

(1) Acquisition of a body shape

(2) Creation of a movable model

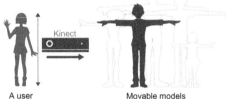

(3) Selection of a movable model based on the height of the user

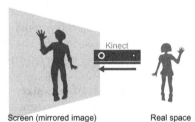

(4) Application of a movable model tothe posture of a user

Fig. 1. Overview of Ima-mirror.

1. Obtain a person's body shape using KinectFusion. Figure 2 (1) shows an example of the acquired body shape.
2. Convert the body shape into a movable model by inserting bones into the model by hand using modeling software. The bones follow the original motion of the model, similar to a bone in the human body. By creating a bone model, it makes it possible to easily deform the model. Place the bones to move the entire body of the model, as shown in Fig. 2 (2), which presents an example of a movable model when you insert a bone. The triangular object in the model is made of bones. There are 22 bones in the body model. The place at which we insert the bone is adjusted to the skeleton acquired using the skeletal recognition function of the Kinect.
3. Measure the provisional height of the user using the Kinect. Figure 3 shows how we obtain the temporary height. From the acquired skeleton information acquired using the Kinect, we obtain the position of the user's midpoint of both legs and head in three-dimensions. The distance between these two

(a) Body shape provider   (b) Molded body shape

(1) Body shape acquisition from a subject

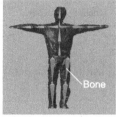

(2) Obtaining a movable model

(a) The movable model who applied   (b) A posture example of a user
the posture of the user

(3) Application of the movable model to the posture of a user

Fig. 2. Example of creating a mobile model and capturing the posture of the user.

points is regarded as the user's provisional height. A user who has entered within view of the Kinect does not necessarily have an upright posture. In this case, it may not be possible to measure the height in the vertical state. Therefore, we set the largest distance among the measured values of the predetermined time as the height. Next, we select the present model from some of the body geometry model, based on the user's height. When swapping the two body models, the system compares their heights, and selects the models of each other person.

4. Obtain the posture of the user from the skeleton recognition function of the Kinect, which is reflected in the bones of the moving model. This process uses the Unity asset "Kinect v2 With MS-SDK". As shown in the figure, the Kinect recognizes the posture of a user facing the screen, and converts it into the model, then horizontally reverses the movement of the model. This image

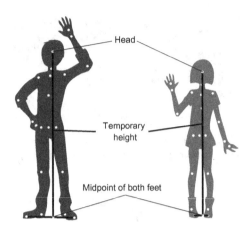

Fig. 3. Acquisition of temporary height.

becomes mirrored when a user sees the screen. Figure 2 shows an example reflecting the posture of the user in (3). The figure shows the body shape being deformed such that it follows the movement of the bones.

4 Evaluation Experiment

To verify the effect of replacing the body with that of another person, we carried out evaluation experiments using Ima-mirror.

4.1 Summary of evaluation experiment

We tested the following hypotheses.

Hypothesis 1: When presenting the self-body shape, it is easy for a user to perform tasks.
Hypothesis 2: A user will be interested in maneuvering the body shape of another person.
Hypothesis 3: A user can experience another person's body sense using the system.

The experimental results are as follows. Figure 4 shows the experimental environment. The width of the experimental field is roughly 3 m, the depth is roughly 3.5 m. The screen of the system is a projection onto a wall at the front. The posture of an experimental subject is recognized using Kinect installed at the front of experimental subjects. The experimental subjects perform tasks while watching the screen.

We focus on the differences in the body attributes between two subjects, who are partners. Therefore, we used a task in which two people must cooperate.

Subjects for an experiment   A screen

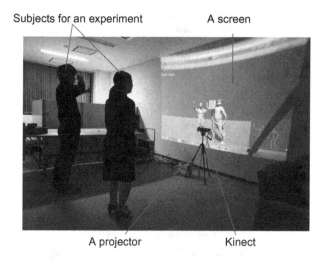

A projector   Kinect

Fig. 4. Experimental environment.

Two experimental subjects were asked to touch an object, which appears on the screen, at the same time.

When the two experimental subjects touch the object at the same time, the object disappears. When the previous object disappears, a new object appears at a different location. The two experimental subjects repeat the task five times. Figure 5 shows the screen of the system. Figure 5 (a) shows the screen just after the experiment has started.

The object appears between the models of the two experimental subjects. The shape of the object is a cube. The object is sized such that one can touch it easily via the hand in the model. Figure 5 (b) shows the locations at which the object can appear.

The location where an object appears is the screen's center; however, the heights at which the center of the cube can appear are 0.6 m, 0.9 m, 1.2 m, 1.5 m, and 1.8 m. We chose these heights based on the heights of the experimental subjects. An experimental subject must stoop or stretch to touch these objects. The appearance order of the object is random. When an experimental subject touches an object, the color changes. When neither experimental subject touches the object, its color is white. When one of them touches it, it becomes red. When both touch it at the same time, the object disappears from the place and appears at a different location. It becomes yellow at the last position at the same time. The number of pairs of experimental subjects is 5. All pairs consist of one man and one woman, because it is easier to see the differences in body features. We acquired the body shape of each experimental subject beforehand. When experimenting, we do not indicate that the shown model belongs to a participant.

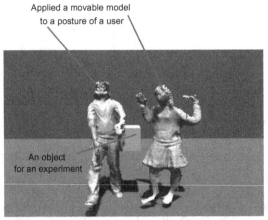

Applied a movable model
to a posture of a user

An object
for an experiment

(a) The screen when the experiment begins

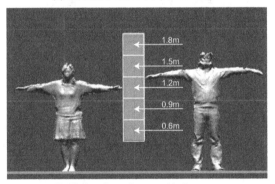

1.8m
1.5m
1.2m
0.9m
0.6m

(b) The locations where an object can appear

Fig. 5. Screenshot of Ima-mirror models. (Color figure online)

Table 1. Time taken to task when each condition.

Pair	One's own model (sec.)	Partner's model (sec.)
A	64	15
B	53	27
C	42	12
D	24	38
E	25	11
Average	41.6	20.6
Std. dev.	15.6	10.4

Table 2. Results of questionnaire for each condition (5-point Likert scale).

Question items	Model	Evaluation					Median value	Mode value	P-value
		1	2	3	4	5			
(1) The experiment was difficult	Own	4	2	1	3	0	2	1	0.895
	Partner	2	5	1	2	0	2	2	
(2) When moving a model, I had the sense that I was moving my body	Own	0	0	1	6	3	4	4	0.0443*
	Partner	0	4	1	4	1	3.5	2,4	
(3) I felt strange when the model was displayed	Own	4	5	1	0	0	2	2	0.00152*
	Partner	0	3	1	3	3	4	2,4,5	

Evaluation value: 1: Strongly disagree, 2: Disagree, 3: Neutral, 4: Agree, 5: Strongly agree
* $p < 0.05$
We performed the Wilcoxon's signed rank test of nonparametric statistics.

Table 3. Results of questionnaire for both conditions (pairwise comparison).

Question items	Evaluation					Median value	Mode value	P-value
	1	2	3	4	5			
(1) Which was easier, the 1st round of the experiment or the 2nd round of the experiment?	1	1	3	5	0	3.5	4	0.257
(2) Which matched your body sense best, the model shown in the 1st round of the experiment or the model shown in the 2nd round of the experiment?	2	6	1	1	0	2	2	0.0196*
(3) Which was more fascinating, the 1st round of the experiment or the 2nd round of the experiment?	0	0	1	3	6	5	5	0.00270*

Evaluation value: 1: First condition, 2: First condition if anything, 3: Neutral, 4: Second condition if anything, 5: Second condition
* $p < 0.05$
We performed the chi-square test.

Table 4. Results of questionnaire on impressions of each model (5-point Likert scale).

Question items	Evaluation					Median value	Mode value	P-value
	1	2	3	4	5			
(1) You noticed that the model shown to you in the 1st round of the experiment is your own body shape	0	0	1	2	7	5	5	0.00270*
(2) [If you answered 4 or 5 in Question (1)] The model was similar to you	0	0	2	4	3	4	4	0.00815*
(3) [If you answered 4 or 5 in Question (1)] I felt that my body was on the screen	0	2	0	3	4	4	5	0.0956
(4) You noticed that the model shown to you in the 2nd round of the experiment is your partner's body shape	0	1	0	3	6	5	5	0.0114*
(5) [If you answered 4 or 5 in Question (4)] The model was similar to your partner	0	0	1	6	2	4	4	0.00468*
(6) [If you answered 4 or 5 in Question (4)] I felt that I became my partner's body on the screen	0	3	2	3	1	3	2,4	0.706

Evaluation value: 1: Strongly disagree, 2: Disagree, 3: Neutral, 4: Agree, 5: Strongly agree

* $p < 0.05$

We performed the chi-square test.

4.2 Results of the experiment

Table 1 shows the time taken to task when each condition. There are the total time which users touch objects that appear in five different locations. For example, first object appears in the height of 1.2 m, and then both users touch it. Next object appears in the height of 1.8 m, and then both users touch it. Times in Table 1 mean the total time spent on five-time touches. Table 2 shows the result of the questionnaire regarding each condition. Table 3 shows the results of the questionnaire regarding both conditions. Table 3 shows the results of paired comparison tests for the questionnaire. Table 4 shows the results of the questionnaire regarding subject impressions of each model.

5   Discussion

5.1   Degree of Difficulty of the Task

We thought that users move precisely for objects on the motion picture when our system shows them in their own model. Because they are accustomed to the movement of their body in the real world. However, Table 3 (1) shows that there is no difference between showing one's own model and showing their partner' model. From the results of the questionnaire, even when being shown a different model, we found out that the experimental subject was experienced in the operation of the system. An experimental subject commented that there was some degree of difficulty due to the difference in the size of the body model. The partner of this experimental subject was taller; therefore, the subject had to perform the movement for a smaller body to be able to touch the object. When the displayed model is tall, the degree of difficulty of the task is low. We did not prove hypothesis 1, i.e., "When presenting the self-body shape, it is easy for a user to perform tasks."

5.2   Interest in Others

The experimental subjects determined that the shown body model can specify one's own body shape or their partner's body shape, as shown in the results in Table 4 (1) and (4). We think that the body shape can express the features of the source body, based on the results in Table 4 (2) and (5). The following comments are the reasoning behind the experimental subjects giving a score of 5 (Strongly agree), see Table 4 (1).

- Because the body shape was akin to my shape, as seen in a mirror.
- Because I recognized myself and my partner from the figures.
- Because we were the same, and the model wore a skirt of the same length.
- Because the model was the same height as myself and wore a skirt.

The following comments are the reasoning behind the experimental subjects giving a score of 5 (Strongly agree), see Table 4 (4).

- Because I found the hair (the model's) to have extended a little.
- Because the figure and clothes of the model were similar.
- Because I was the person's model, which is easy to recognize.

The experimental subjects noticed a change in the body shape. Moreover, they can specify their model and their partner's model from the shape and features of the model, including the clothes and the hairstyle. The experimental subjects replied that the other subject's model was more fascinating than their own model, as shown in the result in Table 3 (3). Therefore, an experimental subject has interest in moving the body shape of another person. We proved hypothesis 2 correct, i.e., "A user will be interested in maneuvering the body shape of another person".

5.3   Another Person's Body Sense Presentation

We found a significant difference between one's own body model and a partner's body model in the results shown in Table 2 (2).

An experimental subject gave a score of 4 for their own model, and a score of 2 for their partner's model. The subject provided the following reasoning. Own model: Because I felt that the model hand was moving to the location one increased. Partner's body model: When I moved my hand, my hand's reach was longer than usual for the distance. This experimental subject felt that the movement became larger for their partner's model than their own model. We think that this difference causes a feeling of strangeness. On the other hand, the partner of this experimental subject gave a score of 5 for their own model, and a score of 4 for their partner's model. The experimental subject provided the following reasoning. Own model: Because the model reflected my movement. Partner's body model: The model reflected my movement. I felt almost no sensory difference.

When comparing their own model and their partner's model, their own model matches better than their partner's, as shown in Table 3 (2). We think that the similarity of body scale produces the feeling that a model matches one's own body sense. Therefore, we found that another person's body sense can be cause a feeling of strangeness when using our system. We proved hypothesis 3 correct, i.e., "A user can experience another person's body sense using the system". When showing one's own model, we found that the system does not always provide an accurate body sense on the screen, as seen in the results shown in Table 4 (3). Moreover, when showing a partner's model, we found that the system does not always provide the sense of experiencing the partner's body, as seen in the results shown in Table 4 (3). The following comments are comments from the experimental subjects who scored the evaluation at 2 (disagree) in Table 4 (6).

– I felt as though I had a new body.
– I thought that the model that was being operated wasn't myself. I didn't feel, "it was my partner's body."

The following comments are comments from the experimental subjects who gave a score of 3 (neutral), see Table 4 (6).

– I felt that I was moving my partner's doll.
– I didn't change my sense of hands and feet very much. I felt I had become relatively big on the screen.

We found that it is necessary to raise an absorbed sense to the screen in future improvements.

6   Conclusion

We have developed the "Ima-mirror," which displays the user's movements using a model that has the physical attributes of someone else on a screen. We obtained the following findings from the evaluation experiments.

1. An experimental subject has great interest in operating the body shape of other people.
2. When the system shows their own body model, the experimental subject experiences a match of body sense.
3. When the system shows another person's body model, the system causes a feeling of strangeness. We found that an improvement would be to raise an absorbed sense to the screen.

We augment the reality of the space and models on the screen to raise an absorbed sense to the screen. We investigate the identifying features (clothes and hairstyle) and the body sense when the height and the figure are changed, and whether a psychological change occurs in the user.

Acknowledgment. This work was supported by JSPS KAKENHI Grant Number 15K12085. We would like to express the deepest appreciation to Dr. Kohei Tokoi of Wakayama University.

References

1. Shibata, K., Hamakawa, R.: Visual change experience system with the head-mounted display. In: Information Processing Society of Japan, Interaction 2015, vol. B52, pp. 623–628 (2015)
2. Nishida, J., Takatori, H., Sato, K., Suzuki, K.: CHILDHOOD: wearable suit for augmented child experience. In: ACM SIGGRAPH 2015 Posters, p. 18 (2015)
3. Tamaki, E., Miyaki, T., Rekimoto, J.: PossessedHand: techniques for controlling human hands using electrical muscles stimuli. In: CHI 2011 Proceedings of the SIGCHI Conference on Human Factors in Computing Systems, pp. 543–552 (2011)
4. Yoshida, A., Miyashita, H.: Video sharing system that overlays body movements for the sense of unity. In: Information Processing Society of Japan, Interaction 2012, pp. 527–532 (2012)
5. Nakamori, R., Aoki, T., Siio, I.: Neighbors' shadow: moderate communication with familiar strangers. In: 7th International Conference on Advances in Computer Entertainment Technology (Creative Showcase), ACE 2010, p. 1 (2010)
6. Morikawa, O., Maesako, T.: HyperMirror: toward pleasant-to-use video mediated communication system. In: Proceeding CSCW 1998 Proceedings of the 1998 ACM Conference on Computer Supported Cooperative Work, pp. 149–158 (1998)
7. Hämäläinen, P.: Interactive video mirrors for sports training. In: Proceedings of the Third Nordic Conference on Human-Computer Interaction, pp. 199–202 (2004)
8. Tomitsch, M., Ackad, C., Dawson, O., Hespanhol, L., Kay, J.: Who cares about the content? An analysis of playful behaviour at a public display. In: Proceedings of the International Symposium on Pervasive Displays, pp. 160–165 (2014)
9. Okamoto, M., Nakanishi, H., Nishimura, T., Ishida, T.: Silhouettell: awareness support for real-world encounter. In: Ishida, T. (ed.) Community Computing and Support Systems. LNCS, vol. 1519, pp. 316–329. Springer, Heidelberg (1998). doi:10.1007/3-540-49247-X_21
10. Jacob, M., Coisne, G., Gupta, A., Sysoev, I., Verma, G.G., Magerko, B.: Viewpoints AI. In: Proceedings of the Ninth AAAI Conference on Artificial Intelligence and Interactive Digital Entertainment, pp. 16–22 (2013)

A Wearable Action Cueing System for Theatrical Performance Practice

Ryosuke Takatsu[1]([✉]), Naoki Katayama[1], Tomoo Inoue[2], Hiroshi Shigeno[3], and Ken-ichi Okada[3]

[1] Graduate School of Science and Technology, Keio University, 3-14-1, Hiyoshi, Minatokita-ku, Yokohama, Kanagawa, Japan
{takatsu,katayama}@mos.ics.keio.ac.jp
[2] Faculty of Library, Information and Media Science, University of Tsukuba, 1-1-1, Tennodai, Tsukuba, Ibaraki, Japan
inoue@slis.tsukuba.ac.jp
[3] Faculty of Science and Technology, Keio University, 3-14-1, Hiyoshi, Minatokita-ku, Yokohama, Kanagawa, Japan
{shigeno,okada}@mos.ics.keio.ac.jp

Abstract. This study focuses on supporting theatrical performances. A system that supports actors learning their acting orders has been already proposed. The system detects actors' speech and cues the next actor to speak. It can however only respond to speech, despite the fact that movement is a very important factor of theatrical performance. Thus this paper proposes to include moving action for cueing the acting order. The evaluation showed that the proof-of-concept prototype system decreased the incidence of both order mistakes and speech mistakes. The findings of this study confirm that the system can efficiently support theatrical performance practice.

Keywords: Acting order · Theatrical performance · Cueing individually · Smart watch · Websocket

1 Introduction

Theatrical performances are a common activity around the world. The theatrical performances are collaborative work, which each person has different role. The most theatrical performances are played according with librettos. Librettos usually have detail instructions, about lines, gesture and who acts it, in timeline format. Actors have to remember a lot of things in addition to the speech lines, including movement, position on-stage, and the flow of the scene. To understand these factors well enough to offer a convincing performance, repeated practice and time are necessary. However, in many case, excessive location costs and schedule coordination make it very difficult to provide enough opportunities to sufficiently learn these elements. Correspondingly, actors compensate for the lack of time and practice with private practices. Actors can refine their own actions like their speech and movement, but it can still be difficult for actors to grasp

© Springer Science+Business Media Singapore 2016
T. Yoshino et al. (Eds.): CollabTech 2016, CCIS 647, pp. 130–145, 2016.
DOI: 10.1007/978-981-10-2618-8_11

their relationship with other actors. Consequently, actors have to hold many group practices to understand this dynamic. Making group practice more efficient can hasten the actors' understanding, thereby reducing costs and improving the quality of performances.

Movement plays an important role in theatrical performances. It shows the audience what the actor is doing and feeling in a way that makes theatrical performance the integrated art of speaking and moving. Just as there is an order to the spoken lines, the movements of the performance also have an order. In some scenes, actors sometime move without speaking, which can then prompt other actors to move or speak. Movement is just as important as speaking. To accurately and sufficiently support theatrical performances, it is necessary to focus on the movement as well as the spoken elements. In addition, the movements of a performance have intentions just like the speaking. As a result, mistakes of movement can impact the actors just as mistakes in the libretto.

The biggest problem in practices is the unwanted interruption from fatal mistakes that cannot be immediately repaired. In these situations, mistakes in the acting order represent the most major problems. Even when actors remember own actions well enough, they can easily make mistakes in the acting order if they lose their relationship with other actors. For example, it is not uncommon for actors to mistakenly speak before another scheduled actor, or forget to move appropriately although it is their turn to act. When these mistakes happen, the director stops the practice, confirms the cause, offers a correction, and the actors replay from a previous point in the scene. It is not only a waste of time, but it also causes stress for the actors. To solve these situations, someone takes on the role of "prompter", who is responsible for keeping the acting ongoing. When actors forget their lines or stammer, the prompter immediately displays the lines on boards for the actors to read. This helps keep the acting smooth, and quickly resolves the stress of the situation. Other actors often take on this role in their free time when they are not involved in the scene. In this way, showing critical information at the appropriate time makes practice more efficient.

In the previous research, which focused on helping actors understand acting order [1], specifically targeting group practice situations. The system detects actor's speech, and then cues each actor in the proper order. The cues are different for each actor depending on their roles and the librettos are stored in the system in advance. By practicing with this system, actors can grasp the flow more easily and concentrate on their own actions. That work focused only on speaking performances, but movement is another very important factor in the theatrical performance. By including movement, we can expect the system to comprehensively support the performance. This study evaluated how this system functions and results confirm a decrease in both order mistakes and acting mistakes. These findings confirm that this system can efficiently support theatrical performance practice.

We describe the flow from the first reading of the librettos to the final rehearsal. The purpose of practice is to enhance the quality of performance. In the beginning, actors get together and read the librettos. In this "read-through", the actors each read their own lines, in order. In this step, the actors have the librettos in hands, and they usually sit on a chair rather than practice the movements. This step allows the actors to grasp a rough image of the story. Next, the actors stand up. They actually move around as they speak along the libretto. In this "Run-through practice", the actors confirm their own movements and standing positions. Finally, they have a "rehearsal" right before the recital. In the rehearsal, the costumes, apparatuses, illumination, and sounds are used exactly as they will be used during the recital.

The Run-through practice is composed of three steps: rough run-through step, extract-step, and sometime-stop-step. In the first step, the actors proceed through the performance without stopping. Even where there are mistakes, the actors continue until the last of libretto, except in the case of extreme failure. Basically, the actors do not focus on their librettos, rather the purpose of this step is to roughly understand the entire flow of the performance. In the second step, the director intermittently stops the actors and instructs them to repeat the libretto or their movements. In the third step, the actors proceed through the performance more smoothly, as long as the director does not mind. If the director notices a mistake that must be corrected, the actors are stopped and briefly corrected before they begin again. After the actors proceed through these steps, they usually only engage in Run-through practice, not rough practice. This is based on the premise that the actors understand their own acting well enough by this step and can correct their own mistakes. In this paper, we focus on these Run-through practice steps.

2   Related Works

In the theatrical performance field, many kinds of works have been researched. Kato et al. proposed an automatic scenario-making system using the information about character and things that have been drawn in preliminary pictures [2]. Sugimoto et al. proposed a scenario making system called "GENTORO" which uses robots and a handy projector [3]. Additionally, there are animation systems called "Pixel Material" [4] for children. In this regard, there is much research supporting story creation.

Much work has also been done on staging. For example, there are systems for presentation apparatuses and illumination on the PC [5], as well as presentation renditions for actors [6]. Kakehi et al. proposed "Tablespace Plus" with which a user can interact with stage information by moving objects [7] A derivative application focuses on the actors' standing positions. In addition, there is a system that deals with 3-dimensional position information [8]. In most of the systems that support staging, computer graphics are used.

In terms of performance planning support systems, there are many types of software being sold. "WYSIWYG" by CAST company [9] focuses on setting stage illumination and spotlights. "Matrix" by Meyer Sound company [10] supports sound needs. Furthermore, there is some research for multi planning collaboration in face-to-face [11] and remote situations [12]. Geigel et al. proposed natural and intuitive interfaces for virtual theatrical performances [13].

Although not specifically designed for theatrical performances, there is the presentation system for a chairperson, activated by using a wearable device. However, this system is only for one chairperson, and not for multiple users.

As described above, many people work to support theatrical performances. However, we cannot find one that focuses on the ordering of moving action in the theatrical field. Moreover, in the field of collaborative work, the same is true.

3   Cueing Speeches and Action Individually

3.1   The Cueing Acting Order System for Theatrical Performance

This study proposed a system of hands-free, wearable devices that individually cues speaking and movement order for each actor. The vibrations of the wearable devices signal the cues, so the actors do not have to see the device's display to know the order. The system sends cues based on the libretto, and provides instructions for each actor individually. In addition, the condition for progress are the actors' speech and movements, so the system clock can measure the relative time, not the absolute time. Both speech and movement factors are incorporated together in order, so this system can comprehensively support the performance. Furthermore, the system can tells when actor makes mistakes in movement, so actors can confirm own their movements. By using this system, actors can concentrate on their own acting and learn the flow in the early stages of theatrical practice.

3.2   Actors' Action Management

Actors can learn and improve their own lines and movements for each performance. However, acting in a relationship with other actors is difficult to understand through solo training. We decided to take libretto in the system to better manage the actors' order of speaking parts. This allows the actors to learn their parts without fully understanding the actions of the other actors. Actors just act when they are cued by system, which enables them to act in the appropriate order every time.

3.3   Efficiency of Run-Through Practices

Mistakes in the acting order happen frequently and can have a huge impact on practice. It stops Run-through practice and applies more stress to the actors, so it is important to make Run-through practices more efficient. Providing better support for Run-through practices will actors to experience the flow of acting more easily.

3.4   Hands Free and Individual Cueing

In the Run-through practice, actors confirm their movements and standing positions. Having to hold the libretto in their hands as they do this creates a hindrance for appropriate training, especially movement practice. Furthermore, each actor has a different role, so they speak different lines and move around the stage differently. As a result, each actor needs different, unique information. To improve Run-through practice, it is necessary to present the appropriate information for each actor individually in a hands-free way. As a good theatrical performance requires the timing of actors' to be synchronized with the movement and libretto of other actors, any system for improving Run-through practice must have a master clock to which all actors' cues are set.

4   Implementation

As a prototype, the proposed system was implemented for three actors. This chapter describe this implementation.

4.1   Hardware Configuration

The system uses WebSocket (described in Sect. 4.2) to connect to a PC server, and Samsung Gear Live as wearable, watch-like devices that can recognize voice and vibrate (Fig. 1). In this system, each actor wears this smart watch to receive acting orders through a vibration and detect the actor's speech with voice recognition.

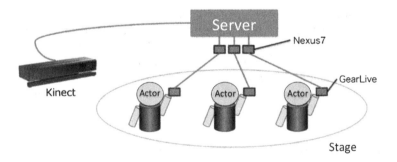

Fig. 1. System configuration

The Samsung Gear Live smart watches are controlled using Nexus 7 tablets. One tablet can control one smart watch, so this prototype system used three tablets connected through Bluetooth. Each table has to be near the actors, but they do not have to wear or carry them. The smart watches use Android Wear 5.0.1 as the implement platform and Android Java API v21.1.2. The processor is a 1.2 GHz Qualcomm Snapdragon 400 and the display is a Super AMOLED

1.63-type. The OS of the tablet is Android Wear 4.4.3, with a 1.3 GHz NVDIA Tegra 3 mobile processor, and an LED backlight 1,280 * 800 type-7 (WXGA) display.

Kinect for Windows API v2.0 was used as a depth camera to recognize each actor's movements. It has a depth camera, an RGB camera, a multi-eye ray-microphone, and a processor. It can recognize gestures to detect the user's position and height. The system used the "Visual Gesture Builder" as a tool for identifying each actor's movements with machine learning. First, we moved in front of the Kinect and taught the system the movements with Kinect Studio. Second, we labeled the data and set threshold parameters. Finally, we confirmed the accuracy of discriminator. After that, the system outputs true or false for each movement that the user acts in front of the Kinect. We can enhance the accuracy of machine learning to use this process for many people, especially those of various heights. This prototype used three people as a model for this process.

4.2   Connection Environment

To connect quickly and support multi devices, the prototype system used Web-Socket, which can keep the socket open in a bidirectional connection. In addition, it supports stable connections in a multi-device environment. This was implemented with node.js and shared with the devices using GitHub and heroku.

4.3   System Function

Connecting Devices. To begin, the server was started and set up to allow access to http://dry-everglades-7373.herokuapp.com. Next, the Kinect (with control PC) and tablets were connected to server. To start program in Kinect and tablets' application, these can be connected to server automatically. IDs are distributed for each device randomly, and each device is manually registered on the server. Next, the tablets are paired to the smart watches using an existing application (Fig. 2). In summary, the procedure for preparing the system is as follows:

1. Accessing the URL (starting server).
2. Starting Kinect program and tablets' app (connecting to server)
3. Pairing tablet and smart watch.
4. Starting smart watch's app.

Management of Actors' Action. The server-control screen is shown in Fig. 3. The librettos were stored as CSV files on the server, which can process and display the data. The relevant libretto information includes the order (number) as well as the corresponding actor, line, and movement. The system can process and transmit three kinds of patterns: line only, movement only, and both line and movement. In cases where actors act at the same time, the system has the same

Fig. 2. Tablet screen for controlling smart watch

order number for these actions and subsequently processes them simultaneously. The corresponding libretto can be matched to the appropriate devices such that the details are displayed on the server and the tablets display each actor's action detail. Until the practice begins, the smart watches display each actor's initial state.

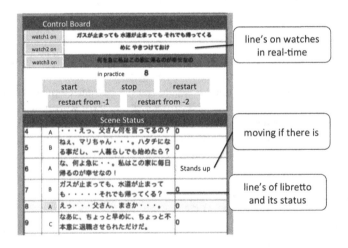

Fig. 3. Server-control screen

Cueing Order for Actors. This system cues acting order for actors using the vibration function of the smart watches. Actors receive information about speaking and movement, so it is necessary for actors to distinguish speaking cues from movement cues. To achieve this, the system uses two vibrations. The smart watch vibrates one time when the actor does not have to move, or twice when actor should move. When cueing movement, the first vibration lasts 500 ms and the second is 700 ms.

The display of smart watch also changes when cued. Although basically stand-by screen is displayed, as shown in Fig. 4(1), when it is cued, display changes to lines screen as shown in Fig. 4(2). If the cue is a movement cue, lines are obviously not shown. This function acts like a prompter and the lines screen changes to the voice input screen within two seconds. The timing is delicate and difficult to judge systematically, so the system allows the actor to freely determine the acting timing.

Fig. 4. Screens of smart watch. 1. Stand-by screen; 2. Lines screen; 3. Voice input screen; and 4. Input result screen

Detection of Speaking and Moving. To cue properly, the system must know the scene the actors are performing in real-time, which it does by detecting both speech and movement. Speech is detected using the smart watch's voice input function, and movement is detected by the depth camera of the Kinect.

After cueing an actor, the smart watches start detecting voice, which is implemented in RecognizeIntent in the Android.Speech package. However, the voice recognition process starts after finishing speech, it takes a moment for the voice input to be recognized.

When the smart watch sends a cue, it displays the lines screen for a short time accompanied by a vibration; two seconds later, it shows the voice input screen. Even when the lines screen is displayed, voice detection has already started. The smart watch then sends the results of this voice detection to the server. The smart watches only perform voice detection for the actor who should be speaking, so the watches worn by other actors are not activated.

To detect voice, the smart watches do not have to be near the actor's mouth. These smart watches can detect voice even if there is certain distance from the mouth, like the natural location of the wrist at the side of the actor's body.

To detect movement, the system used the skeleton detect function of Kinect. Figure 5 shows the PC screen when detecting an actor's movement. This works only in scenes when actors have to move. Kinect can detect max 6 users and it's coverage is max 70° and 4.5 m depth.

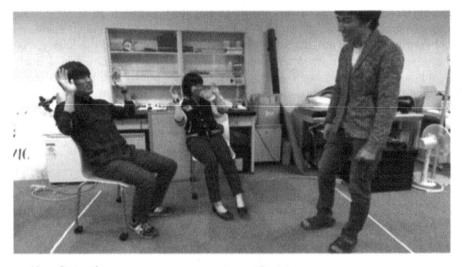

User Detecting

User 1 Detected (0.315365)   User 3 Detected (1)   User 5 Detected (0.20014

Fig. 5. Kinect detecting users

Collation of Detection Result and Notification. If the result of detection is right, the system proceeds to next scene. When recognizing speech, the system only judges whether the actor who is speaking is right, but does not judge the words for accuracy. As long as actors follow this system and do not act without cueing, the actors will not miss the acting order.

The system used the Visual Gesture Builder to recognize gestures. Each actor's movement data is registered in the system in advance. If the actor's movement nearly matches the registered movement, Kinect send a True message to the server.

When actors fail the movement or do not move with seven seconds of the time they should move, the system sends a sound notification.

4.4   Actors' Flow

1. Receive cue by vibration
2. Acting
3. If fail, receive notification by sounds

The actors' process is very simple. The actor receives a cue through a vibration, then performs the speech or movement. If the actor acts properly, the next actor receives the next appropriate cue; if the actor fails, the system stops the practice and the smart watch sounds a notification. To restart the practice, the actor touches the buttons on smart watch display. For this purpose, the smart watch has three buttons: stop, back one step, and back to the beginning, of which the last two can only be used in stop state.

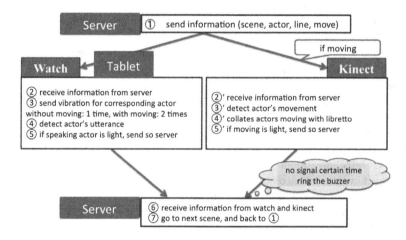

Fig. 6. System flow

4.5 System Flow

The system flow is shown in Fig. 6. For cueing an action to an actor, the server sends the appropriate data, including the order, the actor who should act, the lines, and the movement to each tablet device and Kinect. If the acting has no movement, the server does not send data to Kinect. Next, each smart watch receives the data from the tablet. If the "actor who should act" coincides with the actor registered in the watch, it vibrates. If there is no movement, it vibrates one time; otherwise, it vibrates twice. Then the smart watch changes its mode to detect voice. When the actor speaks, the system determines whether the speaker is light, in which case the smart watch sends "true" to server. If the actor should move, Kinect receives data from the server, and starts recognizing movement. If Kinect finds that "actor who should act" acts light "movement", Kinect sends "true" to server.

The server receives the results from the smart watch and Kinect. If the server sent data to Kinect and does not receive "true" back from Kinect, the server determines that the actor failed to move, and sounds the buzzer. If the server receives true, it proceeds to send data about the next action to each device. This flow continues until the end of the libretto.

An example of a practice timeline is shown in Fig. 7, where the horizontal axis represents time. The colors shown on the right correspond to the line colors in the figure, and white lines represent when the system detects voice or movement. In this example, the flow is as follows:

1. Actor A: speech and movement
   (a) Smart watch vibrates twice.
   (b) Smart watch shows lines and starts voice detection. Kinect starts recognizing movement.
   (c) Smart watch detects speech and Kinect recognizes movement.
   (d) Kinect sends "true" to server.
   (e) Smart watch finishes detecting and sends "true" to server.
   (f) Server goes to the next action.
2. Actor B: only speech
   (a) Smart watch vibrates once.
   (b) Smart watch shows lines and starts voice detection.
   (c) Smart watch detects voice and sends "true" to server.
   (d) Server goes to the next action.
3. Actor C: only movement
   (a) Smart watch vibrates twice.
   (b) Kinect starts recognizing movement.
   (c) Kinect recognizes movement and sends "true" to server.
   (d) Server goes to the next action.
4. Actor A and B: only speech
   (a) Each smart watch simultaneously vibrates once.
   (b) Smart watch shows lines and starts voice detection.
   (c) Smart watch detects voice and sends "true" to server.
   (d) Server goes to the next action.
5. Actor C: speech and movement (mistake)
   (a) Smart watch vibrates twice.
   (b) Smart watch shows lines and starts voice detection. And Kinect starts recognizing movement.
   (c) Smart watch detects speech, however Kinect does not recognize movement.
   (d) Smart watch finishes detecting and sends "true" to server.
   (e) Server does not receive "true" from Kinect, so server determines it has encountered a mistake and sounds buzzer.
   (f) Pause the practice.

5   Evaluation

This chapter provides an evaluation describing whether this system can effectively support theatrical performance practice.

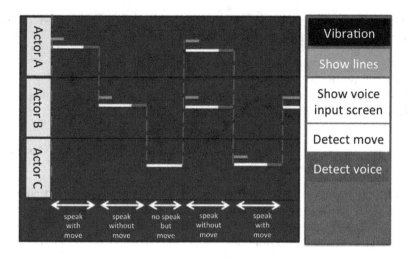

Fig. 7. Timeline of practice with the system (Color figure online)

5.1   Outline

Purpose. The purpose of this analysis is to evaluate whether the system decreases mistakes and facilitates practice.

Method. Participants used the proposed system in actual practice, acted according to the librettos prepared for them, and the number of mistakes of speech and movement were counted.

Participants. This experiment included 24 university and graduate school students, all of whom were novices in theatrical performance. The participants were divided into eight groups of three.

Comparison. The system measures presence or absence. Kinect's recognition and sound buzzer were used to evaluate the effects of cueing, in both environments. The number of mistakes were counted in both environments.

Evaluation Items. This experiment evaluated four types of mistakes: speech order mistakes, speech line mistakes, movement order mistakes, and movement content mistakes. Regarding speech line mistakes, the experimenter allowed actors to make small mistakes as long as they did not change the meaning, and the actors were not required to speak the exact words in the libretto. The number of movement mistakes was compiled with the Kinect's buzzer count.

Librettos. This experiment used librettos, both with three actors, each with 12 – 14 speaking parts and 5 – 7 movements. These librettos were called "Libretto A" and "Libretto B".

Questionnaire. After the experiment, the participants completed a simple questionnaire with the follow questions:

– Which system did you feel easy to practice?
– Please tell us the reason.
– Please score own acting. (from 1–5 for speech and 1–5 for movement)
– Please include other relevant comments.

Procedure. Based on the advice of actual theatrical performers, this experiment set the time for remembering the libretto.

1. Explaining the experiment and how to use the system to the participants.
   First, we explained the experiment. Next, to help the actors become familiar with the system, we explained how to use the system and its flow. Then, we explained that the smart watches cannot detect soft voices and that participants should speak clearly. We also evaluated how the participants remembered the libretto in this experiment, so we told them not to watch their smart watch displays.
2. Participants memorize the libretto in private.
   Roles were determined and the libretto was distributed to the actors, who were then given five minutes to memorize their lines.
3. Read-Run-through practice.
4. Experimenter teaches the participants their movements.
   The libretto also included instruction for movement. However, in this system, Kinect cannot recognize slight differences in the interpretation of the actual movements, so the actors were shown how to move accurately.
5. Participants memorize libretto in private again.
   The actors were given three minutes to memorize the movements that should accompany their lines.
6. The experiment in Run-through practice.
   Participants performed the Run-through practice experiment and the number of mistakes were counted. If participants failed, the practice was paused while they were instructed, and then restarted from the failure point. Participants tried this twice.
7. Repeat steps 2–6 with a second libretto.

Pattern of Experiment for Each Group. To offset the effect of order difference, the experiment proceeded according to the process shown in Table 1.

5.2   Result

The results of this experiment are shown in Fig. 8. The bars in this graph represent the average per Run-through practice. The t test results are as follows:

Table 1. Example of pattern for experiment

	Group 1	Group 2	Group 3	Group 4
Take 1	With system Libretto A practice twice	Without system Libretto A practice twice	With system Libretto B practice twice	Without system Libretto B practice twice
Take 2	Without system Libretto B practice twice	With system Libretto B practice twice	Without system Libretto A practice twice	With system Libretto A practice twice

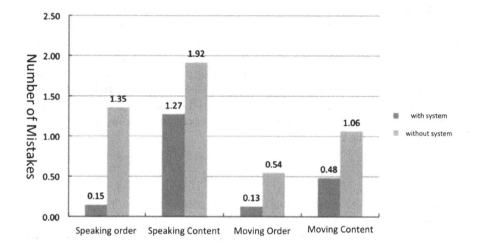

Fig. 8. The result of number of mistakes

- Speaking order mistake: t(47) = 5.58, p < 0.05
- Speaking lines mistake: t(47) = 3.05, p < 0.05
- Moving order mistake: t(47) = 4.19, p < 0.05
- Moving content mistake: t(47) = 3.52, p < 0.05

We confirmed significant difference in all items, and the standard deviation is shown in Table 2. We also confirmed whether we could offset the effects of the experimental order:

Table 2. The results of standard deviation

	Speech order	Speech intent	Moving order	Moving
With system	0.456	1.604	0.331	0.763
Without system	1.534	1.835	0.815	0.852

- Difference of librettos: $t(7) = 0.24$, $p > 0.05$
- Difference of experiment order: $t(7) = 0.46$, $p > 0.05$

These results confirm that we could offset the effects of the experimental order.

5.3 Discussion

The results of the experiment demonstrate that the system can decrease mistakes, so using this system in Run-through practice would allow actors to practice more efficiently. Specifically, this experiment showed a decrease not only in order mistakes but also in line and movement mistakes. Although our system just cues the order (participants did not watch the lines screen), it has an effect on lines and movement content. This means that participants could concentrate on remembering content and not be distracted by remembering acting order. This was noted in some of the comments in the post-experiment questionnaire, which also confirmed a large difference in self-assessment. Participants can act with confidence using the cueing order prepared by the system. These results clearly show that this system can accurately and efficiently coordinate theatrical performance practice in real time.

6 Conclusion

Actors in a theatrical performance are forced to memorize a lot of information in the libretto. To grasp the acting order, actors must understand not only their own acting but also their relationships with other actors. The proposed system helps actors learn to act in the proper order by cueing the order for each actor individually. However, movement is also a very important factor in theatrical performances, so this study extended the functionally of the system to focus on the actor's movements in addition to their speaking parts. This experiment confirmed that using this system lead to a decrease in the number of order mistakes and acting mistakes during Run-through practice. This system allows actors to more fully concentrate on their own acting and grasp the acting flow in the early stages of the practice. Overall, this system was effective in helping actors improve their performance during Run-through practice.

References

1. Ryosuke, T., Naoki, K., Tomoo, I., Hiroshi, S., Ken-ichi, O.: A wearable real-time cueing system for theatrical performance practice. In: 13th IPSJ SIG Digital Contents Creation, No. 8 (2016)
2. Shigeru, K., Takehisa, O.: The support system for story creation using pictures. In: Proceedings of the 2006 International Conference on Game Research and Development, pp. 141–148. Murdoch University (2006)
3. Masanori, S., Toshitaka, I., Tuan, N.N., Shigenori, I.: Gentoro: a system for supporting children's storytelling using handheld projectors and a robot. In: Proceedings of the 8th International Conference on Interaction Design and Children, pp. 214–217. ACM. New York (2009)

4. Tal, D., Michal, R.: Pixel materiali: a system for creating and understanding pixel animations. In: Proceedings of the 6th International Conference on Interaction Design and Children, pp. 157–160. ACM, New York (2007)
5. Matthew, L.: Bowen virtual theater. In: ACM SIGGRAPH 2003 Web Graphics, p. 1. ACM (2003)
6. Mel, S., Howell, J., Steed, A., David-Paul, P., Maia, G.: Acting in virtual reality. In: Proceedings of the Third International Conference on Collaborative Virtual Environments, pp. 103–110. ACM, New York (2000)
7. Yasuaki, K., Takeshi, N., Mitsunori, M.: Tablescape plus: Interactive small-sized vertical displays on a horizontal tabletop display. In: Second Annual IEEE International Workshop on Horizontal Interactive Human-Computer Systems, TABLETOP 2007, pp. 155–162. IEEE (2007)
8. Hanyuool, K., Issei, T., Hiroki, Y., Takayuki, K., Satoshi, M., Takeshi, N.: Mario: mid-air augmented realityinteraction with objects. In: Reidsma, D., Katayose, H., Nijholt, A. (eds.) ACE 2013. LNCS, vol. 8253, pp. 560–563. Springer, Heidelberg (2013)
9. Cast Group of Companies Inc. http://www.cast-soft.com/wysiwyg/overview
10. Meyer Sound Laboratories Inc. http://www.meyersound.com/
11. Daiki, N., Yousuke, H., Tomoo, I., Kenichi, O.: Diamond theater: a system for supproting creative activities. Inf. Process. Soc. Jpn. Jornal **51**(12), 2396–2408 (2010)
12. Christian, D., Denis, L.: Avatar: a virtual reality based tool for collaborative production of theater shows. In: The 3rd Canadian Conference on Computer and Robot Vision, p. 35. IEEE (2006)
13. Joe, G., Marla, S., David, H., Namco, B., Brian, J.: Adapting a virtual world for theatrical performance. Computer **44**(12), 33–38 (2011)

Development of a Cooking Support System Aimed at University Students Living Alone

Takuma Tsujimoto$^{(\boxtimes)}$ and Takashi Yoshino

Graduate School of System Engineering,
Wakayama University, Sakaedani 930, Wakayama, Japan
tsujimoto.takuma@g.wakayama-u.jp, yoshino@sys.wakayama-u.ac.jp
http://www.wakayama-u.ac.jp/en/

Abstract. It is common for people to start cooking for themselves when they go away to university. It is important to acquire knowledge of foods and to experience cooking while young. With this in mind, we have developed "Cookma" a cooking support system using microblog. Cookma supports step-by-step improvement of cooking abillity and increase of recipe repositories by a recipe recommendation function that considers cooking difficulty. Cookma both motivates students to cook, and supports continuation by a dish photo sharing function via microblog and a gamification function. Evaluation experiment results showed the following three points: (1) It is possible for Cookma to motivate users to cook habitually by a recipe recommendations that considers cooking difficulty. (2) Sharing dish photos on a microblog can motivate users to cook habitually. (3) Game-like elements of replies between a user and a Cookma bot can motivate users to cook habitually.

Keywords: Cooking support · Recipe recommendation · Microblog · Gamification

1   Introduction

It is common for people to start cooking for themselves when they go away to university. However, students do not usually make a habit of cooking for themselves on a regular basis. According to a report from the Cabinet Office of Japan, 23.1 % of university students cook once per week or less, and 20.3 % do not cook at all [1]. In other words, 43.4 % of university students almost do not cook.

The reason is that cooking is troublesome for them, and they have no habits of cooking [2]. On the other hand, since only 6.4 % of students actually dislike cooking, there is possibility to make students to cook habitually by some motivation [3].

In recent years, there has been an increase in food outsourcing. It is difficult to keep a nutritional balance by only eating out [4]. Self-management of eating habits is necessary for a healthy life. Therefore, it is important to acquire knowledge of foods and to experience cooking while young.

© Springer Science+Business Media Singapore 2016
T. Yoshino et al. (Eds.): CollabTech 2016, CCIS 647, pp. 146–158, 2016.
DOI: 10.1007/978-981-10-2618-8_12

In recent years, use of social networking services (SNS) has become widespread among young adults. According to a report by the Ministry of Internal Affairs and Communications in 2015, 49.3 % of people in their twenties or younger are using Facebook, and 52.8 % are using Twitter [5].

Thus, we have developed a cooking support system, called Cookma, using microblog. Cookma supports step-by-step improvement of cooking abillity and increase of recipe repositories by a recipe recommendation function considering cooking difficulty. Cookma both motivates students to cook, and supports continuation by a dish photo sharing function via microblog and a gamification function.

2   Related Work

Several studies have been conducted on searching for and recommending cooking recipes. In research by Takahashi et al., there are proposals concerning recipe searches using semantics, ingredient substitutions, and pictures and videos [6].

A recipe recommendation system by Nakaoka et al. aimed at increasing recipe collections, recommends recipes that include inexperienced ingredients and cooking methods with priority [7]. Lertsumruaypun et al. proposed a recipe recommendation system using onomatopoeic words [8]. A system developed by Mizuno et al. focused on property of ingredients [9]. Wakao et al. introduced serendipity-like elements to recipe recommendation [10]. Our system structures a search method focused on cooking difficulty. This method automatically calculates the cooking difficulty of recipes, and then recommends recipes based on the user's cooking ability.

Kuramoto et al. aim to increase working motivation using breeding game [11]. "Habitica" To-Do management service using gamification helps people improve living habits by showing real-life tasks as monsters that have to be conquered [12]. Our system assimilates gamification consulting these examples.

As a system supporting cooking using SNS, there are Cookking by Wiel et al. [13]. Cookking shares recipes and make ranking in collaboration with SNS. Our system aims at motivating students to cook for themselves by photo sharing on SNS, according to their knowledge.

3   Cookma

We describe the Cookma cooking support system in this section. Cookma supports a user's cooking habit through replies between a Cookma bot and users on Twitter. The purpose of Cookma is to help improve cooking ability, to motivate a user to cook, and to support continuation of cooking. A recipe recommendation function that considers cooking difficulty plans step-by-step improvement of user's cooking ability and increase of recipe repositories. A dish photo sharing function and a gamification function plans to motivate users to cook and continuation support.

3.1 Design Policy

The design policy of Cookma is as follows:

User friendliness to encourage daily usage
We need to design Cookma so that users, namely, university students living alone will use this system routinely because Cookma encourages healthy cooking habits. Accordingly, we used Twitter which is widespread among young adults, as the front-end for Cookma.

Adaptation based on diversity and improvement of user's cooking ability
Due to the wide range of cooking ability among students, it is necessary that recipes are recommended that take into account a user's specific ability. Because cooking ability improves with continuous use of Cookma, Cookma must recommend recipes that gradually increase in difficulty in order to raise the user's ability.

Supporting improvement and continuation of cooking motivation
Cookma has to continuously motivate users to cook for themselves. Cookma encourages continuous use by a dish photo sharing function and a gamification function.

3.2 System Configuration

Figure 1 shows system configuration of Cookma. Cookma consists of a "Cookma bot", a "Cookma server", and "Users." The Cookma bot obtains a user's tweet and sends ingredient-related words extracted from the tweet to the Cookma server. The Cookma server receives the words from the Cookma bot and searches for recipes in accordance with the user's cooking ability from a recipe database. Recipe titles and recipe urls are then sent to the user through the Cookma bot. The cooking difficulty calculation module classifies recipes into five groups ranked by difficulty. The users prepares the recommended recipes, and sends dish photos to the Cookma bot. In this study, we used Cookpad data as a source for the recipe data. Cookpad[1] is the most popular recipe sharing service in Japan.

Figure 2 shows an image of the bot in use. In Fig. 2, the bot extracts "Chinese cabbage" as an ingredient, and recommends a recipe using Chinese cabbage. The user prepares the dish and sends photo to the bot.

3.3 Recipe Recommendation Function

This function extracts ingredients from a user's tweet and recommends recipes to the user. There are three processes involved in this function flow. First ingredients words are extracted. Next, the recipe database is searched. Finally recipes are recommended.

----

[1] http://cookpad.com/.

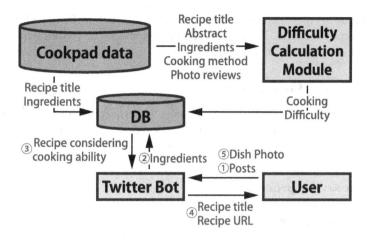

Fig. 1. System configuration.

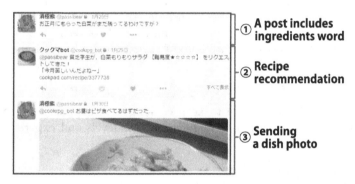

Fig. 2. Usage example.

Ingredients extracting process

In this process, the system extracts words classified as "food" from a user's tweet using morphological analysis. We used the Japanese language morphological analysis JUMAN[2] as a morphological analysis engine for our experiment.

Recipe search process

In this process, the system searches recipes using extracted ingredients words from the recipe database. Because the system considers a user's cooking ability, the difficulty calculation module ensures that recipes of the correct difficulty level are selected for the user.

Recipe recommendation process

In this process, the system selects a recipe from results of recipe search, and recommend recipe title and recipe url to users. Because Cookpad data does

---

[2] http://nlp.ist.i.kyoto-u.ac.jp/index.php?JUMAN.

not include recipe url, the system obtains recipe url on Cookpad website at each recommendation. If users are dissatisfied about the recommended recipe, they can demand other recipes.

3.4 Dish Photo Sharing Function

This function takes dish photos sent by users, and shares them with other users. There are two processes in this flow. First, dish photos are saved. Next the photos are shared with other users. The dish photo sharing function is used to motivate users.

Dish photo saving process
In this process, the system saves on the server dish photos of foods cooked by users. Cookma uses the photos to confirm that users actually cooked the foods.

Dish photo sharing process
In this process, the bot tweets dish photos received from users and shares them with other users. The tweet includes the identification of the person who prepared the dish. Figure 3 shows an example of dish photo sharing. In this case, the bot is tweeting a photo of yogurt received from a user.

3.5 Gamification Function

This function motivates people to keep cooking, and support continuation of cooking by using gamification. This function uses levels and experience points to encourage users to cook.

Levels and experience points
When users send a dish photo, they obtain experience points according to the difficulty of the recipe that was prepared. If users cook often, resulting in raising to new levels, Cookma will recommend more difficult recipes.

Nicknames for cooks
Cookma creates nicknames for users, such as "assistant cook," and "experienced cook." The nicknames change when the user advances to a new level.

Recipe recommendations by imaginary characters
Recipe recommendations from the bot take the form of imaginary characters suggesting dishes for users. For example, "a footballer boy" requesting a dish with the caption "I'm hungry!"

4 Cooking Difficulty

In this study, we used Cookpad data as the data source for recipes provided to users. However, Cookpad data includes no information about cooking difficulty. We have to define difficulty automatically based on recipe information. We describe a method for calculating cooking difficulty in this section. Policies of calculation are as follows:

User name

Dish photo

Fig. 3. Screenshot of a photo sharing function.

1. To easily calculate cooking difficulty easily based on a large number of recipes.
2. To classify cooking difficulty into wide ranges; from easy to difficult.

We use five data items from Cookpad to calculate difficulty. The data used were as follows:

- number of ingredients in a recipe,
- number of steps involved in the preparation of a recipe,
- number of characters of cooking method in a recipe,
- number of photo reviews[3] for a recipe,
- the existence, or nonexistence, of phrases in recipe title and an abstract that indicate easiness.

The above data items were used in the following formula to determine a difficulty score.

$$
\begin{aligned}
Difficulty = \ & MIN(the\ number\ of\ ingredients,\ 20) \\
& + MIN(the\ number\ of\ steps,\ 20) \\
& + MIN(the\ number\ of\ characters,\ 1000)\ /\ 100 \\
& - MIN(the\ number\ of\ photo\ reviews,\ 600)\ /\ 60 \\
& - the\ existence\ of\ phrases\ that\ indicate\ easiness\ *\ 10
\end{aligned}
$$

---

[3] Cookpad users make interested recipes and send photo reviews to recipe authors.

In this formula, values for the number of ingredients, the number of steps, and the number of characters are first added. Then, values for the number of photo reviews, and the existence or nonexistence of phrases that indicate easiness are subtracted.

In case that values about ingredients, steps of cooking method, and characters of cooking method are high, cooking difficulty might be also high because the recipe is complicated. In case that values about photo reviews and phrases which shows easiness are high, cooking difficulty might be low.

If the values for ingredients, steps, and characters are high, the difficulty value may also be high because the recipe will be complicated. If the values for photo reviews and phrases are high, the difficulty value might be low.

Outliers of values for ingredients, steps, characters, and photo reviews (about 1%) are excluded from the formula. Values obtained from the formula for ingredients and steps are calculated in 0–20. Other values are calculated in 0–10. Finally, the cooking difficulty score is calculated in −20 − +50. Cookma classifies recipes into five ranks based on the difficulty score. Classification rules are as follows:

- < −2: rank 1 (easiest), 6,878 recipes
- −2 to < +11: rank 2, 61,087 recipes
- +11 to <+24: rank 3, 49,058 recipes
- +24 to < +37: rank 4, 7,961 recipes
- ≧ +37: rank 5 (most difficult), 1,320 recipes

Most recipes are classified as rank 2. There are 61,087 recipes. Difficulty rank 5 has the fewest number of recipes, only 1,320.

This calculation method was created using investigation results from a difficulty calculation method used in an existing study [14].

5   Evaluation Experiment

5.1   Summary of Evaluation Experiment

The purpose of this experiment was to evaluate whether each function of Cookma could motivate students to do their own cooking, and then support them in efforts to continue cooking for themselves. For this evaluation, we developed the following three hypotheses, and then tested them.

Hypothesis(1). The recipe recommendation function provides recipe recommendations properly.
Hypothesis(2). The dish photo sharing function motivates users to cook.
Hypothesis(3). The gamification function motivates users to cook.

Because the purpose was to evaluate each function, the experiment was carried out for three days: from Friday to Sunday. Participants were university students (eight men, two women) who use Twitter and live alone. The experiment tasks were as follows:

1. Follow the Cookma Twitter bot
2. Tweet a text that includes desired ingredients.
3. Cook recipes recommended by Cookma, and send dish photos once or more times

When the experiment began, we set all participants to level 1 (lowest). Therefore, in the early stages of the experiment, Cookma recommended only easy recipes regardless of the user's cooking ability. When users prepare recipes, some reordering of recipes and substitutions of ingredients are permitted. In the experimental period, one of the co-authors used Cookma, posted tweets with ingredients, and sent dish photos. That is because we plan to inform users how to use the dish photo sharing function. This author was not included as a participant. After the experimental period, we asked each participant to complete a questionnaire using the 5-point Likert scale, and free description.

5.2   Experiment Results and Considerations

In experimental period, all participators tweeted with ingredients words and cooked recommended recipes. Table 1 shows the number of recipe recommendation, the number of demand of other recipes, and the number of cooking recipes. The bot recommended recipes 21 times most. Users cooked recipes 3 times most. Table 2 shows the result of questionnaire survey using the 5-point Likert scale. Figure 4 shows an example of replies between a user and the bot. In this case, recipe recommendation and dish photo sharing were done about recipe using onion.

During the experimental period, all participants tweeted ingredients words and prepared the recommended recipes. Table 1 shows the number of recipe recommendations, the number of demands for other recipes, and the number of recipes cooked by each user. The largest number of recipes recommended by the bot was 21. The largest number of recipes actually cooked by users was three. Table 2 shows the results of the questionnaire survey using the 5-point Likert scale. Figure 4 shows an example of replies between a user and the bot. In the example shown in Fig. 4, the recipe recommendation and cooking, was for a dish that included onions.

Evaluation of the recipe recommendation function. Items (1) to (4) in Table 2 show the evaluation results of the recipe recommendation function.

Survey item (1), "Dialogues with the bot using replies are easily comprehensible," had a median of 4 and a mode of 4, 5. From the free description answers, we obtained the following opinions: "Using Cookma is simple and easy to understand." "It wasn't at all confusing to operate." These remarks show that Cookma is user-friendly.

Survey item (2), "The timing of recipe recommendation is appropriate," had a median of 4 and a mode of 4. From the free description answers, we obtained the following opinion: "There was a response to my tweet after only a short time."

Table 1. The number of recipe recommendations and the number of recipes cooked.

	The number of recommendations	The number of demands for other recipes	The number of recipes cooked
User A	21	8	3
User B	13	3	2
User C	12	5	3
User D	16	1	1
User E	1	1	1
User F	9	0	1
User G	3	1	1
User H	4	1	1
User I	15	9	1
User J	3	2	1

Table 2. Results of questionnaire survey.

	Question items	Evaluation					Median	Mode
		1	2	3	4	5		
(1)	Dialogues with the bot using replies are easily comprehensible	0	1	1	4	4	4	4,5
(2)	The timing of recipe recommendations is appropriate	0	3	1	6	0	4	4
(3)	Recommended recipes are possible to cook	0	0	2	4	4	4	4,5
(4)	You would like to cook recommended recipes	0	0	2	7	1	4	4
(5)	I feel resistant to sharing my dish photo	1	4	1	4	0	2.5	2,4
(6)	Sending dish photos to other users motivate me to cook for myself	1	1	4	3	1	3	3
(7)	Viewing dish photos sent by other users motivate me to cook for myself	0	1	1	5	3	4	4
(8)	Experiment points motivate me to cook for myself	0	2	1	3	4	4	5
(9)	Nicknames motivate me to cook for myself	0	3	1	3	3	4	2,4,5
(10)	Requests by imaginary characters motivate me to cook for myself	0	3	3	2	2	3	2,3
(11)	I want to use Cookma continuously	0	0	1	7	2	4	4

- Evaluation: 1: Strongly disagree, 2: Disagree, 3: Neutral, 4: Agree, 5: Strongly agree.
- "Evaluation" is the number of people.

On the other hand, we also obtained the following opinion: "Recommendations also came to me when I did not want them." These remarks show that we must

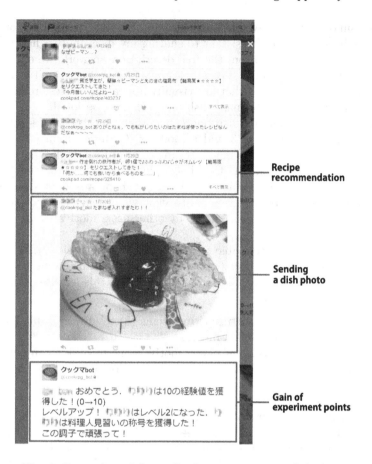

Fig. 4. Screenshot of the replies between a user and the bot.

also use clock time and tweet content when deciding whether Cookma should or should not recommend recipes.

Survey items (3) and (4), "Recommended recipes are possible to cook," and "You would like to cook recommended recipes," had a median of 4 and a mode of 4, 5. From the free description answers to the question item "What recipes do you want to?" we obtained the following opinions from users who are not in the habit of cooking for themselves: "Simple recipes which have a few cooking steps." "Recipes should not require too many ingredients." These remarks show that Cookma recommends recipes appropriately to users who do not normally cook for themselves.

From these results, we were able to prove correct hypothesis (1), "The recipe recommendation function provides recipe recommendations properly."

Evaluation of the dish photo sharing function. Items (5) to (7) in Table 2 show the evaluation results of the dish photo sharing function.

About survey item (5), we obtained the survey results divided like or dislike. The survey item (5), "I feel resistant to sharing my dish photo," had a median of 2.5 and a mode of 2, 4. From the free description answers, we obtained the following contrasting opinions: "I'm a little embarrassed, but I don't worry about it." "I have to prepare dishes that are visually appealing." These remarks show that it would be advisable to make dish photo sharing optional.

Survey item (6), "Sending dish photos to other users motivates me to cook for myself", had a median of 3 and a mode of 3. Survey item (7), "Viewing dish photos sent by other users motivates me to cook for myself," had a median of 4 and a mode of 4. From the free description answers to question item (7), we obtained the following opinions: "Viewing dish photos makes me want to cook something too." "It energizes me to view what other users cook." These remarks show that viewing dish photos by other users motivates users to cook for themselves.

From these result, we were able to prove correct hypothesis (2), "Dish photo sharing function motivates users to cook." However, because some users do not want to share their own dish photos, we should make this feature optional.

Evaluation of gamification function. Items (8) to (10) in Table 2 show the evaluation results of gamification function.

Survey item (8), "Experiment points motivate me to cook for myself," had a median of 4 and a mode of 5. From the free description answers, we obtained the following opinion: "Raising levels is fun." These remarks show that obtaining points through cooking motivates users to cook more.

Survey item (9), "Nicknames motivate me to cook more," had a median of 4 and a mode of 2, 4, 5. From the free description answers, we obtained the following opinions from users who gave low ratings: "Because there is no actual feeling involved with recieving nicknames." "I was not conscious of that." These remarks show that nicknames may motivate users to cook as experiment points. However, it is necessary to improve how nicknames are presented.

Survey item (10), "Requests by imaginary characters motivate me to cook for myself," had a median of 3 and a mode of 2, 3. From the free description answers, we obtained the following opinions from users who gave high ratings: "If the characters recommend recipes, I will try to make the dishes for them." "It was a fun way to get recommendations." On the other hand, users who gave low ratings described following opinions: "I cannot empathize with strangers." "I can't picture in my mind or relate to imaginary characters." These remarks show that imaginary characters can, in some cases, motivate users to cook in some case. However, it is necessary to improve how we present the imaginary characters.

From these result, we were able to partially prove correct hypothesis (3), "The gamification function motivates users to cook" partly. However, we should rethink how to improve the presentation of nicknames and how to represent the characters.

Overall evaluations of cookma. Survey item (11), "I want to use Cookma continuously," had a median of 4 and a mode of 4. From the free description answers, we obtained the following opinions: "I want to raise my level and be challenged with more difficult recipes." "There is no sense of obligation, so I think it's easy to continue." The experiment period was short, however, the results do indicate that Cookma can motivate users to cook for themselves, and Cookma can support users to continue cooking for themselves, and to become better cooks.

6 Conclusion

In this paper, we have developed the "Cookma" cooking support system aimed at university students living alone. The conclusions of this study are as follows:

1. It is possible for Cookma to motivate users to cook habitually by a recipe recommendations that considers cooking difficulty.
2. Sharing dish photos on a microblog can motivate users to cook habitually.
3. Game-like elements on replies between a user and the Cookma bot can motivate users to cook habitually.

Hereafter, we will improve our system, and evaluate over the long term.

Acknowledgment. In this paper, we used recipe data provided by Cookpad and the National Institute of Informatics.

References

1. Cabinet Office of Japan: Report of university students' reality and conscious about food (2009)
2. Momma, K., Washio, S.: Survey on university students toward dietary habits and menu model for one day. Bull. Paper Kyoto Women's University Department of Living and Welfare **10**, 11–20 (2014)
3. Hori, M., Hirashima, M., Isobe, Y., Nagano, H.: Research on the cooking habits among college students. Bull. Paper Gifu City Women's Coll. **57**, 61–65 (2008)
4. Process of food outsourcing rate. http://www.anan-zaidan.or.jp/data/
5. Ministry of Internal Affairs, Communications of Japan: Effect of social media spreading, White Paper Information and Communications in Japan, 209 (2015)
6. Takahashi, T., Ide, I.: Food and Computing: 2 recipe and menu search. IPSJ Mag. **52**(11), 1376–1381 (2011)
7. Nakaoka, Y., Satoh, T.: Proposal of a recipe recommendation system for the increase of a repository based on ingredients bias and cooking methods. In: Proceedings of Multimedia. Distributed, Cooperative, and Mobile Symposium (DICOMO 2014), pp. 1653–1660. IPSJ, Japan (2014)
8. Lertsumruaypun, K., Watanabe, C., Nakamura, S.: Onomatoperori: Recipe Recommendation System Using Onomatopoeic Words, IPSJ SIG Technical Report, 2009-DD-73, 6, 1–7 (2009)

9. Mizuno, Y., Kojiri, T., Yokoi, S., Ide, I., Seta, K.: Alternative ingredient generation support based on similar recipe presentation. In: Proceedings of the 75th National Convention of IPSJ. 6ZE-8, 4, pp. 779–780. IPSJ, Japan (2013)

10. Wakao, K., Oku, K., Hattori, F.: Fusion-based approach for serendipity-oriented recipe recommendations. In: Proceedings of the 75th National Convention of IPSJ. 3P–2, 1, pp. 681–682. IPSJ, Japan (2013)

11. Kuramoto, I., Katayama, T., Shibuya, Y., Tsujino, Y.: A virtual aquarium based on EELF with subjective competition for keeping workers' motivation. IPSJ J. **50**(12), 2807–2818 (2009)

12. Habitica. https://habitica.com/static/front

13. Eelco, W., Martin, M., Suleman, S.: CookKing: a king of healthy, fun and social cooking. In: Proceedings of the 7th International Conference on Advances in Computer Entertainment Technology (ACE 2010), pp. 110–111. ACM, New York (2010)

14. Tsujimoto, T., Yoshino, T.: Proposal of self-cooking support system using microblog. In: Proceedings of IPSJ Kansai-Branch Convention 2016. G-08, pp. 1–4. IPSJ, Japan (2015)

Collaborative Web Search Using Tablet Terminals on a Virtual Tabletop Environment

Tadashi Inoue, Ian Piumarta, and Hideyuki Takada[✉]

College of Information Science and Engineering, Ritsumeikan University,
1-1-1 Noji-Higashi, Kusatsu, Shiga 525-8577, Japan
htakada@cs.ritsumei.ac.jp
http://www.cm.is.ritsumei.ac.jp/~htakada/index_e.html

Abstract. The *Virtual Tabletop Environment* (VTE) is a tablet-based framework that simulates an interactive tabletop environment suitable for collaborative work. We present a VTE application that supports collaborative Web search. Web views are placed on the virtual tabletop. Users have tablet terminals that provide windows onto the VTE, through which the Web views can be seen and manipulated. Four groups of three users participated in an evaluation of the effectiveness of the system. The results show that discussion and information sharing is more likely compared with collaboration using traditional desktop Web browsers.

Keywords: Collaborative web search · Tablet terminals · Virtual tabletop Environment

1 Introduction

As tablet computer and 'smart-phone' technology advances, these mobile devices become increasingly capable of supporting collaborative work. 'Collaborative Web search' is conducted by multiple users, each using a mobile device to individually search for Web content. Search results are shared among the users as they work towards a common goal.

A user can share their individual search results physically by showing the screen of their mobile device to other users. This is disruptive because it interrupts the search activities of the other users. Results can also be shared electronically by sending search result URLs to other users via an information sharing tool such as Apple's AirDrop. This is also disruptive because the sender must open an information sharing application that is not related to their ongoing search activity.

Useful results can also be lost because sharing is initiated by a single user; if a user does not proactively share a potentially useful result, it will not be seen by the other collaborators. To maximize the benefit of collaborative search, and to minimize the risk of losing useful information, the methods for group communication should encourage instant sharing of individual results within the group.

© Springer Science+Business Media Singapore 2016
T. Yoshino et al. (Eds.): CollabTech 2016, CCIS 647, pp. 159–173, 2016.
DOI: 10.1007/978-981-10-2618-8_13

Users engaged in collaborative search on a desktop computer can immediately see every search result on a large, shared display. To obtain a similar degree of communication when working with mobile devices we have developed the *Virtual Tabletop Environment* (VTE) [3]. Communication and sharing are encouraged by placing all collaborators' documents on single, shared virtual tabletop surface.

This paper presents an evaluation of a collaborative Web search system, built on the virtual tabletop environment, in which users share information rapidly and with little disruption. Related work is reviewed in Sect. 2. The collaborative Web search system is described in Sect. 3. Section 4 presents our evaluation of the system's effectiveness, compared with users working with traditional Web browsers. Section 5 offers some concluding remarks.

2   Related Work

This section introduces work related to collaborative Web search. We also briefly describe the virtual tabletop environment.

2.1   Collaborative Web Search

Web search has traditionally been a solitary activity, and major Web browsers are designed based on this assumption. Many systems have nevertheless been proposed to support collaborative Web search [5,9] in which members of a group share information while searching the Web to achieve a common goal. Possible scenario of a collaborative Web search task is to plan a travel with friends, decide a product of furniture to purchase with family members and find related research works with laboratory colleagues.

Examples of systems supporting collaborative Web search include Group-Web [2] which is a Web browser allowing group members to remotely share and navigate Web sites, SearchTogether [6] and Coagmento [10] which target remote users, CoSearch [1] and a collaborative exploratory search system [8] which target co-located users, Maekawa's page partitioning system for hand-held mobile devices [4], and WeSearch [7] which uses a shared tabletop display. Among these, WeSearch is the closest in approach to our system.

WeSearch provides collaborative Web search on a large, shared, tabletop display. Two overhead projectors provide content on a specially-constructed 1.2×1.8 meter touch-sensitive surface. Users collaborate on a search activity simultaneously, standing around the display. Unlike Web search with individual mobile devices, they can easily see what other users are doing during the search process. Users can therefore share not only their results but also the process of Web searching with the other group members.

2.2   Virtual Tabletop Environment

Here we briefly describe the virtual tabletop environment in which a Web search system is built as an application. Detailed design, implementation and analysis of the VTE can be found in a separate article [3].

The VTE provides a shared workspace extended virtually over a normal tabletop, whose content is viewed on the displays of mobile tablet computers. Direct manipulation using gestures on the touch-sensitive tablet screens provides interaction with the shared objects in the virtual workspace.

Figure 1 illustrates how collaborative work is conducted on the VTE. Each tablet acts as a peephole, giving its user a moving window onto the much larger virtual space. When the user slides the tablet across the tabletop, the tablet display scrolls so that the content appears stationary on the tabletop. Synchronization among the tablets ensures that, for a given position on the tabletop, the same content will be displayed on any terminal moved to that position.

Preliminary experiments show that VTE users have good situational awareness and understanding of their working area's location within the entire virtual workspace. Spatial relationships between objects are easily understood. Users employ spoken explanations and physical gestures, such as pointing, to communicate information about object relationships within the workspace efficiently.

Our collaborative Web search application lets users immediately share their individual search results within the large common workspace of a VTE. Being able to see and share information within other users' working areas is the key characteristic that the VTE brings to a tablet-based Web search system.

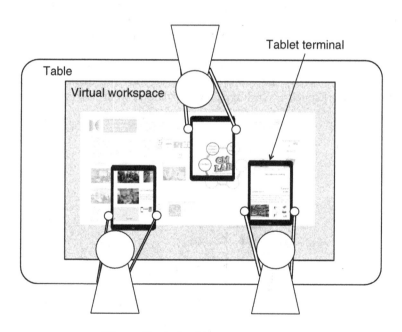

Fig. 1. Virtual tabletop environment

3   The Collaborative Web Search System

This section presents the design and implementation of our collaborative Web search application running on the VTE.

3.1   Functional Design

Shared Workspace. As shown in Fig. 2, users collaborate on a search activity within a large virtual workspace. Each user holds a tablet PC which displays a small portion of the much larger virtual workspace. The portion displayed depends on its physical position of the tablet on the tabletop.

Within the workspace the contents of Web pages are displayed in Web views. Views can be moved around within the workspace. Changes to the number and positions of views in the workspace are synchronized among the tablets; when a new Web view is created on one tablet, the same view is created locally on the other terminals at the same position within the workspace. Contents of Web views are also synchronized; if the content of a Web view changes after following a hyperlink, the view is updated accordingly on the other terminals.

The number of terminals in use need not equal the number of collaborating users. Terminals are not 'owned' by a specific user; users are expected to operate whichever terminal is the most convenient at any given moment.

Users can perform the following actions in the shared workspace:

1. *Change the displayed portion of the workspace*
   Sliding a tablet across the tabletop surface scrolls the displayed portion of the virtual workspace accordingly. (When the system starts up, the initial

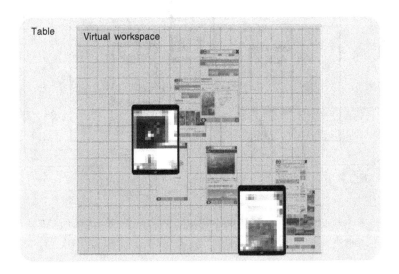

Fig. 2. Shared workspace

physical position of each terminal can be synchronized to one of the four corners of the virtual workspace.)

2. *Display the entire workspace*

   Pressing the 'whole view' button lets a user see the entire virtual workspace, as shown in Fig. 3. Seeing the whole workspace gives users situational awareness of where Web views are placed relative to each other, and what Web pages are currently open. Web pages cannot be scrolled in the whole view mode; to see details of the Web page of interest or to interact with it, users need to move the terminal to the location of its Web view while in 'normal view' mode.

3. *Invert the Web view*

   Showing a terminal to a user located on the opposite side of the table will present an inverted view of the Web pages' contents. When the 'upside-down view' button is pressed, the contents of all Web views are rotated 180 degrees so that they have the correct orientation for users viewing from the other side of the tabletop.

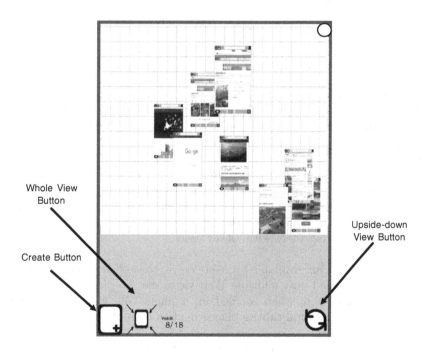

Fig. 3. Whole view

Web Views. Figure 4 shows an example of a Web view. The major functions of Web views are described below.

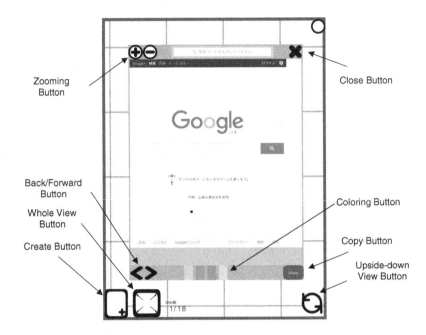

Fig. 4. Web view

1. *Create a Web view*

   Pressing the 'create' button adds a new Web view to the virtual workspace at the currently-displayed location. Web views provide the usual browser functions such as 'back', 'forward', and 'close'.

2. *Move the Web view*

   Tapping and dragging the colored frame of a Web view allows it to be moved within the workspace. Moving the terminal while dragging a Web view causes the Web view to follow the movement of the terminal. Web views can thus be moved easily to any position on the tabletop, which is essential for showing them to, and sharing them with, other users.

3. *Zoom in or out*

   Six levels of zoom are available for Web views, controlled by the 'zoom' buttons. When zoomed out, multiple Web views can be displayed on a single tablet for comparison; when zoomed in, a single Web view can be seen in great detail using several tablets placed next to each other.

4. *Change frame color*

   Every Web view has a frame. The color of the frame can be changed using the 'color' buttons. Frame colors can be used to tag and then easily identify Web views classified according to characteristics such as content, the person who found the Web page, and so on.

5. *Copy the Web view*

   Pressing the 'copy' button creates a new Web view containing the same Web content. Copying is needed to duplicate a view before passing it to a another user. It is also a way to 'bookmark' a search result by storing its content in a new view before moving on to another Web page within the original view.

3.2 Implementation

We use Apple's iPad with 9.7 in. screen for our implementation. The *Multipeer Connectivity* framework is used to synchronize the virtual workspace among multiple iPads. This framework provides server-less communication over Wi-Fi and Bluetooth.

When a Web view is created or moved, its coordinates are transferred to all the terminals. When the content of a Web view is updated, the corresponding URL is sent to all the terminals. Every terminal's model of the workspace content is therefore synchronized so that users can observe the same workspace contents, with the same spatial relationships, regardless of which terminal they use.

Scrolling the displayed portion of the workspace when a tablet is moved requires a mechanism to measure physical movement on the tabletop surface. In our provisional implementation we use a wireless mouse to measure the movement of each tablet. Figure 5 shows how a mouse is attached to a tablet to detect movement. Movement information is sent to a PC (MacBook) via Bluetooth and forwarded to the tablet via Wi-Fi. The Web view application running on the tablet scrolls the workspace accordingly.

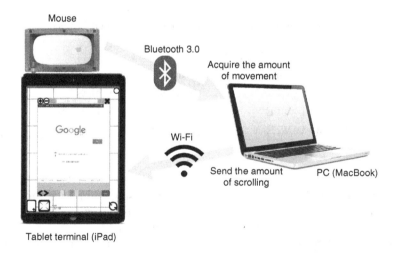

Fig. 5. System structure for scrolling the workspace

Several mice can be connected to a single PC. (Our current implementation allows up to four mice per PC.) A tool running on the PC associates the MAC address of each mouse with the IP address of the physically-corresponding tablet. When movement information is received from a mouse, it is forwarded to the corresponding tablet.

In this provisional implementation, users cannot lift or rotate their tablet because a mouse is attached. We plan to develop a device using a color sensor to detect the absolute position on a colored surface to overcome this limitation.

4   Evaluation

This section presents an experiment to evaluate the effectiveness of multiple-tablet interfaces for virtual tabletop environments by performing collaborative Web search using our prototype VTE system.

4.1   Purpose

The experiment is designed to answer the following two questions:

- How useful is a VTE-based system for collaborative Web search, compared to a traditional Web browser?
- Does changing the number of tablets available to the users affect how they perform the task?

To answer these questions we asked experimental participants to perform a task using three different environments. Table 1 summarizes these environments, each of which is described in detail below.

Table 1. Working environments for the experimental tasks

Task	Working Environment	
Task 1	Safari+AirDrop	N users with N tablets
Task 2	VTE	N users with N tablets
Task 3+1	VTE	N users with $N + 1$ tablets
Task 3−1	VTE	N users with $N - 1$ tablets

Safari+AirDrop: Participants perform the task using Safari, a standard Web browser on iPad. Search results are shared between users using AirDrop, an information-sharing tool provided on Apple devices.

VTE system with N users and N tablets: Participants perform the task using the VTE-based collaborative Web search system, with the same number of tablets as users. The usefulness of this environment is compared with that of the Safari+AirDrop environment.

VTE system with N users and $N \pm 1$ tablets: Participants use the VTE-based system with either one more tablet than the number of users, or one fewer than the number of users. With $N + 1$ tablets we evaluate how a surplus of tablets might be used for the task. With $N - 1$ tablets we evaluate how the participants might overcome a small deficit of tablets.

4.2   Experimental Method

Twelve students participated in the experiment. They formed four groups of three participants to perform a collaborative Web search in each of the working environments. In all cases the participants were seated around the same physical tabletop.

The topics of the collaborative search tasks were "find the three best places to visit in western Japan", "find the three best places to visit in eastern Japan", and "find the three best places to visit in the world".

Each group first performed the search task using Safari+AirDrop (Task 1). All groups then performed the same search with the VTE-based system using three tablets (Task 2). The first two groups then performed the search using the VTE-based system using four tablets (Task 3+1), whereas the last two groups performed the search using two tablets (Task 3−1). Before using the VTE-based system, each group was explained how to use the system and given three minutes to become familiar with its user interface. Twenty minutes were allotted for the completion of each task. Figure 6 shows an experiment in progress.

Fig. 6. A scene of the experiment

4.3   Evaluation

Evaluation was based on observation of the participants while they performed the tasks, and analysis of a questionnaire they completed after the task. Tables 2 and 3 list the contents of the questionnaires. Questions shown in Table 2 are designed to evaluate whether participants could share information easily and collaborate effectively. Questions shown in Table 3 are designed to assess the effects of a surplus or deficit of tablets, by asking participants how they used an additional tablet or overcame a shortage of them.

Table 2. Questionnaire comparing Task 1 with Task 2

	Questions	Answer format
Q1	For Task 2, did the chance of seeing Web pages that other users were searching increase?	multiple choice
Q2	(For those who answered "yes" for Q1) Was the sharing of Web information also improved?	multiple choice, and free description
Q3	For Task 2, did placing the Web views on a surface make it easier to compare multiple Web pages?	multiple choice, and free description
Q4	For Task 2, did using "whole view" make it easier to understand the relative positions of Web views?	multiple choice
Q5	(For those who answered "yes" for Q4) How did you use the "whole view" function?	free description
Q6	Comparing Task 1 with Task 2, which did you feel gave more satisfactory search results?	multiple choice, and free description

Table 3. Questionnaire comparing Task 2 with Task 3

	Questions	Answer format
Q7	Compared with Task 2, how did you use the tablets in Task 3?	free description
Q8	Compared with Task 2, was it easy to perform the collaborative search in Task 3?	multiple choice, and free description

4.4   Results

Experimental results concern the two aspects mentioned above: comparing a VTE-based system with the more traditional Safari+AirDrop, and analyzing the effects of increasing or decreasing the number of tablets available to the participants.

VTE compared to Safari+AirDrop

Observations. Participants using Safari+AirDrop first performed Web searches individually using their own tablet. During the task, they showed their tablet directly to others, or exchanged URLs using AirDrop when they found Web pages they wanted to share. Little discussion occurred while performing the individual searches, except in some cases when showing a Web page to another user.

Participants using the VTE-based system first performed Web search individually using their own tablet, as in the case for Safari+AirDrop. When they found a Web page of interest, they shared Web views by moving their terminals across the table or simply by showing their tablet to other users. All of the groups shared Web views of interest by collecting the views together in the center of the workspace. They looked at other users' tablets more frequently than in the case of Safari+AirDrop. They were able to share Web pages rapidly by positioning their terminals over a similar area.

Questionnaires. Table 4 shows the answers to Q1, asking whether the chance of looking at other users' terminals increased. More than half of the participants answered that the chance increased. Participants who answered "yes" to this question also answered Q2, asking whether the sharing of Web pages was improved; the results are shown in Table 5. Typical reasons given in the 'free description' part of the answer were "because we were able to see easily other users' terminals like a shared screen" and "because we were able to look at the other terminals just by moving the terminal a little, and to talk easily".

Table 4. Chances of looking at others' tablets

Greatly decreased	Somewhat decreased	No difference	Somewhat increased	Greatly increased
1	1	2	6	2

Table 5. Experience of sharing Web pages

Not enhanced	Somewhat enhanced	Greatly enhanced
0	4	4

Table 6 shows the results for Q3, asking about the ease of comparing Web pages in the VTE-based system. Five participants answered "somewhat easy" or "very easy". Reasons given for the ease of comparison included "Web pages could be related visually" and "the whole workspace could be inspected". Other participants said it was less easy, expressing difficulties with using the system such as "it was difficult to find a target Web page because of the inaccuracy of scrolling by moving the tablet" and "tablet movement had to be performed carefully". One of the participants answered "it is possible to have a 'whole view' in Safari too".

Table 6. Comparing Web pages

Very difficult	Somewhat difficult	No difference	Somewhat easy	Very easy
0	5	2	2	3

As shown in Table 7, most participants answered Q4 by saying that it was easy to relate the positions of views within the workspace. Answers to Q5 revealed that participants used the 'whole view' function to see Web pages opened by other users and to know the positions of Web pages within the workspace. Because only a small portion of the workspace is normally visible, the 'whole view' function was used frequently by the participants.

Table 8 shows the results for Q6. Eight out of the twelve participants answered that they were satisfied with the results of collaborative Web search using the VTE-based system. Their opinions included "everyone could work without being isolated" and "discussion was encouraged because of the increased chances of looking at other users' Web pages". Those users who preferred the standard browser answered "time ran out without becoming familiar with moving the terminal correctly" and "AirDrop was easier to use". During the tasks, some groups obtained good results because of the ease of looking at each others' Web pages and having discussion encouraged, while others spent most of the allotted 20 min familiarizing themselves with the operation of the system and were left with insufficient time to work on the search task.

Table 7. Understanding the position of Web views

Very difficult	Somewhat difficult	No difference	Somewhat easy	Very easy
0	2	0	5	5

Table 8. Satisfaction with search results

Task 1 (Safari+AirDrop)	Task 2 (VTE-based system)
4	8

Surplus or Deficit of Tablets

Observations. Giving four tablets to a group of three users produced different patterns of behavior for different groups. One group used the additional tablet to display the 'whole view', facilitating the comparison of Web pages; individual users continued to use a single tablet of their own. Another group did not use the additional tablet at all. In neither case was any significant change to the amount of discussion, compared with providing exactly one tablet per user, seen.

Giving just two tablets to a group of 3 users resulted in each tablet being used for individual searches, but with two of the users having to share one tablet. Users sharing a single tablet engaged in active communication with each other to perform the Web search. When sharing Web pages with the group, the pages of interest were collected in the center of the workspace as in the case of one tablet per user. Tablets tended not to be moved around the workspace very much, staying close to the participants and their small visible area of the virtual workspace. No significant change was seen in the level of discussion between the users of the two tablets; the tablets themselves were never exchanged while performing the task.

Questionnaires. Question 7 asked users how they handled the tablets when a surplus or deficit of tablets was provided. Participants with an additional tablet answered "the additional tablet was used for the 'whole view' to understand the overall locations of views" and "the additional tablet was not used for much at all". Participants with too few tablets answered that "two users performed most of the searching, with the third user mainly observing the screen" and "the range of tablet movement became restricted".

Table 9. Surplus or deficit of tablets

	Harder	No difference	Easier
$N + 1$: 3 users with 4 tablets	0	4	2
$N - 1$: 3 users with 2 tablets	3	2	1

Table 9 shows the results of Q8, asking how easy it was to perform the collaborative search. The groups with an additional tablet answered "one of the tablets was used for the whole view" and "we couldn't think of a way to use the additional tablet". The groups with only two tablets answered "the tablet screen was too small for two users to use together" and "only a part of the virtual workspace could be used".

4.5   Discussion

VTE Compared with Standard Browser. Compared with the standard Safari+AirDrop environment, the results show that a VTE-based system increases the chances that users share Web pages with each other and leads to increased user satisfaction with their performance of the task. This is because users can perform the task collaboratively, easily sharing both the process and the results of their searches. Sharing is easy because of several characteristics of a virtual tabletop environment; in particular, being able to see other users' terminal screens and being able to share Web pages instantly within the shared virtual workspace.

A problem arose because of inaccuracies in tracking tablet movement. Difficulties were experienced when trying to move a tablet to a position of interest in the virtual workspace, which consequently reduced the ease with which Web pages could be compared. These difficulties arose from the tracking mechanism used in our prototype environment, and would not be present to the same degree in a VTE using more sophisticated mechanisms. The results do however demonstrate the importance of minimizing the scrolling and positioning errors experienced by users of a VTE.

Number of Available Tablets. When given a surplus of tablets, one group used the additional tablet as a shared 'workspace overview' display while the other group did not use the additional tablet at all. In both cases each user performed the collaborative task using only one of the available tablets. We can conclude that users tend to use a single tablet to perform their searches, and that different uses (including none) can be found by different groups for an additional tablet. With a deficit of tablets, one of the users simply did not use a tablet and instead became an observer of one of the other users. While the communication with their 'tablet partner' was increased, it was difficult for them to contribute as much to the collaborative work.

Users continued to use a single tablet throughout the task, never exchanging their tablet with another user. This suggests that users identify personally with the tablet that they are initially given.

5   Conclusion

We presented a collaborative Web search system built as an application in a virtual tabletop environment, using multiple tablet terminals for display and interaction. Practical experiments evaluated users' use and reaction to the system, to determine the usefulness of a VTE and the effect of changing the number of tablets to create a surplus or deficit. The experimental results show that our VTE-based system promotes discussion and information sharing compared with collaboration using traditional desktop Web browsers.

Future work will include improving the movement tracking in our prototype, with the aim of developing a compact and inexpensive device that can be attached to a tablet to accurately track its location on a tabletop surface.

Acknowledgments. This work was supported by the Japan Society for the Promotion of Science (JSPS) KAKENHI Grant Number 25330249.

References

1. Amershi, S., Morris, M.R.: CoSearch: a system for co-located collaborative Web search. In: Proceedings of the SIGCHI Conference on Human Factors in Computing Systems, pp. 1647–1656. ACM (2008)
2. Greenberg, S., Roseman, M.: Groupweb: A WWW browser as real time groupware. In: Conference Companion on Human Factors in Computing Systems, pp. 271–272. CHI 1996, ACM (1996)
3. Ito, N., Takada, H., Piumarta, I.: Effectiveness of tabletop interaction using tablet terminals in a shared virtual workspace. In: International Conference on Collaboration and Technology. Springer, Heidelberg (2016) (to appear)

4. Maekawa, T., Hara, T., Nishio, S.: A collaborative Web browsing system for multiple mobile users. In: Proceedings of Fourth Annual IEEE International Conference on Pervasive Computing and Communications, pp. 12–35, March 2006

5. Morris, M.R.: A survey of collaborative Web search practices. In: Proceedings of the SIGCHI Conference on Human Factors in Computing Systems, pp. 1657–1660. ACM (2008)

6. Morris, M.R., Horvitz, E.: SearchTogether: an interface for collaborative Web search. In: Proceedings of the 20th annual ACM symposium on User interface software and technology, pp. 3–12. ACM (2007)

7. Morris, M.R., Lombardo, J., Wigdor, D.: WeSearch: supporting collaborative search and sensemaking on a tabletop display. In: Proceedings of the 2010 ACM conference on Computer Supported Cooperative Work, pp. 401–410. ACM (2010)

8. Pickens, J., Golovchinsky, G., Shah, C., Qvarfordt, P., Back, M.: Algorithmic mediation for collaborative exploratory search. In: Proceedings of the 31st Annual International ACM SIGIR Conference on Research and Development in Information Retrieval, pp. 315–322. SIGIR 2008, ACM (2008)

9. Shah, C., Capra, R., Hansen, P.: Collaborative information seeking [guest editors' introduction]. Computer **47**(3), 22–25 (2014)

10. Shah, C.: Coagmento–a collaborative information seeking, synthesis and sensemaking framework. In: Integrated demo at CSCW, pp. 6–11 (2010)

Social Presence Visualizer: Development of the Collaboration Facilitation Module on CSCL

Masanori Yamada[1]([⊠]), Kosuke Kaneko[2], and Yoshiko Goda[3]

[1] Faculty of Arts and Science, Kyushu University,
744, Motooka, Nishiku, Fukuoka, Japan
mark@mark-lab.net
[2] Cyber Security Center, Kyushu University,
744, Motooka, Nishiku, Fukuoka, Japan
kosukekonako@kyudai.jp
[3] Graduate School of Instructional Systems,
Kumamoto University, 2-39-1, Kurokami,
Kumamoto 860-8555, Japan
ygoda@kumamoto-u.ac.jp

Abstract. This study aims to develop and evaluate a visualization function of CSCL that is based on social presence. This function automatically categorizes the postings from learners and visually presents social interaction following a social presence indicator. Furthermore, this function seems to enhance social presence and encourage learning behavior, such as active discussion. In order to investigate the validity of auto-categorization, the inter-rater agreement rate and the ability to predict the quality of the discussion were analyzed and compared to the human-categorized data. The results demonstrated that there are several social presence indicators that have high and low inter-rater agreement, but the categorization of the function developed in this study had more prediction power than the human-conducted categorization.

Keywords: Community of inquiry · Social interaction · Social presence · Computer-Supported Collaborative Learning (CSCL) · Visualization

1 Introduction

There has been growing interest in collaborative learning in higher education. Collaborative learning requires the active participation of students, and thus fosters high-end learning skills. However, there are several challenges to the implementation of collaborative learning in educational settings: Nishimori et al. [1], for example, have pointed out the difficulty in tailoring collaborative learning schedules around the various other class commitments of learners, as doing so poses a potential threat to group cohesion and delays the progress of learning.

In the age of technological innovation, one increasingly popular solution to this problem is the use of computer networks for Computer-Supported Collaborative Learning (CSCL). Computer-Mediated Communication (CMC) tools, such as Bulletin

© Springer Science+Business Media Singapore 2016
T. Yoshino et al. (Eds.): CollabTech 2016, CCIS 647, pp. 174–189, 2016.
DOI: 10.1007/978-981-10-2618-8_14

Board Systems (BBS) are particularly useful in supporting collaborative learning outside of the classroom.

The background of CSCL is based in socio-constructivist pedagogical theory, which posits that knowledge should be constructed and re-constructed through inter-action between learners, or between learners and artifacts [2]. In support of this per-spective, it is important to consider how one may enhance interaction between learners who work collaboratively in a virtual setting when designing CSCL. This study aims to develop the visualization tool for CSCL based on social presence in order to contribute to the enhancement of learning motivation and achievement in support of collaborative learning programs.

2 Community of Inquiry (CoI) Framework

2.1 Definition of CoI Framework

Garrison and Anderson [3] constructed a "Community of Inquiry (CoI)" framework in which teachers and learners interact in text-based, online communication. The CoI framework consists of three elements: social presence, cognitive presence, and teaching presence. Social presence is defined as "the ability of participants to identify with the community, communicate purposefully in a trusting environment, and develop inter-personal relationships by way of projecting their individual personalities" [3]. Social presence is regarded as a necessary element for creating a secure environment for interpersonal communication in order to foster an open environment that is con-ducive to discussion. Shea and Bidjerano [4] suggest that social presence is an important factor in predicting the level of cognitive behaviors. They reported that learners who are regarded as high-level cognitive learners treated low-level cognitive learners by responding to them using social presence. Cognitive presence is defined as "a vital element in critical thinking, a process and outcome that is frequently presented as the ostensible goal of all higher education" [5]. Teaching presence is defined as the design, facilitation, and direction of cognition and social processes for the purpose of realizing personally meaningful and educationally worthwhile learning outcomes [6]. Two of the three CoI elements and indicators. CoI is enhanced by integrating the three presences in the teaching of projected learners [7], as doing so promotes metacognition for collaborative learning [8]. Goda and Yamada [9] investigated the relationship between these three presences in Asynchronous Computer-Mediated Communications (ACMC). Their findings reveal that the teaching and cognitive presence were signifi-cantly correlated with discussion satisfaction, and social presence was positively associated with the number of utterances.

Many researchers used the CoI framework for the evaluation and investigation of the effects of the learning community (e.g., [10, 11]), but this framework can also be applied to collaborative learning environment designs. Several studies have tried to design and develop a CSCL system that is either based on CoI or that is comprised of CoI components (e.g., [12]). The present study aims to develop the function, in par-ticular, of visualization, which is based on the "Social Presence" CoI element.

2.2 Social Presence and Its Role in CMC

Social presence is a crucial factor in learning with CMC, in denoting perceptions of oneself and others, as well as in supporting social interactions within a community, promoting trust relationships, and playing an important role in the effective implementation of CSCL. Learners' perception of presence is affected by social presence, which Short, Williams, and Christie [13] describe as the "degree of salience of the other person in the interaction and the consequent salience of the interpersonal relationship." In other words, social presence promotes the perceived proximity to real-time communication in a face-to-face setting, depending on the type of CMC tool used. Short, Williams, and Christie [13] further suggest that the two dominant factors in social presence are "immediacy," which is defined as the psychological proximity of the interlocutors, conveyed, for example, through facial expressions, and "intimacy," which is defined as the perceived familiarity evoked by social behavior, such as eye contact and smiling.

Researchers have interpreted social presence in different ways, both in their experiments and in their practical applications. Gunawardena and Zittle [6] conducted a research project in which they investigated the effect of social presence on learning satisfaction, from the perspective of facilitating and moderating discussion and the perspective of the perception of interactivity in online discussions. Their research revealed that a high awareness of social presence has positive effects on learning satisfaction. According to this view, which focuses on the notion of interactivity rather than on perceived proximity to real-time communication, social presence depends on interaction between groups using the same CMC tool in their learning.

Other researchers have concentrated on the expressive functions of social presence, which is thereby framed as a type of communication ability. Garrison and Anderson [3] redefined social presence according to its expressive function in the establishment of group cohesion in asynchronous text-based communication. Garrison and Anderson [3], meanwhile, describe social presence as one of the elements in a "Community of Inquiry (COI)," in which teachers and learners interact in text-based online communication. Social presence is regarded as a necessary element for creating a secure environment for interpersonal communication and for developing an atmosphere that is open to discussion. Their study further proposes specific indicators of social presence in the asynchronous, text-based CMC, which serve to bridge cognitive behaviors for learning.

Enhancing social presence is effective not only in promoting learning satisfaction [6], but also in the promotion of cognitive learning behavior. Shea and Bidjerano [4] suggest that social presence is one of the most important factors in predicting the level of cognitive behavior. They reported that learners who are regarded as high-level cognitive learners treated low-level cognitive learners by interacting with them using social presence. In order to enhance social presence, a system in which learners reflect and adjust the current degree of social presence is needed. However, social presence is an unconscious feature; that is, learners are not always engaged in collaborative learning with the consciousness of social presence. Social perspectives, such as social awareness (e.g., "What role will I take in this group?" and "How will I interact with this group?"), which are formed in collaboration are difficult features to support using groupware [14]. Several researchers tackled this challenge by using visualization (e.g., [15, 16]). Mochizuki et al. [16] developed and evaluated a visualization system called "ProBo Portable" which visualizes the situation and progress of each group member's task on a mobile phone. This research reveals that the visualization of situation and progress in collaborative circumstances is effective in monitoring each other and in enhancing the learning community, as reflective feature.

The perspectives on social presence discussed above are useful in designing a CMC tool that enhances interaction between learners. An integrated view of social presence seems necessary for the purpose of designing and evaluating a CMC tool for collaborative learning, in which the system design can enhance social presence for the encouragement of learning behavior. This study aims to develop a social presence visualization system for CSCL. Thus, another aim of this study was to point out future directions for designing a function that promotes learning through the enhancement of social presence.

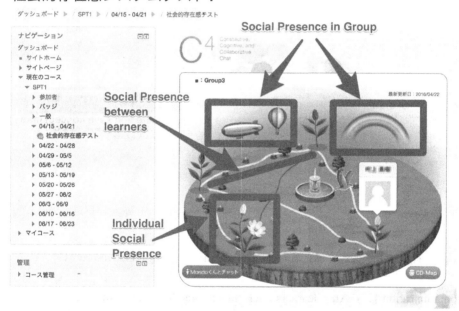

Fig. 1. Interface of social presence visualization

3   System

A visualization module was developed for the extend function of the chat tool with the permission of extension development from the researchers [17], which is also developed as the LMS "Moodle" module 2.9.X. Figure 1 shows the interface of this module. Figure 2 shows the fundamental functions for the support of social and cognitive

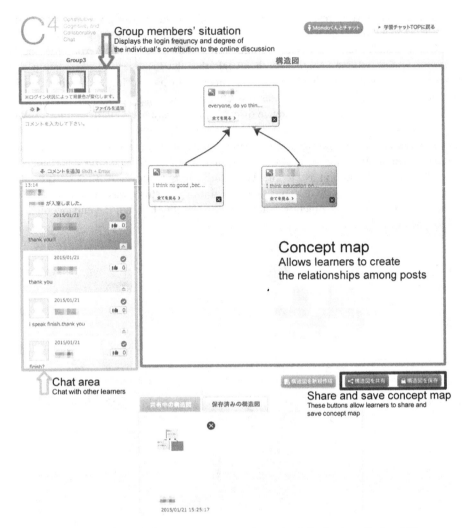

Fig. 2. Interface of chat, concept map and member's login time display [17].

communication [17]. After learners click the chat module link in the course, learners can move to the group chat entrance page displayed in Fig. 1. When learners click the "CD-Map" button, learners can move to chat page shown in Fig. 2.

This system consists of two functions; chat and concept map. Chat function allows learners to post their massages using emoticon and share the file. Learners can mark other posts as "favorite" by pushing "like" button. In concept map, leaners can click and drag a posting object in the chat area to the concept map area, and then show relationships between postings using arrow lines. Concept map function as a group cognitive tool allows learners to index the information on the concept map, thus is effective on the improvement of group memory [18]. The researchers indicated that the system used in this research may be effective to enhance social presence and improve the discussion quality [17].

3.1 Calculation Method for Social Presence Scores

3.1.1 System Overview

Figure 3 presents an overview of our proposed system that evaluates the Social Presence Scores from users' comments in a chat group. The system stores every comment written by each user into a chat group thread and calculates the three types of Social Presence Scores: (a): Score of a user to a group, (b): Score of a user's reply to another user; and (c): Score of a whole group. The calculation of score (a) is based on every comment written by a user in a chat group thread. The calculation of score (b) is based on every reply made by one user in response to the comment of another user. For the calculation of score (b), the visualization system collects the data of the user name that sent the messages as variable name "MENTION." That is, the "Reply Symbol" in Table 1 means a kind of symbol appears in a text when a user replies to another user's comment in the proposed system. Only when the symbol appears in a text, the first value in the score is set as 1; otherwise, the value is 0. The calculations of score (c) are based on every comment written by every user in a chat group.

The proposed system has a national language processing (NLP) module for analyzing a text written by each user as a comment in a chat group. The core part of the system is implemented by using PHP so that the system can be easily implemented to cooperate with Moodle developed by PHP. Only the module is implemented by using Python because Python has many helpful libraries that support NLP. "Stanford CoreNLP" [19], a popular NLP library for analyzing documents written by English, is used in the module for the text analysis. The procedure that is used to calculate the Social Presence Scores starts with the core system's passing of one text written by a user into the module, which is followed by the module's calculation of a Social Presence Score of the text, which is based on several rules and is explained in the next section. After

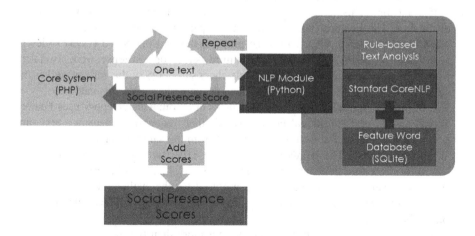

Fig. 3. Overview of the proposed system

this score is calculated, the score is returned to the core system. The returned score is expressed as a 19-value sequence (social presence and mention) of 0 or 1, separated with commas, e.g. 0,1,0,0,1,0,0,0,0,0,0,0,0,0,0,0,1,1,1. The 0 or 1 in the sequential value means a 1 is set on the bit flag only when the text contains a factor related to each category supporting the Social Presence Theory. Otherwise, 0 is set on the bit flag. The 17 categories of Social Presence are listed in Table 1. The core system repeats the pass-and-receive process until every comment in a chat group is checked. After the process, the system adds up every returned score and presents the Social Presence Scores.

3.1.2   Procedures of Rule-Based Text Analysis

The NLP module analyzes the texts by using rule-based procedures. Table 1 presents the rules that determine whether or not the text contains a factor that supports each category. The description of "Feature Word" in Table 1 shows that a text contains a feature word that supports the categories. The feature words were extracted in the pre-process phase from several sample chat data, which had 3,570 comments in 10 groups, and were also extracted from the WordNet database [20, 21]. The method used to extract these feature words is described in the next section. The description of the "Feature Phrase" in Table 1 refers to a certain phrase that frequently appears in a text supporting the categories. The phrases are selected by an expert who researches Social Presence based on his experiences by investigating phrase patterns of the sample chat data. Different from the case of the "Feature Word," the module checks the dependencies of each word on constructing the phrase. The following list explains in further detail the rule-based procedures for each category.

- Expressing emotions: an Emoticon Symbol appears in a text when a user uses an emoticon in their comment. This symbol is one factor supporting this category. Another factor is that of Feature Words extracted from WordNet Affect 1.1 [22].
- Use of humor: This category uses Feature Words and Feature Phrases to judge whether or not a text contains a factor supporting this category. There are only two Feature Phrases: "it is funny" and "it is humorous."
- Self-disclosure: This category also uses Feature Words and Feature Phrases for the evaluation. The Feature Phrases follow three patterns: "I am XXX", "I was born XXX" and "I live in XXX". In these phrases, the part-of-speech (POS) styles of verbs, namely the Present Tense Verbs in third-person or past-tense, were also taken into account for this category. The module checks the POS of the verb as well as the subject. Only when the subject is "I" does the module enable this category.
- Use of unconventional expressions to express emotion: This category uses Feature Words and several Additional Feature Words that frequently appear in a text supporting this category but cannot be extracted from the sample chat data or from the WordNet database. The words selected by the expert are only words that are followed by these five punctuation marks: "!", "• • •", "…", "~", "—".
- Expressing value: Only Feature Words are used for the evaluation.
- Continuing a thread: The module sets 1 on the sixth position of the sequential value only when users
- continuously reply to another one's comment more than two times.

- Referring explicitly to others' messages: The Feature Phrase of this category is "XXX said ∼". XXX is a subject in a text. At first, the module, checks a verb in a text, and if the verb is "say", present-tense verbs in third-person or past-tense are taken into account. Next, the dependency modifier of "nsubj" or "nsubjpass" is checked. These technical terms express a relationship of dependency according to "Stanford typed dependencies" [23]. Lastly, the module checks the POS of the subject for the evaluation. Only when the POS is a PRP (Personal Pronoun) or a NNP (Proper Noun, singular), is the module set on 1 in the seventh position in the sequential value.
- Quoting from another's message: This category is enabled when a user writes a comment containing the same comment written by another user within the previous 20 comments. The 20 comments do not take into account comments constructed in less than five words or comment supporting the SALUTATION category.
- Asking questions: The only factor that can enable this category is a question mark.
- Complimenting expressing appreciation: This category uses Feature Words for the judgment.
- Expressing agreement: The module uses Feature Words for the judgment and also checks dependency relationships to decide whether a text contains Positive, Negative or Neutral sentence. This category becomes enabled when a text contains a feature word and is a positive sentence, or when a text contains a feature word of DIS-AGREEMENT and is a negative sentence. Two additional phrases, "me, too" and "me too", were also taken into consideration for the evaluation.
- Expressing disagreement: This category is the counterpart of the AGREEMENT category.
- Personal advice: This category is enabled when a text is a positive sentence and contains Feature Words supporting this category.
- Vocatives: For the evaluation of this category, the module extracts the subject in a text based first on a dependency analysis, and then checks whether or not the subject is the Named Entity of a person. This category sets 1 in the fifteenth position in the sequential value only when the subject is named entry of a person and depending on if the word is "Mr." or "Ms." As for "nickname," it is enabled when a text contains a Reply Symbol because the proposed system adds the nickname of a user in a text when a user replies to the user's comment.
- Addresses or refers to the group using inclusive pronouns. Only six words, namely "we," "our," "us," "they," "their," and "them," are factors supporting this category.
- Phatics, salutations, and greetings: This category uses Feature Words for the evaluation. "How are you" is the additional feature phrase for this category.
- Course reflection: The module set 1 on the last position of the sequential value when a text is a positive sentence and contains Feature Words supporting this category.

Social Sharing, which is one of the social presence indicators, was not implemented for the visualization because there is no data in the categorization result, thus implying that there is no feature word.

3.1.3　Extraction Methods for Feature Words

The feature words introduced in the previous section are extracted based on two types of methods: (a): the Statistical Method and (b): the WordNet database. Method (a) uses the tf–idf (term frequency–inverse document frequency) method, which is one of the popular statistical methods to extract feature words in documents. The feature words extracted from the sample chat data containing 3.570 comments in 10 groups comprised of university students. Every comment in the sample data has the Social Presence Score evaluated by several experts. For example, 0,1,0,0,0,0,0,0,0,0,0,0,0,1,0,0,0,1,0,1 is the same format of the score returned from the module. In this research, the extracted feature words for a certain category show that the word appears in 6 times in a text supporting the category in the whole document and appears less than 70 % of the time in texts throughout the entire document. A total of 345 words were extracted by the statistical method. However, several extracted words were removed by the experts because these words were influenced by the topic of the sample data.

Finally, 132 words were registered as feature words using method (a). Method (b) is a method that extracts feature words from the WordNet 3.0 database, which is a popular database that describes the relationship between words. In the first step of the procedure, the expert selected several seed words that frequently appear in a text supporting a certain category, and then he or she extracted feature words contained in the same "Synset" of the seed words. The "Synset" is a kind of Synonym group defined in WordNet. The list of seed words supporting each category is shown in Table 2. A total of 279 words were extracted by this method. But, similar to the procedure of method (a), several extracted words were removed by the expert because the word contained different meanings across the seed words. For example, the seed word "reflect" has four Synsets. The actual Synset ID and typical word in the Synset are here: 2136892 (reflect), 630380 (think_over), 2136271 (reverberate), 2765924 (shine). The seed word "reflect" does not contain the meanings "reverberate" and "shine." Therefore, these words in the Synset ID, namely 2136271 and 2765924 were removed by the expert. Finally 268 words were extracted this procedure. Feature words supporting the EMOTION category were extracted from WordNet-Affect 1.6. A total of 2,272 words were extracted from the database. In the WordNet database, phrase words are expressed as the format that connects each word by underscores. These words are separated and registered as a feather phrase. As a result, 2,540 words were registered in the WordNet database. Additionally, 21 words, which frequently appear in a text supporting a certain category but which could not be extracted by employing the above procedures, were selected by the expert and combined with the feature words. The 21 words are also shown in Table 2. Finally, 2,693 words were registered as feature words.

The system developed in this study visualizes the social presence based on the flow mentioned above in three types (a, b, c), displayed in Fig. 1. This system visualizes each type of social presence score in several levels; five levels in two score types, from a user to a group and a use's reply to another user, and three levels in a score type, a whole group.

Table 1. Rule-based procedures for text analysis

Category	Indicator	Rule-based procedure
Affective	Expressing emotions	a Emoticon appears in a text a Feature Word appears in a text
	Use of humor	a Feature Word appears in a text a Feature Phrase appears in a text
	Self-disclosure	a Feature Word appears in a text a Feature Phrase appears in a text
	Use of unconventional expressions to express emotion	a Feature Word appears in a text an Additional Feature Word appears in a text
	Expressing value	a Feature Word appears in a text
Open communication	Continuing a thread	a Reply Symbol appears over 2 times in group chats
	Quoting from others' message	the Same Comment in past 20 comments
	Referring explicitly to others' messages	a Feature Phrase appears in a text
	Asking questions	a Question Mark appears in a text
	Complimenting expressing appreciation	a Feature Word appears in a text
	Expressing agreement	a Feature Word appears in a Positive sentence a Feature Word of DISAGREEMENT appears in a Negative sentence an Additional Feature Phrase appears in a text
	Expressing disagreement	a Feature Word appears in a Positive sentence a Feature Word of AGREEMENT appears in a Negative sentence
	Personal advice	a Feature Word appears in a Positive sentence.
Cohesive	Vocatives	Mr./Ms. depended a Named Entry of a Person appears in a text. a Reply Symbol appears in a text
	Addresses or refers to the group using inclusive pronouns	The Feature Words, "we", "our", "us", "they", "their" and "them" appear in a text
	Phatics, salutations, and greetings	a Feature Word appears in a text the phrase of "how are you" appears in a text
	Course reflection	a Feature Word appears in a Positive sentence

Table 2. The 26 seed words and 21 additional words supporting each category.

Category	Seed words	Additional words
Expressing emotions	–	
Use of humor	–	
Self-disclosure	remember, experience	
Use of unconventional expressions to express emotion	–	!, • • •,…, ~, —
Expressing value	important, good, better, best, worse, bad, worst, poor, wonderful, beautiful, great	
Continuing a thread	–	
Referring explicitly to others' messages	–	
Quoting from others' message	–	
Asking questions	–	
Complimenting expressing appreciation	thank, appreciate, thankful	
Expressing agreement	agree, follow	I think so, "me, too", me too
Expressing disagreement	disagree	
Personal advice	advice	
Vocatives	–	
Addresses or refers to the group using inclusive pronouns	–	we, our, us, they, their, them
Phatics, salutations, and greetings	hello, hi, good-bye, bye, sorry	good morning, good afternoon, good evening, good night, good-night, ohayo
Course reflection	reflect	hey

4   Method

In order to evaluate the validity of auto-categorization, a comparison was made between the results of human-conducted categorization versus this system. Utterance data were collected in a university English class using the chat tool module as mentioned above. The procedure is explained in detail below.

4.1 Data Collection

Utterance data were collected in a Computer-Assisted Language Learning class. A total of 60 sophomores (42 males and 18 females) in the Informatics Department attended this class. The students were required to participate in an online English discussion for 40 min. The students were divided into 15 groups, each consisting of three or four students.

The discussion topic was "What is the ideal university-entrance test?", and it assessed students' interest in learning. The online discussion was conducted using the chat system [18], which has several integrated functions, such as a concept-map tool.

4.2 Analysis Procedure

The collected utterance data was stored in the database, after which the visualization module read the utterance data from the database and categorized them according to each social presence item. As for the human-conducted categorization, one researcher in educational technology and one in psychology independently categorized each learner's utterance into social and cognitive presence items. When the post contained a social and cognitive presence feature in each indicator, raters wrote down a 1, when they did not contain either feature, raters wrote a 0. Then, two researchers shared the categorization results and discussed the differences in categorization in order to combine results separated according to individual categorizations.

5 Results

5.1 Inter-rater Agreement

The number of utterances for the analysis was 371. In order to evaluate the validity of the automatic social presence categorization, Cohen's Kappa coefficient (K) [24], which is used to measure the agreement between two raters, was calculated. The range of Kappa is −1 to 1. When there is perfect agreement, Kappa is 1. The criteria of Kappa [24] are, below 0.000: Poor, 0.000–0.200: Slight, 0.210–0.400: Fair, 0.410–0.600: Moderate, 0.610–0.800: Substantial, 0.810–0.999: Almost perfect, and 1.000: Perfect. The results are shown in Table 1. The results of "social sharing" and "course reflection" were eliminated because there was not data in both the visualization module and human categorization results. Table 3 shows the results of Kappa coefficient calculation. The results indicate the moderate agreement rate between the module and human in several indicators; however, there are indicators in which the inter-rater reliability is very low. Question has the highest coefficient (0.900), which indicates almost perfect agreement. The Paralanguage, Value, and Salutation indicator items are at a moderate level, while Agreement, Name and Inclusive pronoun are at fair level. The remaining eleven indicators are very low.

Table 3. Cohen's Kappa coefficient

Indicator item	K
Expressing emotions	0.013
Use of humor	0.000
Self disclosure	0.021
Use of unconventional expressions to express emotion	0.558
Expressing value	0.441
Continuing a thread	−0.007
Referring explicitly to others' messages	0.000
Quoting from others' message	0.000
Asking questions	0.900
Complimenting expressing appreciation	0.068
Expressing agreement	0.326
Expressing disagreement	0.046
Personal advice	0.000
Vocatives	0.201
Inclusive pronoun	0.375
Phatics, salutations, and greetings	0.432

5.2   The Relationship with Cognitive Presence

In order to investigate the power to predict the cognitive presence that indicates the discussion quality, a multiple regression analysis was conducted in which cognitive presence was established as the dependent variable, and the sum-up frequency data of module categorization and human categorization were established as the independent variables. The results are displayed in Table 4.

The results showed that the social presence frequency calculated by the module developed in this study had a positive causal relationship on cognitive presence; however, the social presence frequency calculated by humans had a negative relationship on cognitive presence. Thus, the prediction rate of the module was better than the human prediction rate.

Table 4. The results of multiple regression analysis

Indicator	Coef.	SE	β	p
Module	0.181	0.018	0.461	p < 0.001
Human	−0.172	0.588	−0.137	p < 0.01

Note: $F(2, 368) = 50.70$, $p < 0.001$,
$R^2 = 0.216$, Adjusted $R^2 = 0.212$.

6 Discussion and Conclusion

This research developed a social presence visualization system for CSCL. In order to evaluate the validity of automated categorization of learners' postings following the social presence indicator, two statistical methods were employed to compare the module with the human-conducted categorization. First, the Kappa coefficient was calculated. Second, a multiple regression analysis was conducted to investigate the power of the prediction for the discussion quality. The results showed that there are indicator items that have high and low agreement rates. The indicator items of criteria that were easy to categorize, such as questions, tend to have high agreement rates. Kappa coefficients of several items were almost zero because there were very few posts categorized as low-rate indicator items, such as "Quoting."

Interestingly, according to the results of the multiple regression analysis, the categorization results of the module had superior prediction power compared to the results of the human-conducted categorization. Including the results in the inter-rater agreement measurement, the accuracy and validity of auto-categorization should be improved in future works. The evaluation of auto-categorization and of extracting and adding featured words shall be required after collecting the utterance data in a long-term investigation.

The results showed that the social presence frequency calculated by the module developed in this study had a positive causal relationship on cognitive presence; however, the social presence frequency calculated by humans had a negative relationship on cognitive presence. Thus, the prediction rate of the module was better than the human prediction rate.

Acknowledgement. This research is financially supported by Grant-in-Aids for Young Scientist A (25702008) and for Scientific Research (B) (16H03080)

References

1. Nishimori, T., Kato, H., Mochizuki, T., Yaegashi, K., Hisamatsu, S., Ozawa, S.: Development and trial of project-based learning support system in higher education. J. Jpn. Soc. Educ. Technol. **29**(3), 289–297 (2005)
2. Scardamalia, M., Bereiter, C.: Technologies for knowledge-building discourse. Commun. ACM **36**(5), 37–41 (1993)
3. Garrison, D.R., Anderson, T.: E-learning in the 21st Century: A Framework for Research and Practice. Routledge Falmer, London (2003)
4. Shea, P., Bidjerano, T.: Community of inquiry as a theoretical framework to faster epistemic engagement and cognitive presence in online education. Comput. Educ. **52**(3), 543–553 (2009)
5. Garrison, D.R., Anderson, T., Archer, W.: Critical inquiry in a text-based environment: computer conferencing in higher education. Internet High. Educ. **2**(2–3), 87–105 (2000)

6. Gunawardena, C.N., Zittle, F.J.: Social presence as a predictor of satisfaction within a computer-mediated conferencing environment. Am. J. Distance Educ. **11**(3), 8–26 (1997)

7. Shea, P., Hayes, S., Vickers, J., Gozza-Cohen, M., Uzuner, S., Mehta, R., Valchova, A., Rangan, P.: A re-examination of the community of inquiry framework: social network and content analysis. Internet High. Educ. **13**, 10–21 (2010)

8. Akyol, Z., Garrison, D.R.: Assessing metacognition in an online community of inquiry. Internet High. Educ. **14**, 183–190 (2012)

9. Goda, Y., Yamada, M.: Application of CoI to design CSCL for EFL online asynchronous discussion. In: Akyol, Z., Garrison, D.R. (eds.) Educational Community of Inquiry: Theoretical Framework, Research and Practice, pp. 295–316. IGI Global (2012)

10. Yamada, M.: The role of social presence in learner-centered communicative language learning using synchronous computer-mediated communication: experimental study. Comp. Educ. **52**, 820–833 (2009)

11. Yamada, M., Goda, Y.: Application of social presence principles to CSCL design for quality interactions. In: Jia, J.: (ed.) Educational Stages and Interactive Learning: From Kindergarten to Workplace Training, pp. 31–48. IGI Global (2012)

12. Yamada, M.: Development and Evaluation of CSCL Based on Social Presence. In: Sanchez, J., Zhang, K. (eds.) Proceedings of the World Conference on E-learning in Corporate, Government, Healthcare, and Higher Education, pp. 2304–2309. Association for the Advancement of Computing in Education (2010). http://www.editlib.org/p/35889

13. Short, J., Williams, E., Christie, B.: The Social Psychology of Telecommunications. Wiley, London (1976)

14. Phielix, C., Prins, F.J., Kirschner, P.A.: Group awareness of social and cognitive behavior in a CSCL environment. In: ICLS 2010 Proceedings of the 9th International Conference of the Learning Sciences, vol. 1, pp. 230–237 (2010)

15. Janssen, J., Erkens, G., Kanselaar, G.: Visualization of agreement and discussion processes during computer-supported collaborative learning. Comput. Hum. Behav. **23**, 1105–1125 (2007)

16. Mochizuki, T., Kato, H., Yaegashi, K., Nishimori, T., Nagamori, Y., Fujita, S.: ProBoPortable: does the cellular phone software promote emergent division of labor in project-based learning? In: CSCL 2007 Proceedings in the 8th International Conference on Computer-Supported Collaborative Learning, pp. 516–518 (2007)

17. Yamada, M., Goda, Y., Matsukawa, H., Hata, K., Yasunami, S.: A computer-supported collaborative learning design for quality interaction. IEEE Multimedia **23**, 48–59 (2016)

18. Hoppe, U.H., Gaßner, K.: Integrating collaborative concept mapping tools with group memory and retrieval functions. In: CSCL 2002 Proceedings of the Conference on Computer Support for Collaborative Learning, pp. 716–725 (2002)

19. Manning, C.D., Surdeanu, M., Bauer, J., Finkel, J., Bethard, S.J., McClosky, D.: The stanford CoreNLP natural language processing toolkit. In: Proceedings of the 52nd Annual Meeting of the Association for Computational Linguistics: System Demonstrations, pp. 55–60 (2014)

20. Miller, G.A.: WordNet: a lexical database for English. Commun. ACM **38**(11), 39–41 (1995)

21. Fellbaum, C.: WordNet: An Electronic Lexical Database. MIT Press, Cambridge (1998)

22. Strapparava, C., Valitutti, A.: WordNet-affect: an affective extension of WordNet. In: Proceedings of the 4th International Conference on Language Resources and Evaluation (LREC 2004), Lisbon, pp. 1083–1086, May 2004

23. de Marneffe, M.C., Manning, C.D.: Stanford typed dependencies manual, September 2008 (Revised for the Stanford Parser v. 3.5.2 in April 2015). http://nlp.stanford.edu/software/dependencies_manual.pdf
24. Landis, J.R., Koch, G.G.: The measurement of observer agreement for categorical data. Biometrics **33**(1), 159–174 (1977)

Face-to-Face Collaborative Learning by Enhancing Viewpoint-Sharing of Learning Materials

Tessai Hayama[1]([✉]), Koji Hasegawa[2], and Kazushi Hoshiya[2]

[1] Department of Information and Management Systems Engneering,
Nagaoka University of Technology,
1603-1 Kamitomioka, Nagaoka-shi, Niigata 940-2188, Japan
t-hayama@kjs.nagaokaut.ac.jp
[2] Department of Information and Computer Science,
Kanazawa Institute of Techonogy,
7-1 Ohgigaoka, Nonoichi-shi, Ishikawa 921-8501, Japan
http://www.nagaokaut.ac.jp/

Abstract. In face-to-face collaborative learning, learners develop an argument about a common learning theme in a small group to understand the subject more deeply. Forming a more convincing argument often involves individual study, in which the learners study additional materials about the theme prior to the collaborative learning session. However, it is difficult for learners without sufficient argumentative skills to incorporate learned knowledge, which is acquired in individual study, into an argument. Therefore, we developed a system that supports face-to-face collaborative learning by enhancing viewpoint-sharing of learning materials. The proposed system provides visual representations of different viewpoints of each learning material for the learners while they discuss the theme. In our experiment, we confirmed the usefulness of the proposed system by comparing it with collaborative learning sessions without a system.

Keywords: CSCL · Face-to-face collaborative learning · Supporting an argument · Viewpoint sharing

1 Introduction

In recent years, student-driven learning has been used extensively for the improvement of education at schools. Project-based learning (PBL) is often adopted as a method for student-driven learning. PBL is an instructional method in which students learn through facilitated problem-solving in student teams. The team-activity exercises provide students with learning effects such as improving their own learning style and understanding learning contents more deeply [10]. It is very important for the students to have productive experiences through the team activities in PBL.

© Springer Science+Business Media Singapore 2016
T. Yoshino et al. (Eds.): CollabTech 2016, CCIS 647, pp. 190–202, 2016.
DOI: 10.1007/978-981-10-2618-8_15

In face-to-face collaborative learning, learners develop an argument about a common learning theme in their small group. This often involves individual study, in which the learners study learning materials about the theme prior to the collaborative learning session, e.g., via the LTD method [8] or the Jigsaw method [1]. Even though the learners can use learned knowledge, which is acquired during individual study, to develop a convincing argument about the theme, it is difficult for learners without sufficient argumentative skills to appropriately incorporate their learned knowledge into the argument [9].

Several researchers have studied argument support systems for collaborative learning and have proposed systems comprising embedding argument models such as IBIS [5] and DRL [6]. The major argument models comprise several nodes, such as "problem," "comment," "issue," and "other," and relationships between the nodes. Even though argument models are useful in finding solutions for complex [11] or ill-defined problems in an argument [2], it is necessary for the learners to understand the complex rules of an argument model and to have the skills to make use of the rules. Therefore, it is difficult for learners without sufficient argumentative skills to manipulate a system embedding an argument model in argumentative collaborative learning. Several other Computer-Supported Collaborative Learning (CSCL) researchers have developed system environments to enhance group arguments in distanced collaborative learning. For example, there are systems that make learners aware of the knowledge and existence of another learner(s) [7] and the degree of a learner's contribution generated using notes of the other learner's in order to facilitate learner sharing and communication between them [3]. Moreover, there are systems that provide favorable feedback on learners' remarks using original speech templates [7]. These researchers have also reported the effectiveness of their systems in their respective experiments. We focus on enhancing the incorporation of the knowledge that each learner has acquired via individual learning into arguments during face-to-face collaborative learning. The present study is different from the previous studies because of its method of support.

We developed a system that supports face-to-face collaborative learning by enhancing viewpoint-sharing of learning materials. This system provides visual representations of different viewpoints of each learning material for the learners while they discuss the theme. In our experiment, we confirmed the usefulness of the proposed system by comparing it with collaborative learning sessions without a system.

2   System Implementation

2.1   Overview

We developed a web-based system that enables each learner to submit evaluations of learning material via a Web browser and that confirms differences in the evaluation of the learning material within the learning group. The system consists of two modes: an individual learning mode and a collaborative learning mode.

The system interface of the individual learning mode is shown in Fig. 1. A learner uploads files with learning materials after logging in. The uploaded files are shared on the system within the learning group of the learner. The learner studies the given theme as an individual using the learning materials. After studying the learning material, the learner can submit an evaluation score for each learning material through the system interface. The evaluation score consists of the following five items: "Comprehensible," "Association with theme," "Importance", "Originality", and "Interesting." The five items were chosen to enhance the following effectiveness of argumentative collaborative learning.

- Confirming their comprehensible and interest to each learning material, the learners know their impression of the learning materials before discussing them.
- Discussing importance to each learning material, key-points of each learning material are likely to be brought out in the argument.
- Showing the originality and association with theme of each learning material, the key-point(s) of each learning material and the theme are likely to be effectively associated in the argument.
- The argument is encouraged to be well-organized through above processes.
- Confirming their comprehensible and interest to each learning material, the learners can know impression of the learning materials before discussing them.
- Discussing importance to each learning material, key-points of each learning material are likely to be brought out in the argument.
- Showing originality and association with theme of each learning material, the key-point(s) of each learning material and the theme are likely to be effectively associated in the argument.
- The argument is encouraged to be well-organized through above confirmation processes.

In the evaluation, a questionnaire with a five-Likert scale was used.

The system interface in the collaborative learning mode is shown in Fig. 2. The system provides a radar chart of the learning material, which is shared in the learning group. The radar chart of each learning material is summarized by the evaluation scores that the group members have assigned to the learning material. In the radar chart, each line with a different color shows the evaluation scores that each learner has assigned to the evaluation items of the learning material. Therefore, the learners can immediately recognize differences in the evaluation of the learning material between the group members by referencing the radar chart of the learning material. The order that the radar charts of the shared learning materials is provided in is determined by an algorithm, which is explained in detail in Sect. 2.2, to initiate a debatable argument. The radar chart on the system interface is manually switched to the next one by the learners.

2.2   Calculating the Order to Provide the Radar-Charts of the Learning Materials

To calculate the order in which to provide the radar-charts of the learning materials, differences between the evaluation values, which the group members have

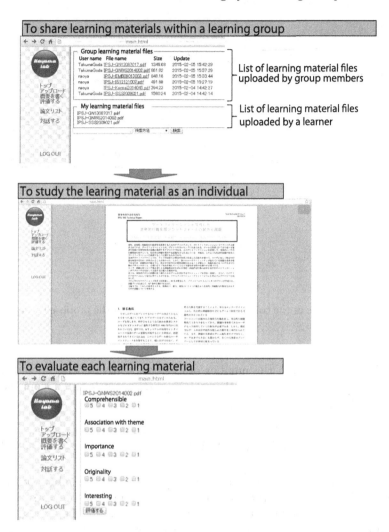

Fig. 1. System interface in the individual learning mode of the proposed system.

assigned to each learning material, are used. The greater the difference between the evaluation values of a learning material, the more room there is for discussion about the learning material. The difference between the evaluation values of a learning material is determined by the following equation:

$$Dis(d, G) = \frac{1}{n(I)} \sum_{i \in I} Var(d, i, G). \tag{1}$$

Here, d, G, and $Dis(d, G)$ indicate a certain learning material, certain learning group, and difference degree of the evaluation of the learning material d in the learning group G, respectively. I, i, and $n(I)$ indicate the set of evaluation items,

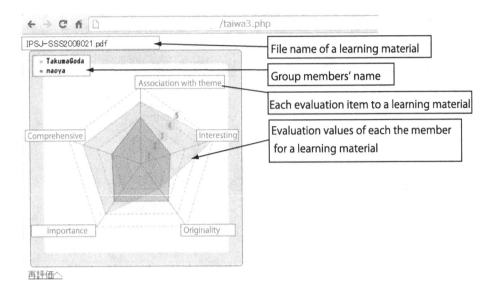

Fig. 2. The system interface in the collaborative learning mode of the proposed system. (Color figure online)

a certain evaluation item, and the number of evaluation items being included in the set of evaluation items I, respectively. $Var(d, i, G)$ is calculated from the following equation:

$$Var(d, i, G) = \sqrt{\frac{1}{n(G)} \sum_{u \in G} (E(u, d, i) - \overline{E(G, d, i)})^2}. \tag{2}$$

Here, $n(G)$, u, $E(u, d, i)$, and $\overline{E(G, d, i)}$ indicate the number of members of the learning group G, a certain learner, the evaluation value that the learner u assigned to the evaluation item i of the learning material d, and the average of evaluation values that every member of the learning group G assigned to the evaluation item i of the learning material d.

An example of the calculated order of provided radar-charts of learning materials is shown in Fig. 3. Two learners in a learning group evaluated three learning materials: A, B, and C. The evaluation values that the two learners assigned to each evaluation item ("Association to theme," "Interesting," "Originality," "Importance," and "Comprehensive") for the three learning materials (A, B, and C) are represented by ([4,2], [3,1], [3,3], [4,2], [4,4]), ([3,2], [4,4], [4,4], [3,2], [2,2]), and ([5,5], [5,5], [4,4], [4,4], [4,4]), respectively. The difference degrees of each evaluation item of the learning materials A, B, and C are calculated as (1, 1, 0, 1, 0), (0.5, 0, 0, 0.5, 0.5), and (0, 0, 0, 0, 0), respectively, from the evaluation values using Eq. (2). Then, the differences between the evaluation of each learning material (A, B, and C) are determined to be 0.6, 0.3, and 0, respectively, from the difference degrees of the evaluation items using Eq. (1). Therefore, the

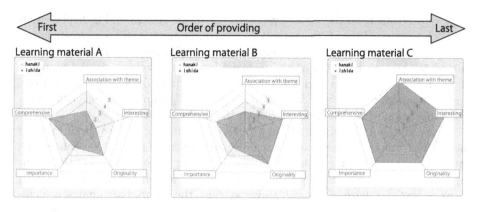

Fig. 3. An example of the calculated order to provide radar-charts of the learning materials.

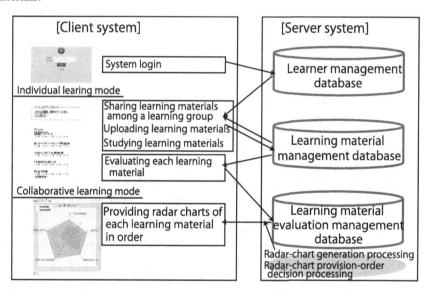

Fig. 4. Composition of the proposed system

radar-charts of the learning materials in the example are established in the order A, B, and then C.

3   System Composition

The composition of the proposed system is shown in Fig. 4. The system is implemented as a Web application so that learners can easily access the system from a distributed environment during the individual learning mode of the system.

A learner begins in the individual learning mode of the system by logging into the system via a Web browser. The list of learning materials that are shared in the group is sent from the server system to the client system and is displayed on the Web browser of the client system. As a learning material file is uploaded onto the server system or the evaluation information of a learning material is submitted to the server system, they are saved into the learning-material management and the learning-material-evaluation management databases, respectively. Learners can share information with their learning group via the asynchronous communication of the client system with the server system.

In the collaborative mode of the proposed system, the client system requires radar-chart images of the shared learning materials and information concerning the provision order of the radar-chart images. Using the evaluation of the learning materials by the learning group members in the learning-material-evaluation management database of the web server system, the radar-chart images are created from the database and the provision order is determined. The charts are processed when any group member logs-in for the first time in the collaborative learning mode.

4   Evaluation

4.1   Overview

We conducted an experiment to investigate whether the proposed system can support learners in making good arguments based on learning materials in face-to-face collaborative learning. We compared an environment with the proposed system with an environment without the system. For the comparison, changes in the differences of evaluations of the learning materials between the before-and-after arguments and the satisfaction degree of each learner's own arguments were used. If the changes in the differences of the evaluation of the learning materials between before and after arguments were smaller in an environment with the proposed system than in one without the system and learner satisfaction was higher in an environment with the proposed system than in one without the system, the proposed system would be deemed to support a satisfactory argument by bridging the gap of the evaluation of each learning material in the learning group. Therefore, the arguments in the face-to-face collaborative learning would increase in quality when using the proposed system.

The experiment was performed by four learner pairs, and each of which studied a similar graduate research theme. The procedure of the experiment included three steps: (1) each learner selected six research papers over six pages long as learning material according to their group theme and uploaded them; (2) each learner studied the 12 learning materials, which were shared within the group individually and then evaluated each learning material using the system; and (3) the learners discussed the group theme in their group in a face-to-face environment by referring to handouts of the learning materials, as shown in Fig. 5. In step 3, the argumentation occurred over approximately 15 min and was executed two times in environments with the proposed system and without the system using six learning materials that were different in every round.

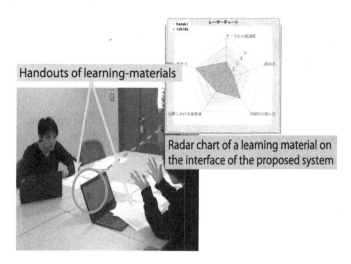

Fig. 5. A picture of the experimental environment.

To investigate changes in the evaluations of each learning material, a re-evaluation was performed after each argument via the system interface, as shown in Fig. 6. Questionnaires concerning the argument and the system usability were given before and after the experiment.

4.2   Results

Average argument times in the experiment, questionnaire results concerning the learner's own argument, changes in the evaluation of each learning material from before and after the arguments, questionnaire results concerning the usability of the proposed system, and the questionnaire result for the ranking of useful evaluation items in the proposed system are shown in Fig. 7, Tables 1, 2, and 3, and Fig. 8, respectively.

An average time of 18 min and 13 s was spent in argument in an environment with the proposed system, while an average time of 18 min and 46 s was spent in an environment without the system; the p-value for this difference is below $p = 0.15$, meaning there was not a statistically significant difference. In the questionnaire results about the argument, the average of all items were high scores, over 3.6. In particular, the questionnaire scores for "easy to talk about learning materials," "satisfaction of learner's own argument," "satisfaction of learner's own behavior," and "comprehensive discussion about the theme" were larger for arguments with the proposed system than for arguments without the system; the F-values for these differences are 7.45 ($> F(1, 14)$, $p < 0.05$), 4.20 ($> F(1, 14)$, $p < 0.05$), 5.93 ($> F(1, 14)$, $p < 0.05$), and 3.31 ($> F(1, 14)$, $p < 0.15$), respectively, meaning that there were statistically significant differences. However, the questionnaire score for "Consciousness of learning materials" was smaller for arguments with the proposed system than for arguments without the

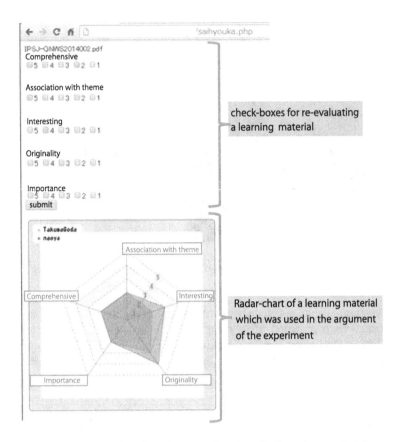

Fig. 6. System interface for re-evaluating the learning material.

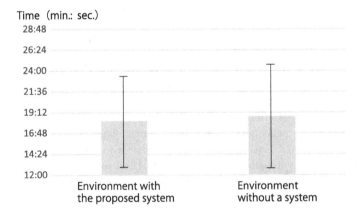

Fig. 7. Average argument times in the experiment.

Table 1. Questionnaire results concerning the learner's own argument for the experiment (each item on the 5 point Likert scale)

	Environment with the proposed system		Environment without the system	
	Ave.	Var.	Ave.	Var.
Consciousness of learning materials	3.75	0.79	4.25	0.21
Easy to talk about learning materials*	3.63	0.84	2.38	0.84
Satisfaction about own argument*	4.13	0.98	3.00	1.43
Satisfaction about learner's own behavior during the argument*	3.88	1.55	2.63	0.55
Comprehensive about own theme**	4.25	0.21	3.88	0.13

*: ANOVA, $p < 0.05$.
**: ANOVA, $p < 0.15$.

system; the F-value for this difference is 2.00 ($> F(1, 14)$, $p < 0.15$), meaning that there was not a statistically significant difference between the two results. However, the scores in both the arguments were very high, over 4.25.

The differences in the evaluation of the learning material within a group in the experiment are summarized in Table 2. In arguments with the proposed system, the average difference value of the evaluation of each learning material, 0.17, before an argument became smaller than the average value, 0.61, after an argument; the F-value for this difference is 13.36 ($> F(1, 22)$, $p < 0.01$), meaning that there was a statistically significant difference. On the other hand, in an argument without the system, the average value of 0.39 before the argument was similar to the average value of 0.37 after the argument; the F-value for the difference is 0.10 ($< F(1, 22)$, $p < 0.05$), meaning that there was not a statistically significant difference between the scores before and after the argument. In comparing the differences of the evaluation of each learning material between an argument without the system and one with the proposed system, the differences in the evaluation of each learning material before the arguments with the proposed system and without the system were on average 0.61 and 0.37, respectively; the F-value for the difference is 0.10 ($< F(1, 22)$, $p < 0.05$), meaning that there was not a statistically significant difference. The differences after the arguments with the proposed system and without the system were on average 0.17 and 3.90, respectively; the F-value for the difference is 12.47 ($> F(1, 22)$, $p < 0.01$), meaning that there was a statistically significant difference. In the changes from the differences in the evaluation of each learning material before an argument to those after an argument, the changes in the argument with the proposed system and without the system were on average 0.44 points closer and -0.33 farther apart, respectively, meaning that using the proposed system makes evaluations of the learning materials in the group closer. On the other hand, the change in the argument without the system had an average of -0.33; the F-value for the difference is 13.36 ($> F(1, 22)$, $p < 0.01$), meaning there was a statistically significant difference. For arguments with the proposed system,

Table 2. Changes in the differences of evaluation for each learning material (LM) between before and after an argument.

	Environment with the proposed system		Environment without the system	
	Ave.	SD	Ave.	SD
Differences in the evaluation of each LM in the group				
(1) before the argument	0.61	0.12	0.37	0.06
(2) after the argument*	0.17	0.03	0.39	0.02
Change from (1) to (2)*	0.44	0.11	−0.03	0.09
Number of LMs that have smaller differences of evaluation in the group after an argument	11		3	
Number of LMs that have larger differences of evaluation in the group after an argument	0		4	
Number of LMs that have no differences of evaluation in the group after an argument	1		5	

*: ANOVA, p < 0.01.

Table 3. Questionnaire results concerning the usability of the proposed system (each item on a 5 point Likert scale)

	Ave.	SD
Operational	3.88	0.83
Sense of burden	2.00	0.93
Convenience during argument	4.75	0.46
Presentation on system interface	4.50	0.53

11 of the learning materials had closer evaluations and 1 learning material had greater scatter in its evaluation. For arguments without the system, 3 learning materials had closer evaluations, 4 learning materials had the same evaluation, and 5 learning materials had greater scatter in their evaluations. Therefore, the proposed system supports sharing evaluation viewpoints of learning materials in a group in face-to-face collaborative learning.

In the questionnaire results concerning the usability of the proposed system, the evaluation values for "Operational," "Convenience during argumentation", and "Presentation of system interface" had high average scores of over 3.88. In the positive opinions of the proposed system from the learners, there were comments such as "Radar-charts were useful to get a lead on the argumentation," "we could build arguments in which our own opinions on the theme became clearer", and "I am likely to ask the other learner because the differences in the viewpoints of each learning material are shown during the argumentation." On

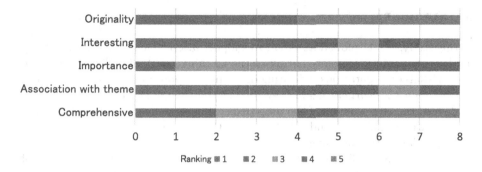

Fig. 8. Questionnaire results ranking the useful evaluation items of the proposed system.

the other hand, the evaluation value for the "Sense of burden" had a low average score of 2.00. The reason for this low score was likely "I could not get used to arguing while watching a monitor" according to the learners' negative opinions of the proposed system.

In the ranking of the useful viewpoint items of the learning materials for the argumentation, the items of "Interesting" and "Association with theme" were assigned to ranks 1 or 2 by over half the subjects, and the other items were assigned to positive or negative ranks. In the opinions about the items from the learners, there was a comment that "More items for evaluating viewpoints of learning materials could be added."

4.3   Discussion

In the experimental results, argument time and degree of learners' conscious of learning-materials during the argument were not significant difference between an environment with the proposed system and an environment without a system. On the other hand, offering evaluation scores of each learning material by the proposed system made the learners improved easy to talk about learning materials and satisfaction of learner's own argument. In the changes from the differences in the evaluation of each learning material between the before-and-after argument, using the proposed system makes evaluations of the learning materials in the group closer. As the reason for this, the learners who were in the environment with the proposed system could build the argument based on basic argument act; building argument in which learners' own opinions on the theme became clearer and asking the other learner because of the differences in the viewpoints of the learning contents. So that the learners could effectively share evaluation viewpoints of learning materials in a group.

Therefore, the proposed system, which supports sharing evaluation viewpoints of learning materials in a group, is useful for building a satisfactory argument by bridging the gap of the evaluation of each learning material in the learning group.

5   Summary

In this study, we developed a system to support face-to-face collaborative learning by enhancing viewpoint-sharing of the learning materials. The system provides visual representations indicating different viewpoints of each learning material between the learners while they discuss the theme. In our experiment, we confirmed the effectiveness of the proposed system to enhance viewpoint-sharing of the learning materials and satisfaction of the learner's own argument in face-to-face collaborative learning.

In our future studies, we will include more items for viewpoint evaluation of learning materials and investigate the effectiveness of the proposed system by conducting an experiment for groups comprising at least 4 people.

Acknowledgement. This work was supported by JSPS KAKENHI Grant Number 25730210 and 15K16107.

References

1. Aronson, E., Blaney, N., Stephin, C., Sikes, J., Snapp, M.: The Jigsaw Classroom. Sage Publishing Company (1978)
2. Carr, C.S.: Using computer supported argument visualization to teach legal argumentation. In: Kirschner, P.A., Shum, S.J.B., Carr, C.S. (eds.) Visualizing Argumentation, pp. 75–96. Springer, London (2003)
3. Hayashi, Y., Kojiri, T., Watanabe, T.: Interaction based on contribution awareness in collaborative learning. In: König, A., Dengel, A., Hinkelmann, K., Kise, K., Howlett, R.J., Jain, L.C. (eds.) KES 2011. LNCS (LNAI), vol. 6882, pp. 104–113. Springer, Heidelberg (2011). doi:10.1007/978-3-642-23863-5_11
4. Kotani, T., Seki, K., Matsui, T., Okamoto, T.: Development of discussion supporting system based on the "Value of Favorable Words' Influence". Trans. Jpn. Soc. Artif. Intell. **19**(2), 95–104 (2004). (in Japanese)
5. Kunz, W., Rittel, H.W.J.: Issues as elements of information systems, Working paper. University of California at Berkeley, pp. 1–9 (1970)
6. Lee, J.: How can groups communicate when they use different languages? Translating between partially shared type hierarchies, Technical report SSM W, pp. 3076–89-MS, MIT (1989)
7. Ogata, H., Matsuura, K., Yano, Y.: Knowledge awareness: bridging between shared knowledge and collaboration in sharlok. In: Proceedings of Educational-Telecommunications 1996, pp. 232–237 (1996)
8. Rabow, J.M., Charness, A., Kipperman, J., Radcliffe-Vasile, S.: William Fawcett Hill's Learning Through Discussion, 3rd edn. Sage Publications, Inc., Thousand Oaks (1994)
9. Toulmin, S.: The Uses of Argument. Cambridge University Press, Cambridge (1958)
10. Wolfe, J.: Efffects of annotations on student readers and writers. In: Proceedings of the 5th ACM Conference on Digital Libraries, pp. 19–26 (2000)
11. Zumbach, J., Reimann, P.: Combining computer-supoorted collaborative argumentation and problem-based learning: an approach for designing online learning environments. In: Proceedings of Computer Supported Collaborative Learning 1999 (1999)

Analysis of Non-verbal Behaviors by Students in Cooperative Learning

Eiji Watanabe[1(✉)], Takashi Ozeki[2], and Takeshi Kohama[3]

[1] Konan University, Kobe 658-8501, Japan
e_wata@konan-u.ac.jp
[2] Fukuyama University, Fukuyama, Hiroshima 729-0292, Japan
[3] Kindai University, Kinokawa, Wakayama 649-6493, Japan
http://we-www.is.konan-u.ac.jp/Welcome.html

Abstract. In this paper, we discuss the relationship between non-verbal behaviors and understandings by students in the cooperative learning. First, we detect non-verbal behaviors by students by using image processing methods. Next, we propose a modeling method for non-verbal behaviors. Furthermore, we discuss the relationship between non-verbal behaviors and understandings by students based on the above models.

Keywords: Cooperative learning · Student · Non-verbal behavior · · Understanding

1 Introduction

In the cooperative learning, students teach other students and vice versa. It is becoming one of the hot topics to be researched [1,2]. The object of the cooperative learning is to improve the cooperation of the group and the understanding for given contents. Moreover, in [3], the following fundamental factors to be effective among the learning group which is listed as follows; (i) mutually beneficial cooperation, (ii) roles and responsibilities of the individual, (iii) stimulatory interaction. However, one teacher cannot grasp the cooperation and understanding of all groups and can note evaluate the above fundamental factors in real time. Therefore, it is very important to construct methods for the estimation of the cooperation and understand the group based on the non-verbal behaviors by students by using such approaches [4,5].

In this paper, we discuss the relationship between non-verbal behaviors and understandings by students in the cooperative learning. First, we detect non-verbal behaviors by students by using image processing methods. Next, we propose a modeling method for non-verbal behaviors. Furthermore, we discuss the relationship between non-verbal behaviors and understandings (notes and before/after tests) by students based on the above models.

T. Yoshino et al. (Eds.): CollabTech 2016, CCIS 647, pp. 203–211, 2016.
DOI: 10.1007/978-981-10-2618-8_16

2　Detection of Non-verbal Behaviors by Students

In this paper, we treat the learning environment using a whiteboard as shown in Fig. 1. Figure 1(a) shows the non-verbal behaviors (writing in the whiteboard and the explanation to "learning" students) by "teaching" students. Moreover, Fig. 1(b) shows the non-verbal behaviors (looking at the whiteboard and "teaching" student) by "learning" students. In this section, we describe image processing methods for the detection of non-verbal behaviors by students.

(a) "Teaching" student　　(b) "Learning" student

Fig. 1. Non-verbal behaviors by students in the cooperative learning using whiteboard.

2.1　Detection of Non-verbal Behaviors by "Teaching" Students

As shown in Fig. 1(a), when "teaching" student teaches to "learning" students with the contents using the whiteboard, we can see the two types of behaviors; (i) writing the contents to the whiteboard, (ii) explaining the contents to "learning" students. In this section, we describe the methods for the detection of non-verbal behaviors and the classification for the two above behaviors.

First, skin-colored (face and hands) and black-colored (hair) regions can be extracted by the images processing [6, 7]. Next, the two types of the above behaviors by "teaching" student can be classified based on the number $x_{Skin}^{Teaching}(t)$ of skin-colored pixels and the number $x_{Black}^{Teaching}(t)$ of black-colored pixels. We define the feature $x^{Teaching}(t)$ for the behaviors by "teaching" student by Eq. 1.

$$x^{Teaching}(t) = \frac{x_{Black}^{Teaching}(t)}{x_{Skin}^{Teaching}(t) + x_{Black}^{Teaching}(t) + 1}. \tag{1}$$

By using the above features $x^{Teaching}(t)$, the behaviors by "teaching" student can be classified as follows;

(i) $x^{Teaching}(t) \geq \varepsilon^{Teaching}$: Writing to the whiteboard,
(ii) $0 < x^{Teaching}(t) < \varepsilon^{Teaching}$: Explaining to "learning" students,
(iii) $x_{Skin}^{Teaching}(t) = 0$, $x_{Black}^{Teaching}(t) = 0$, $x^{Teaching}(t) = 0$: "Teaching" student cannot be detected.

2.2   Detection of Non-verbal Behaviors by "Learning" Students

As shown in Fig. 1(b), "learning" students have the following non-verbal behaviors; (i) looking at "teaching" students and the whiteboard, (ii) taking a note, (iii) looking at other "learning" students.

First, the face regions of students can be detected from the movie recorded by a camcorder in the center of students [6,7]. Next, we count up the number of skin-colored in each divided region (Upper-Left, Upper-Right, Lower-Left, Lower-Right) of the face region and we obtain the rate of skin-colored pixels in each divide region as follows;

$$\begin{cases} R_{UL} = \dfrac{1}{S} \sum_{x,y \in UL} f_{face}(x,y), \ R_{UR} = \dfrac{1}{S} \sum_{x,y \in UR} f_{face}(x,y), \\ R_{LL} = \dfrac{1}{S} \sum_{x,y \in LL} f_{face}(x,y), \ R_{LR} = \dfrac{1}{S} \sum_{x,y \in LR} f_{face}(x,y). \end{cases} \tag{2}$$

When the object pixel $f(x,y)$ is skin-colored, $f_{face}(x,y)$ is set to 1. Moreover, S denotes the size of the face region.

Furthermore, we define the feature $R^{Learning}$ concerning on the face direction of "learning" students by Eq. 3.

$$R^{Learning} = R_{UL} - R_{UR} \tag{3}$$

Here, we can classify the non-verbal behaviors by "learning" students by using the feature $R^{Learning}$. Therefore, if $R^{Learning} \neq 0$ and $R_{UL} + R_{UR} \neq 0$, the non-verbal behaviors (looking at "teaching" and other "learning" students) can be detected. On the other hand, if $R^{Learning} = 0$ and $R_{UL} + R_{UR} = 0$, the non-verbal behaviors (noting or teaching) can be detected.

3   Modeling of Non-verbal Behaviors by "Learning" Students

In the cooperative learning, the non-verbal behaviors by "learning" students has strong relations with the understandings and interests for the given contents and the explanation by "teaching" students. In this section, we discuss the method for the modeling the above relations.

First, we introduce the following non-linear time-series model for the feature $R^{Learning}(t)$ for "learning" students. Here, we define $x_p^{Learning}(t) = R^{Learning}(t)$.

$$x_p^{Learning}(t) = \sum_q \alpha_{p,q} f\left(\sum_{\ell=1}^{L} w_{p,q,\ell}^{Learning} x_q^{Learning}(t-\ell)\right)$$

$$+ \beta_p f\left(\sum_{\ell=1}^{L} w_{p,\ell}^{Teaching} x^{Teaching}(t-\ell)\right) + e(t), \tag{4}$$

where $\alpha_{p,q}$ denotes the influence of the non-verbal behavior $x_q^{Learning}(t)$ by other "learning" students on the "learning" student and β_p denotes the influence of the non-verbal behavior $x_p^{Learning}(t)$ by the "teaching" student on the "learning" student. Moreover, $w_{p,q,\ell}$ denotes the correlation for the non-verbal behavior $x_q^{Learning}(t)$ by other "learning" students. Furthermore, $f(\cdot)$ denotes the sigmoid function. Here, the non-linear time-series model defined by Eq. 4 can be represented by the neural network model [8] shown in Fig. 2.

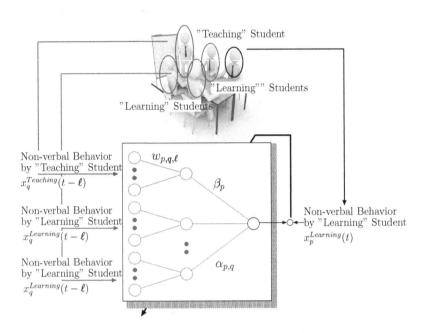

Fig. 2. Neural network model for Eq. 4

Next, the learning object for a neural network model shown in Fig. 2 is to minimize the following error function E.

$$E = \sum_{t=1}^{T} E_t = \sum_{t=1}^{T} (x_p^{Learning}(t) - \hat{x}_p^{Learning}(t))^2, \tag{5}$$

where $\hat{x}_p^{Learning}(t)$ denotes the prediction value for the feature $x_p^{Learning}(t)$ by "learning" students. First, the learning law for weights $\alpha_{p,q}$ can be represented by

$$\alpha_{p,q} = \alpha_{p.q} - \eta \frac{\partial E_t}{\partial \alpha_{p,q}}, \tag{6}$$

where η denotes the learning coefficient. The differential coefficient $\partial E_t/\partial \alpha_{p,q}$ can be calculated by

$$
\frac{\partial E_t}{\partial \alpha_{p,q}} = \frac{\partial E_t}{\partial \hat{x}_q^{Learning}(t)} \frac{\partial \hat{x}_q^{Learning}(t)}{\partial \alpha_{p,q}}
$$
$$
= (x_p^{Learning}(t) - \hat{x}_p^{Learning}(t)) f(\sum_\ell w_{p,q,\ell} x_q^{Learning}(t - \ell)). \qquad (7)
$$

Next, the learning law for weights $w_{p,q,\ell}^{Learning}$ can be represented by

$$
w_{p,q,\ell}^{Learning} = w_{p,q,\ell}^{Learning} - \eta \frac{\partial E_t}{\partial w_{p,q,\ell}^{Learning}}. \qquad (8)
$$

Here, the differential coefficient $\partial E_t / \partial w_{p,q,\ell}^{Learning}$ can be calculated by

$$
\frac{\partial E_t}{\partial w_{p,q,\ell}^{Learning}} = \frac{\partial E_t}{\partial \hat{x}_q^{Learning}(t)} \frac{\partial \hat{x}_q^{Learning}(t)}{\partial w_{p,q,\ell}^{Learning}}
$$
$$
= (x_p^{Learning}(t) - \hat{x}_p^{Learning}(t)) f'(\sum_\ell w_{p,q,\ell}^{Learning} x_q^{Learning}(t - \ell))
$$
$$
\times \alpha_{p,q} x_q^{Learning}(t - \ell), \qquad (9)
$$

where $o_q = \sum_\ell w_{p,q,\ell}^{Learning} x_q^{Learning}(t - \ell)$.

4   Experimental Results

We record movies for "learning" students by "Meeting Recorder" (Kingjim Co. Ltd.) and movies for "teaching" students by MacBook Air (Apple Co. Ltd.) as shown in Fig. 3. "Teaching" and "learning" students have the two lectures concerning on the derivation of the formula for some trigonometric functions.

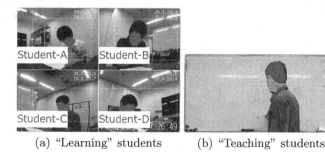

(a) "Learning" students   (b) "Teaching" students

Fig. 3. "Learning" and "Teaching" students

The experimental procedure are as follows; (i) before-test, (ii) taking video lectures and taking notes, (iii) cooperative learning, (iv) after-test. Table 1 shows

Table 1. Scores (1:best, 4:worst) of before/after tests and evaluation of notes

Student	Lecture-1 Test (Before/After)	Note	Lecture-2 Test (Before/After)	Note
A	1.33/1.33	1.67	2.00/1.67	1.33
B	3.67/1.00	2.67	4.00/1.00	1.67
C	3.67/2.00	3.00	3.33/2.67	1.33
D	3.33/3.33	2.33	1.67/4.00	2.33

scores of before and after-tests and evaluation of notes taken by students for given video lectures. Such scores for tests and notes are evaluated by the three authors.

4.1   Features for Non-verbal Behaviors by Students

Figure 4 shows the feature $x^{Teaching}(t)$ by "teaching" students and the feature $R^{Learning}(t)$ by "learning" students in Lecture-1.

- In Fig. 4(a), we can see that the feature $x^{Teaching}(t)$ changes according to the non-verbal behaviors by "teaching" students. Similarly, in Fig. 4(b), we can see that the feature $R^{Learning}$ changes according to the non-verbal behaviors by "learning" students.
- In Fig. 4(b), student-A moves to the whiteboard at 180 [sec] and the behavior by student-A cannot be detected. On the other hand, in Fig. 4(a), the behavior by "teaching" student can be detected.

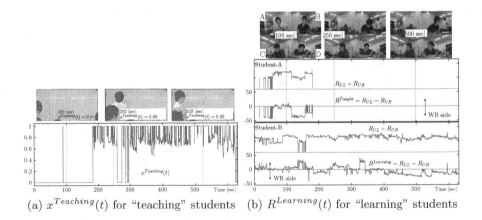

(a) $x^{Teaching}(t)$ for "teaching" students   (b) $R^{Learning}(t)$ for "learning" students

Fig. 4. Features for non-verbal behaviors by students (Lecture-1)

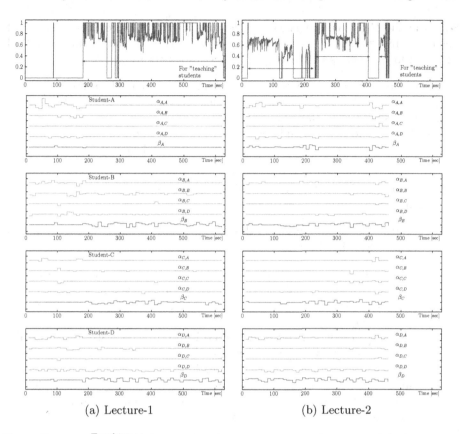

(a) Lecture-1   (b) Lecture-2

Fig. 5. Feature $x^{Teaching}(t)$ for "teaching" students and weights $\alpha_{p,q}$ and β_p for "learning" students for Lecture-1 and Lecture-2

4.2 Modeling of the Non-verbal Behaviors by "Learning" Students

In Fig. 5(a), we show the feature $x^{Teaching}(t)$ for the non-verbal behaviors by "teaching" students and the weights $\alpha_{p,q}$ and β_p in the model (Eq. (4)) for the non-verbal behaviors by "learning" students for Lecture-1. Here, we set as $T = 10$ for the section for the modeling.

- The Student-A is standing at the whiteboard at 180 [sec] and the feature $x^{Teaching}(t)$ changes according to the non-verbal behavior by "teaching" student (the Student-A). As a result, the weights $\alpha_{A,q}$ and β_A for Student-A have a small value. Therefore, we can see that the Student-A is not effected by the other students based on the values of the above weights.
- The weight $\alpha_{p,p}$ denotes the influence of the non-verbal behavior by the Student-p on oneself and the weight β_p denotes the influence of the non-verbal by "teaching" student on the non-verbal behaviors by Student-p.
- Weights β_B and β_D change largely and the Student-B and the Student-D have influence by the non-verbal behaviors by "learning" student.

Similarly, in Fig. 5(a), we show the feature $x^{Teaching}(t)$ for the non-verbal behaviors by "teaching" students and the weights $\alpha_{p,q}$ and β_p in the model (Eq. (4)) for behaviors by "learning" students for Lecture-2.

- In Lecture-2, Student-A becomes "teaching" student in the sections of [240-405] and [450-470] and Student-C becomes "teaching" student in the sections of [20–238] and [430–450].
- Weights β_B and β_D change largely and Student-B and Student-D have influence by the non-verbal behaviors by "learning" student just like Lecture-1.

4.3   Relationship Between the Non-verbal Behaviors and Understandings by Students

We discuss the relationship between the non-verbal behaviors (Fig. 5) and understandings (Table 1) by the students.

- **Understandings by the students**: In Table 1, we can see that the Student-A and the Student-B have high scores for after-tests in Lecture-1 and Lecture-2. On the other hand, we can see that the Student-C and the Student-D have low scores for after-tests.
- **Relationship between the non-verbal behaviors and understandings by the students**: In Fig. 5, the weight β_D change largely compared with other "learning" students. Here, the weight β_p represents the influence by "teaching" student. Therefore, "learning" students having large weights β_p are affected by "teaching" students and the understandings by such "learning" students depend on the "teaching" behavior.

5   Conclusions

In this paper, we have discussed the non-verbal behaviors and understandings by students in the cooperative learning. We have proposed image processing methods for the detection of non-verbal behaviors by students and modeling methods for the non-verbal behaviors by "learning" students. From experimental results for the two lectures, we have discussed the relationship between non-verbal behaviors and understandings by "learning" students based on the weights in the above models. Moreover, we have shown that the behaviors by the students could be classified into the two types based on the weights β_p. Furthermore, we can list future works as follows; (i) detection of nodding behaviors, (ii) hearing for students, (iii) discussion on other groups, (iv) speech by students.

References

1. International Conference on Interactive Collaborative Learning (2014). http://www.icl-conference.org/icl2014
2. Sugie, S.: An invitation to cooperative learning. Nakanishiya, Kyoto (2011)

3. Johnson, D.W., et al.: Circles of learning: cooperation in the classroom. Interaction Book Co., Edina (1993)
4. Otsuka, K., et al.: A Realtime multimodal system for analyzing group meetings by combining face pose tracking and speaker diarization. In: Proceedings of ICMI, pp. 257–264 (2008)
5. Shinnishi, M., et al.: Wi-Wi-Meter : A prototype system of evaluating meeting by measuring of activity. IEICE Technical Report. HCS2014-63, 19–24 (2014)
6. Watanabe, E., et al.: Analysis of behaviors by participants in brainstorming. ITE Technical Report. AIT2015-100, 9–12 (2015)
7. Watanabe, E., et al.: Analysis of behaviors by participants in meetings for decision making. IEICE Technical Report. HCS2015-56, 89–94 (2015)
8. Rumelhart, D.E., et al.: Parallel Distributed Processing. MIT Press, Cambridge (1986)

Browsing Methods for Multiple Online Handwritten Note Animations

Yuuki Maeda[1](✉) and Motoki Miura[2]

[1] Department of Applied Science for Integrated System Engineering,
Kyushu Institute of Technology, 1-1 Sensui, Tobata,
Kitakyushu, Fukuoka 804-8550, Japan
maeda@ist.mns.kyutech.ac.jp
[2] Faculty of Basic Sciences, Kyushu Institute of Technology, 1-1 Sensui, Tobata,
Kitakyushu, Fukuoka 804-8550, Japan
miuramo@mns.kyutech.ac.jp
http://istlab.mns.kyutech.ac.jp/~maeda/

Abstract. We proposed a student note-sharing system to facilitate collaborative and interactive learning in conventional classrooms. Student notes can already be immediately shared by the students and teacher, using a projection screen. However, the resolution is currently insufficient to allow each student note to be shown in detail, which lessens the learning benefits. To address this issue, we proposed two browsing methods that allow simultaneous viewing of multiple online handwritten note animations. In both methods, the zoom rates were determined automatically. Experiments were conducted on the readability of texts, the visibility of figures, and the intuitiveness of animations. The results demonstrated that the animations produced by the ConstantZoom method were more intuitive than those produced by the VariableZoom method.

Keywords: Multiple handwritten notes · Digital pen system · Simultaneous note animations

1 Introduction

Popularization of digital devices such as tablets and smartphones is changing lifestyles. Users can collect information from online resources and exchange ideas and thoughts through their devices. There is an accelerating movement to use digital devices for learning and teaching in classrooms, allowing teachers to collect student responses, and share them with other students [1].

Tablets and smartphones are versatile tools. However, their usability depends on the interface with the application. These devices may also require drastic changes in our approach to learning and teaching. Such changes may place extra burdens on students, who must learn the usage of each application.

To minimize this burden, Miura et al. have proposed AirTransNote, a student note-sharing system that facilitates collaborative and interactive learning in

© Springer Science+Business Media Singapore 2016
T. Yoshino et al. (Eds.): CollabTech 2016, CCIS 647, pp. 212–219, 2016.
DOI: 10.1007/978-981-10-2618-8_17

Fig. 1. Anoto-based pen and the special paper

conventional classrooms [2]. AirTransNote uses digital pens (Anoto) and paper (shown in Fig. 1) to collect ideas and responses from students. Since these notes are transmitted wirelessly, the teacher can immediately share them with the rest of the class using a projection screen. This can enhance group learning. As students are familiar with the use of pen and paper, the interface is intuitive, lessening the burden on the students. Prieto et al. [3] reviewed similar augmented paper systems in educational applications.

One of the primary effects of note sharing during a lecture is the enhancement of interaction between students [4]. The browsing method used for the collected notes is therefore crucial. A system can be introduced in which a personal tablet allows each student to browse the notes of other students. However, in this study, we focus on the use of a projection screen as a shared display.

The existing AirTransNote system provides two view modes for note browsing: a thumbnail view and a focused view. The thumbnail view (Fig. 2 left) displays all the student sheets at reduced size, allowing the teacher to assess the progress of each student from the volume of writing. However, teachers find it difficult to comprehend the details of each note due to the low resolution. The focused view (Fig. 2 right) enlarges an area selected by the teacher from the thumbnail view. The focused view is helpful for checking student answers at a glance and has an appropriate resolution for allowing notes to be understood. The OpenNOTE system of DNP [5] provides similar view modes. However, to improve the focused view, teachers are required to decide in advance the areas to be focused on. Because the location of the focused area is the same across all student sheets, if the teacher wishes to focus on real-time handwriting using free format sheets, the focus region must be moved to track the latest notes.

To improve the effectiveness of sharing real-time student handwriting, we introduced an alternative method of browsing that tracks the latest student notes using the AirTransNote system.

Fig. 2. Conventional view modes in AirTransNote: Thumbnail view (left) and Focused view (right). When the teacher hovers the mouse pointer over the focused view, both views are highlighted.

1.1 Design Criteria

We set the following criteria for the design of an alternative view mode for tracking the latest student notes.

- The view mode displays multiple student notes at an appropriate zoom rate.
- To track the handwriting activities of each student, the view mode focuses on the latest notes.
- Both the teacher and students can read the note content without controlling the zoom rate or position. Panning and zooming are determined automatically.
- To improve awareness of handwriting, the view mode displays handwritten notes with pens.
- The view mode allows both texts and figures to be read.

2 Alternative Browsing Methods

To meet these criteria, we considered two alternative browsing methods: constant zoom and variable zoom.

In this section, we describe our method of calculating zoom areas and zoom rates.

2.1 Format of Digital Pen Data

Before explaining how the zoom areas and zoom rates are calculated, we introduce the basic format of digital pen data. Digital pen data comprises multiple strokes, in which each stroke represents a line generated by the continuous movement of the pen-tip on the paper. The stroke data comprises (1) the coordinates of the pen-tip (x,y), sampled at a frequency of 75 times per second, and (2) the start time of the stroke. The size of the bounding box of the stroke is calculated as shown in Fig. 3. The height of the bounding box is used to estimate the size of the characters used in texts or formulae. It can also be used to determine whether the writing is text, formulae, or figures. In our initial designs, we used the height of the bounding box to determine zoom rates.

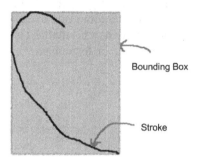

Fig. 3. Bounding box of a stroke

2.2 Constant Zoom

To determine the appropriate zoom rate for each note, the following parameters were considered: (1) the size of the browsing area, (2) the resolution of the display, and (3) the size of the written characters. The first parameter is based on the number of browsing areas, the aspect ratio of the area, and the layout of the browsing areas. The second parameter is determined by the specification of the projector. The third parameter varies from student to student. We therefore estimated the size of the characters by averaging the height of the bounding boxes of the previous strokes. From preliminary experiments, we determined the zoom rate by the following formula:

$$ZoomRate = \frac{27.58}{3 \times AvgHeight_{BoundingBox}} \tag{1}$$

Here, the zoom rate is based on a display resolution of 700 pixels in width and 990 pixels in height for a whole A4-sized sheet. This display resolution allows most of the note to be recognized on the screen. The base line height of the pixels is 27.58, corresponding to 5 mm on the display. This value was based on the guidelines of Japan's Ministry of Health, Labour and Welfare[1]. The denominator is based on the average line height of the main handwritten text in the pixel unit. In our experiment, as described in Sect. 3, a heuristic method was used to determine the denominator part, by introducing a magnification parameter of three that converted the average height of the bounding box to the line height

---

[1] http://www.mhlw.go.jp/houdou/2002/04/h0405-4.html.

based on target note data. Strictly, the denominator part should be determined by analyzing the height of the main texts in each note.

Figure 4 shows a screenshot of the ConstantZoom view. Each browsing area displays a corresponding student note with the calculated zoom rate and handwriting animations. The pen is moving in the browsing area, and the position of the focused area is automatically updated (panned) based on the latest handwriting position. In ConstantZoom, the zoom rate of each browsing area is almost fixed if the number of large height strokes is smaller than the number of strokes that are generated when writing texts or formulae.

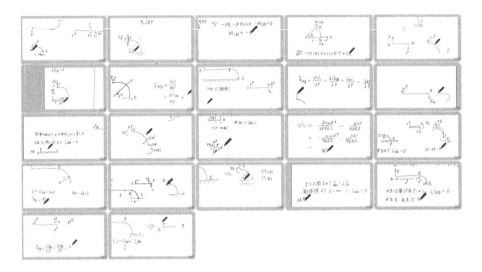

Fig. 4. Screenshot of the ConstantZoom view. The number and layout of the browsing areas were held constant in the experiment.

2.3   VariableZoom

The ConstantZoom method is suitable for notes that consist of texts and formulae. However, a handwritten note often contains figures and graphs. Generally, when the figures and graphs are larger than the texts and formulae, they cannot be displayed using the ConstantZoom method.

To allow display of both texts/formulae and figures/graphs, we introduced the Variable-Zoom method. The VariableZoom method determines the zoom rate by analyzing the average height of the last fifteen strokes. This allows the whole figure and graph to be displayed by zooming out.

3   Experiments

Experiments were conducted to investigate the usability of the proposed browsing method and to explore its characteristics.

Handwritten notes were collected from forty undergraduate students in a lecture on material mechanics. The students were asked to answer questions in the course of the lecture using Anoto digital pens and paper. The notes contained both formulae and figures, at a different ratio for each student. The timestamp data of several of the student notes were defective, and our analysis was confined to notes for which the timestamp data were correct. Notes with few or limited drawings were also eliminated. A total of 22 student notes were used in the analysis.

Eight further participants (all male, ages from 20 to 24) were asked to browse the selected notes on a PC, with a view similar to that shown in Fig. 4. Each participant browsed the notes alone and one by one. The display of the PC was 348 mm in width and 197 mm in height, with a resolution of 1920 × 1080 pixels. The size of each browsing area was 64 mm in width and 32 mm in height, with a resolution of 353 × 175 pixels. An LCD display was used in place of the projection screen to reduce the effect of brightness.

To avoid participants becoming confused when browsing multiple notes simultaneously, we asked them to focus on one specified browsing area. Four student notes with similar average stroke heights and containing both formulae and figures were selected. Figure 5 shows one of the notes used in the experiment. Each participant browsed the notes four times, using the ConstantZoom and VariableZoom methods. The order of presentation was counterbalanced by area and method.

After four browsing sessions, participants were asked to evaluate the online handwriting note animations from three viewpoints: (1) readability of texts, (2) visibility of figures, and (3) intuitiveness of representation/animation. A 5-point Likert scale (1: worst; 5: best) was used.

3.1   Results and Discussion

Figure 6 shows the actual zoom rates for an example note (Fig. 5). The "ConstantZoom" and "VariableZoom" represent the zoom rates of the ConstantZoom and VariableZoom, respectively. This confirmed that the transition of zoom rates was more moderate when using ConstantZoom.

Figure 7 gives the results of the questionnaire. A Mann-Whitney U-test was conducted, with a 5 % significance cutoff. Table 1 shows the results. In terms of readability of texts and visibility of figures, there was no significant difference between the ConstantZoom and the VariableZoom methods. However, the intuitiveness of animation of the ConstantZoom method was rated significantly higher than that of VariableZoom. The participants found frequent and rapid changes in the zoom rate unintuitive, which reduced their evaluations of the browsing method. However, some participants reported that the zoom change helped a mode change to be recognized. Several participants also noted that the readability of the text was significantly affected by the neatness of the handwriting.

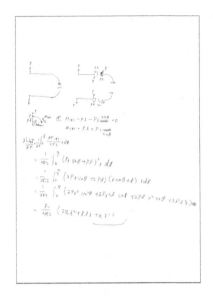

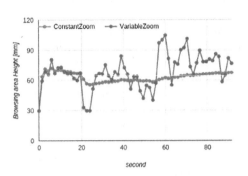

Fig. 5. Example note

Fig. 6. Actual zoom rates of Constant-Zoom/VariableZoom methods for the example note

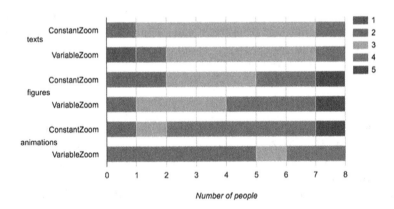

Fig. 7. The results of the questionnaire

Table 1. Mann-Whitney U-test for the result of the questionnaire (significance level was 5%)

	U	p
texts	28	0.61
figures	13.5	0.58
animations	11.5	0.03

4   Conclusions and Future Work

In this paper, we proposed two browsing methods for simultaneous viewing of multiple online handwritten note animations. In the ConstantZoom method, the zoom rate was determined by averaging the previous handwriting strokes. VariableZoom used a similar approach, except that only the last 15 strokes were used to determine the zoom rate. Experiments were conducted to evaluate the readability of texts, the visibility of figures, and the intuitiveness of animations. The results showed that there were no significant differences in the readability of texts or the visibility of figures. However, the ConstantZoom method was superior to VariableZoom in terms of the intuitiveness of animations.

In future work, we will evaluate a refined VariableZoom method in which the zoom rate is changed more smoothly. We will also try to improve the ease of distinguishing texts and figures by appropriate zooming. Our browsing methods can be used to enhance classroom communication and interactions between students and with teachers by improving the interpretability of handwritten notes.

Acknowledgements. The part of this research was supported by the fund of JSPS KAKENHI Grant-in-Aid for Scientific Research (C): Grant Number 15K00485 and the fund of Telecommunication Advancement Foundation.

References

1. Enriquez, A.G.: Enhancing student performance using tablet computers. Coll. Teach. **58**(3), 77–84 (2010)
2. Miura, M., Sugihara, T., Kunifuji, S.: Improvement of digital pen learning system for daily use in classrooms. Educ. Technol. Res. **34**, 49–57 (2011)
3. Prieto, L.P., Wen, Y., Caballero, D., Dillenbourg, P.: Review of augmented paper systems in education: an orchestration perspective. Educ. Technol. Soc. **17**(4), 169–185 (2014)
4. Sugihara, T., Miura, M., Kunifuji, S.: Practicing on stage: increasing transparency and interaction in class activity with digital pen system. In: König, A., Dengel, A., Hinkelmann, K., Kise, K., Howlett, R.J., Jain, L.C. (eds.) KES 2011. Lecture Notes in Artificial Intelligence (LNAI), vol. 6884, pp. 457–464. Springer, Heidelberg (2010). doi:10.1007/978-3-642-15384-6_49
5. DNP: OpenNOTE.   http://www.dnp.co.jp/works/detail/10111269_18925.html (2016/2/12 accessed)

Development of a GeoTour Support System Using a Microblog

Shogo Taniguchi[✉] and Takashi Yoshino

Graduate School of System Engineering, Wakayama University, Wakayama, Japan
taniguchi.shogo@g.wakayama-u.jp, yoshino@sys.wakayama-u.ac.jp
https://www.sys.wakayama-u.ac.jp/

Abstract. A GeoTour is a tour around natural terrains and landscapes. The problems with GeoTours are mainly of the following three types: participants often have difficulties in understanding technical terms that are used by Geoguides; since the distance between Geosites is often relatively large, the destination indicated by the Geoguide can be difficult for participants to discern; GeoTours currently have a relatively low profile. Therefore, in this study, we have developed a GeoTour support system using a microblog entitled Twi-Geo. The main purposes of Twi-Geo are to support participants' understanding, and to increase the profile of GeoTours. Twi-Geo contains two main functions. Firstly, it offers a guide-explanation function to support Geoguides in delivering their photographs and explanatory text of Geosites to the participants. Secondly, there is a tagging function to support participants when they post Tweets through the Twi-Geo system; the hashtag #GeoTour is added automatically to the Tweet, which advertises GeoTours subtly to the participant's followers. Evaluation of our experimental results showed that the guide-explanation function of Twi-Geo helps to improve the understanding of Geoguide material, and that participants' automatically tagged Tweets are likely to increase the visibility of GeoTours.

Keywords: GeoTour · Increasing of the visibility · Microblog · Twitter · Communication support

1 Introduction

The nine municipalities in the southern part of Wakayama contain within them the Nanki Kumano Geopark. In August 2014, the area was recognized as a Geopark by the Japanese Geoparks Committee[1], which concerns itself with recognizing valuable geology and terrain[2]. Since then, many people in the Wakayama Prefecture have become interested in Geoparks and Geosites[3]. Geoparks are areas

---

[1] Accreditation organization of Geoparks in Japan.

[2] AGARA Kii Minpo http://www.agara.co.jp/news/daily/?i=279635 (reference 2016-4-17).

[3] http://www.nankikumanogeo.jp (reference 2016-4-17).

© Springer Science+Business Media Singapore 2016
T. Yoshino et al. (Eds.): CollabTech 2016, CCIS 647, pp. 220–230, 2016.
DOI: 10.1007/978-981-10-2618-8_18

of the natural environment that contain attractive and interesting features, such as valuable terrain or geological heritage. Geosites are points of particular interest within a Geopark. A GeoTour is a journey around a collection of Geosites that is curated and directed by a Geoguide. The main purpose of a GeoTour is to promote economic development, as well as to attract people's attention to a particular geographical area. However, GeoTours have three particular problems associated with them. (1) When a Geoguide attempts to introduce a new Geosite to a participant, the relatively large distance to that site can make familiarization difficult. (2) Participants often have difficulties in understanding technical terms that are used by Geoguides. (3) GeoTours currently have a relatively low profile. Therefore, in this study, we have developed a GeoTour support system using a microblog entitled Twi-Geo. In this paper, we give an overview of Twi-Geo and describe an experiment that was carried out to assess its utility.

2 Related Work

Saitou et al. carried out a study on tourism using Twitter[4] [1]. They created a Geoguide named Twitter-GeoTour, which explained Geosites to its Twitter followers. They examined the method and its effect. However, in that study, the majority of participants did not actually visit any of the Geosites. Furthermore, the participants were of an unspecified large number from among followers of Twitter. In contrast, we consider the situation where participants use a Geoguide to visit the actual Geosites themselves. Tanaka et al. developed a system for recommending tourist attractions by using Twitter [2]. In that study, the target participants were foreign Twitter users who were tourists in Japan. This system is that make recommendations via the removal and utility of determining the user unsuitable for language decision and recommendation. In the present case, we consider that our system is intended for Japanese Twitter users. Giorgos et al. studied the use of data from social networking services (SNS[5]) in tourism support [3]. In that study, their system combined the SNS evaluation information about various tourist attractions, analyzed it, and then recommended a suitable destination for the user. The system used a function to add position information to an associated Tweet. Here, we consider a system that uses a Twitter tagging function, supports communication between Geoguides and participants, and improves the profile of GeoTours by promoting them to the Twitter followers of the participants. Nagao et al. developed a tourism-support system based on smartphone technology [4]. In that study, they performed tourism support by using a smartphone with both GPS and camera functions. However, the purpose of the present system is to promote local experiences. We also consider that it is necessary for participants to have the necessary motivation to take the actual GeoTour in person. Sawada et al. studied GeoTours [5]. In that study, which involved an experimental investigation of a GeoTour directed by a Geoguide of Hokkaido, the results were used to describe the necessary plan required for a

---

[4] https://twitter.com.

[5] Abbreviation Social Networking Service.

GeoTour. We have used some of the ideas that were discussed in the conclusion of [5] to develop the functions of the present system.

3   Twi-Geo

In this section, we describe a GeoTour support system based on a microblog that is entitled Twi-Geo.

3.1   Outline of Twi-Geo

When Geoguides and participants engage in a GeoTour, Twi-Geo is a Web application that they can use on their smartphones. Twi-Geo has the following two main functions. (1) A guide-explanation function supports a human guide in delivering photographs and explanatory text of a Geosite for the participants. (2) A tagging function supports participants by allowing them to post Tweets directly from the system, while adding the hashtag #GeoTour automatically to the tweet. In this way, participants advertise GeoTours subtly to their Twitter followers. We intend that Twi-Geo should not burden Geoguides and participants unduly. We achieve this by easy operation and an auto-update function during a GeoTour.

3.2   Policy

The ideas that motivated the development of Twi-Geo are as follows.

(1) Support for participants' understanding

Since the distances between Geosites can be relatively large, it is sometimes difficult for a Geoguide to introduce participants to a new site. In addition, some participants may not understand certain technical terms that are used in a Geoguide explanation. Therefore, Geoguides and participants can use Twi-Geo on their own smartphones to allow participants to receive and understand a detailed Geoguide explanation.

(2) Increased visibility support for GeoTours

Since GeoTours and Geosites currently have relatively low profiles, it can be difficult to use them to promote sustainable social and economic development. We can address the problem of low visibility in part by using the participants themselves to transmit information about GeoTours. When considering the transmission of information, we noted the increasing number of users of SNS in recent years. According to the Nakayama report [6], Twitter had 12.44 million Japanese users as of November 2010. Therefore, we decided to use Twitter as the means of transmitting the information that is intended to increase of the visibility of GeoTours.

(3) Communication support

A GeoTour consists of several Geoguides and tens of participants, and the Geoguides tend to be fewer in number than the participants. Many participants would meet each other at a GeoTour for the first time. Therefore, there can be communication difficulties between Geoguides and participants, or between the participants themselves. Therefore, we intend that the present system should offer communication support by using the medium of Twitter.

3.3 System Configuration

Figure 1 shows the system configuration for Twi-Geo. It comprises the smartphone of each user, and a server to transmit the explanations of the Geosites by a Geoguide. Firstly, the Geoguide and the participants enter the Twi-Geo URL directly into their web browsers. The Geoguide in Fig. 1(a) performs a transmission of information to the participants in Fig. 1(c) by means of the server in Fig. 1(b), from the main page of Twi-Geo. Thereafter, the participants in Fig. 1(d) post Geosite information on Twitter by means of a tweet-posting function. The friends and acquaintances of the participants in Fig. 1(e) read these Tweets, thereby increasing of the visibility of GeoTours. In addition, the Geoguide and the participants can communicate with each other by reading all the respective Tweets. Furthermore, because Twi-Geo uses Twitter as its external system, the appeal of Twi-Geo can extend to many more people than were engaged in that particular GeoTour.

3.4 Explanation of Individual Functions

In this section, we give further details about Twi-Geo's three main functions.

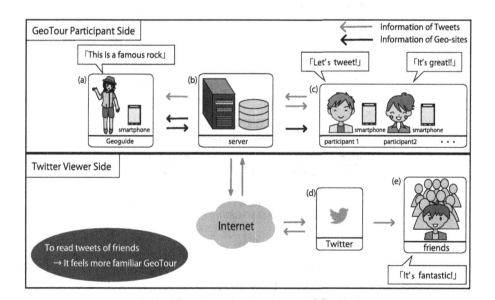

Fig. 1. System configuration

A Guide-Explanation Function. Figure 2 shows an example of the guide-explanation function that we developed on the basis of the policy discussed in Sect. 3.2 (1). This function can show participants the explanations that a Geoguide has pre-registered on the system. Figure 2(a) shows the screen display for the Geoguide, while Figs. 2(b) and (c) show the screen for the participants.

Firstly, a Geoguide selects one of the pre-registered Geosites in Fig. 2(a-1). Next, the Geoguide presses the explanation display button of Fig. 2(a-2). Then, the Geoguide can show the participants the explanation that the Geoguide has pre-registered, as shown in Figs. 2(b) and (c). Participants can then see the explanation in the form of text and photographs that are displayed automatically on each individual smartphone. This automatic-display process is intended to help the participants concentrate on the explanations being provided by the Geoguide.

Tweet-Posting Function. Figure 3 shows an example of the Tweet-posting function that we developed on the basis of the policy discussed in Sect. 3.2 (2). This function can post Tweets that participants have composed in the textbox shown in Fig. 3(1). Participants can add an optional photograph by using the photo-selecting button shown in Fig. 3(2). Finally, the function appends the

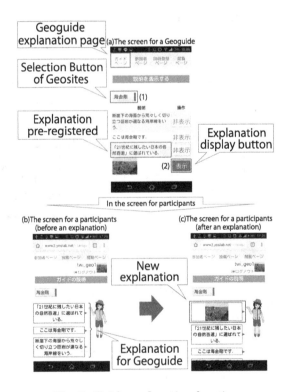

Fig. 2. Guide-explanation function.

Fig. 3. Tweet-posting function.

hashtag #GeoTour automatically when participants post Tweets using the posting button shown in Fig. 3(3). In this way, participants are effectively advertising the GeoTour concept each time they Tweet about a particular GeoTour using the Twi-Geo web application.

Tweet-Reading Function. Figure 4 shows an example of the tweet-reading function that we developed on the basis of the policy discussed in Sect. 3.2 (3). This function displays Tweets with the hashtag #GeoTour from participants in the window shown in Fig. 4(1). The username, user ID, date, time, text and (optional) photograph of the tweet are all displayed. Our hypothesis is that, by seeing such Tweets, the Geoguide can gauge the moods and opinions of the participants, and that this will provide an opportunity for informative dialogue. We hypothesize further that, when participants see each other's Tweets, they can similarly gauge the moods and opinions in the group and establish some form of supportive communication.

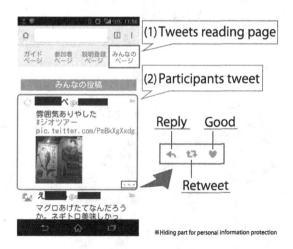

Fig. 4. Tweet-reading function.

4   Experimental Methodology

4.1   Verification Points and Goal

We performed experimental tests on the following three hypotheses.

1. When a Geoguide uses the guide-explanation function, the degree of understanding of the participants improves.
2. When participants post using the Tweet-posting function, there is a likelihood of Twitter users developing an interest in GeoTours.
3. When participants read posts using the Tweet-reading function, there is a likelihood of improved inter-participant communication.

4.2   Verification Overview

One of the authors performed the role of the tour guide (Geoguide) in this experiment, since it represents a stage of the experimental process that is prior an actual GeoTour. The participants in the experiment were 31 students from Wakayama University, 10 of whom were the Geotourists, and 21 of whom were the viewers who looked at Twitter while the Geotourists performed the tour. Incidentally, the Twitter viewers did not know in advance any details of the tour

Fig. 5. Photograph of an experiment.

that was being performed. The 10 Geotourists were divided into three groups and given the task of posting more than one Tweet during their GeoTour. The location of the experiment was Tuna Land Kuroshio Market and Porto Europa in Wakayama Marina City[6]. We performed questionnaire-based surveys after the end of the GeoTour, and we considered the effect of the order of the experiments. Incidentally, we gave the same explanations regardless of whether Twi-Geo was used. Figure 5 shows a photograph of the guide and some of the tourists performing the tour while using the system.

5   Experimental Evaluation and Discussion

We now present the results of the questionnaire-based survey. We used a five-point Likert scale for evaluation, in which the individual responses were 1: Strongly disagree, 2: Disagree, 3: Neutral, 4: Agree, and 5: Strongly agree.

5.1   Guide-Explanation Function: Results and Discussion

Table 1(1) (i.e., statement (1) in Table 1) shows that the median and mode scores were both 5 for the statement "When explanations for Geoguides are been showed, I became easy to understand the explanations for Geoguides." We obtained the following two opinions from the experimental participants, which were classed as being favorable: "The explanation for Geoguides was clearly visible and could be looking back it", and "I can prevent missed hear."

Table 1(2) shows that the median score was 4 and the mode score was 4 and 5 for the statement "When explanations for Geoguides are been showed by sentences, I think that I could be understand more information of the tourist spot." We obtained the following two opinions from the experimental participants, which were classed as being favorable: "It was convenient that I could have looked up unknown words using a web-site because explanations for Geoguide was text", and "If I missed hear the explanations for Geoguides once, I could

Table 1. Results of questionnaire about the guide-explanation function (5-point Likert scale).

	Question items	Evaluations					Median	Mode
		1	2	3	4	5		
(1)	When explanations for Geoguides are been showed, I became easy to understand the explanations for Geoguides	0	1	0	2	7	5	5
(2)	When explanations for Geoguides are been showed by sentences, I think that I could be understand more information of the tourist spot	0	2	2	3	3	4	4,5
(3)	When explanations for Geoguides are been showed by photos, I think that I could be understand more information of the tourist spot	0	0	0	5	5	4.5	4,5

- Evaluation: 1: Strongly disagree, 2: Disagree, 3: Neutral, 4: Agree, 5: Strongly agree.
- "Evaluation" is the number of people.

---

[6] A famous tourist spot in both Wakayama Prefecture.

not understand the explanations for Geoguides in details. But, I could understand it because it was possible to look it by this function." However, we also obtained the following two opinions that were classed as being unfavorable: "I was able to understand only listen, and I thought that it became neglected that I listen the explanations for Geoguides if I used the system", and "I have to scroll until the screen's bottom when the explanations for Geoguides is long."

Table 1(3) shows that the median score was 4.5 and the mode score was 4,5 for the statement "When explanations for Geoguides are been showed by photos, I think that I could be understand more information of the tourist spot". We obtained the following two opinions from the experimental participants, which were classed as being favorable: "It was convenient that I could look at the photo at hand", and "Because I can zoom everywhere, I felt that it is beneficial as a function of the order to understand the explanations for Geoguides".

Thus, we conclude that the guide-explanation function does help to improve the degree to which participants understanding the GeoTour, but that the form of the user-interface screen must be considered further.

5.2   Tweet-Posting Function: Results and Discussion

Table 2(1) shows that the median and mode scores were both 4 for the statement "It has become an opportunity to promote communication with other participants by looking at the tweets of other participants." We obtained the following opinion from the experimental collaborators, which was classed as being favorable: "When I looked at the tweets posted, it was possible to communicate to tell my thoughts." However, we also obtained the following opinion that was classed as being unfavorable: "I was talking directly to other participants without looking at a tweet."

Thus, we conclude that the Tweet-reading function is likely to promote communication with other participants from the Tweets posted, except in cases where there are other participants within talking distance.

Table 2(2) shows that the median and mode scores were both 4 for the statement "My tweet motivation has improved by looking at the tweets of other participants." We obtained the following two opinions from the experimental participants, which were classed as being favorable: "I thought that I want to post a photo that other participants did not post", and "I thought that I want

Table 2. Results of questionnaire about the tweet-reading function (5-point Likert scale).

	Question items	Evaluations					Median	Mode
		1	2	3	4	5		
(1)	It has become an opportunity to promote communication with other participants by looking at the tweets of other participants	0	3	0	6	1	4	4
(2)	My tweet motivation has improved by looking at the tweets of other participants	0	0	1	5	4	4	4

- Evaluation: 1: Strongly disagree, 2: Disagree, 3: Neutral, 4: Agree, 5: Strongly agree.
- "Evaluation" is the number of people.

to tweets together because other participants were posting tweets." However, we obtained the following an opinion that was classed as being unfavorable: "I was fun just to look at the tweet of the other participants."

Thus, we conclude that the Tweet-reading function is likely to prompt the participants to post their own Tweets.

5.3   Questionnaire of Twitter Readers: Results and Discussion

Table 3(1) shows that the median and mode scores were both 4 for the statement "When I looked at the tweets with "#GeoTour", I was interested in the tweet." We obtained the following opinion from the experimental participants, which was classed as being favorable: "I thought it looks like fun because my friend posted the tweet with a photo." However, we obtained the following opinion from the experimental collaborators, which has a low mark. "Because it was the place that I knew, I was not interested."

Table 3(2) shows that the median score was 3 and the mode score was 4 for the statement "When I looked at the tweets with "#GeoTour", I was interested in the GeoTour and Geosites." We obtained the following two opinions from the experimental participants, which were classed as being favorable: "I looked like a good mood", and "I thought I want to go because the buildings in the photo was beautiful." However, we also obtained the following two opinions that were classed as being unfavorable: "I saw that my friend posted the tweets only exclamatory sentence such as 'fun!' and 'good!' and I could not understand the goodness of the tour", and "I did not know the meaning of the word 'GeoTour'."

Table 3(3) shows that the median and mode scores were both 4 for the statement "When I looked at the tweets with "#GeoTour", I thought that I also want to participate the tour next time." We obtained the following two opinions from the experimental participants, which were classed as being favorable: "It looked like fun anyway", and "I want to go there because I do not have been to tourist spot in Wakayama." However, we also obtained the following opinion that was classed as being unfavorable: "Because there was not a Geosites", and "I do not know GeoTour well."

Table 3. Results of questionnaire for Twitter readers (5-point Likert scale).

	Question items	Evaluations					Median	Mode
		1	2	3	4	5		
(1)	When I looked at the tweets with "#GeoTour", I was interested in the tweet	0	3	2	11	5	4	4
(2)	When I looked at the tweets with "#GeoTour", I was interested in the GeoTour and Geosites	0	6	5	8	1	3	4
(3)	When I looked at the tweets with "#GeoTour", I thought that I also want to participate the tour next time	0	5	4	7	5	4	4

- Evaluation: 1: Strongly disagree, 2: Disagree, 3: Neutral, 4: Agree, 5: Strongly agree.
- "Evaluation" is the number of people.

Thus, we conclude that it is necessary for participants to tell their Twitter followers the meaning of the word 'GeoTour'. However, we consider that it is likely that participants will raise the awareness of followers who do not know about GeoTours by posting Tweets using Twi-Geo about their enjoyable Geo-Tour experiences.

6   Conclusions

In this study, we have developed a GeoTour support system using a microblog entitled Twi-Geo. We described the results of the experimental evaluation and discussion of this system. The results of the evaluation experiments revealed the following two points.

1. The guide-explanation function can make it easier for GeoTour participants to understand the experience by means of the explanations and photographs that are displayed by the Geoguides.
2. During a GeoTour, participants have the possibility to advertise to their Twitter readers who do not know about GeoTours by posting Tweets of their enjoyable experiences using Twi-Geo.

In future work, we intend to evaluate further the design and function of the user interface that is used by the Geoguide. We should compare with Twi-Geo and a regular Twitter client. We also aim to use the Twi-Geo system on an actual GeoTour.

Acknowledgments. This work was supported partly by JSPS KAKENHI Grant Number 25242037 and an Original Research Support Project at Wakayama University during 2012–2016.

References

1. Saito, C., Komine, S., Ito, T., Amano, K.: Attempt of new geotour using Twitter, The Geological Society of Japan, p. 97 (2010)
2. Tanaka, H., Seki, Y.: Recommendation of Twitter users who use English for the foreign tourists, Society for Tourism Informatics. In: 11th Proceedings of the Annual Conference of the Japan Society, pp. 21–24 (2015)
3. Papadimitriou, G., Komninos, A., Garofalakis, J.: An investigation of the suitability of heterogeneous social network data for use in mobile tourist guides. In: Proceedings of the 19th Panhellenic Conference on Informatics PCI 2015, pp. 283–288 (2015)
4. Nagao, S., Katou, F., Urada, M., Yasuda, T.: Developed a tourism support system using a smartphone. In: 2013 PC Conference, pp. 321–324 (2013)
5. Sawada, Y., Takeda, K., Kawabe, M., Fujiyama, H.: Ideas for designing a geotour: suggestions from experimental geotour for professional nature guides in Hokkaido Island, Japan. J. Geogr. **120**(5), 853–863 (2011)
6. Nakayama, K.: Connecting social media/Study and health to change we think the Twitter as an example."Nursing study" Med. Study **44**(1), pp. 86–93 (2011)

A Microtask Drawing Generation System that Links with a Commercial Crowdsourcing Site

Akira Hirata[1(✉)], Kousuke Sasaki[1], He Ban[1], and Tomoo Inoue[2]

[1] Graduate School of Library, Information and Media Studies,
University of Tsukuba, Tsukuba, Japan
{hirata,ksasaki,heban}@slis.tsukuba.ac.jp
[2] Faculty of Library, Information and Media Science,
University of Tsukuba, 1-2, Kasuga, Tsukuba, Ibaraki 305-8550, Japan
inoue@slis.tsukuba.ac.jp

Abstract. Crowdsourcing has been gaining attention. Microtasking is a specially featured way of distributing work among crowd workers. With the combination of a number of microtasks which is simple and need short period of time, goal objective is achieved. Because it typically shows advantages in time and money costs, methods to achieve variety of goals by the combination of microtasks have been studied. At present, some Web sites provide microtask-type crowdsourcing. However the kind of work that can be placed is very limited. Thus we propose a novel crowdsourcing platform in this paper. By using an existing microtask crowdsourcing service as literally a source of crowd workers, various work can be placed in the proposed system and can be achieved. We show application of the system to the microtask drawing generation method, which cannot be placed in the existing services.

Keywords: Crowdsourcing · Microtask · Drawing generation

1 Introduction

Creating content (such as novels and music, etc.) with multiple workers through a network has grown more popular with the development of content production on the Internet. Research on how to support remote workers to create contents together is increasing and such research makes it possible for anyone to engage in the production contents easily with the use of a support system. If ability for anyone to be able to create contents can improve the content industry. Therefore, there is a high demand for a system that supports everyone creating contents.

In this paper, we focus on generating illustration as a kind of creative contents which is supported by a system. Illustration is a key factor to attract document readers. Illustrations can improve the readability of texts [7]. In addition, remote environment workspaces to collaborate with workers in generating illustration is suggested until now [3,11]. Real-time collaboration Web systems to generate

© Springer Science+Business Media Singapore 2016
T. Yoshino et al. (Eds.): CollabTech 2016, CCIS 647, pp. 231–245, 2016.
DOI: 10.1007/978-981-10-2618-8_19

illustration, such as FlockDraw, have been developed [9]. These systems work in real-time. However real-time systems compel workers to work together at the same time. Yet this makes gathering workers harder. Therefore, we use crowd-sourcing to recruit workers easily in contrast to the real time method.

Moreover, when we create creative contents such as illustration, we need to have the technical knowledge to make each content. For example, when a creator makes an illustration, they need skills in sketching, painting, determining composition, and so on. Previously, professional creators generally made contents. In recent years, however, studies have been conducted that support workers who do not have the technical knowledge to engage in creating illustrations, such as Sketch-sketch Revolution [17] or ShadowDraw [16]. If generating creative contents does not require technical knowledge, then the number of workers who concern themselves with drawing illustrations can increase.

A system of drawing generation by crowdsourcing has been suggested, whose worker are free from time constraints and do not have to have technical knowledge. In this method, microtasks are used to enable any worker regardless of skill in drawing to work on drawing tasks. Using microtasks makes workers contribute the tasks without time constraints. In addition, many workers can crowd to contribute the microtasks by using crowdsourcing Web site because of lighter strain on the tasks [22].

It is also being discussed that features of the generated drawings by using proposed method. It is reported that not inferior drawings were obtained as compared to the ones which were created by a single worker, and this method can make diversity in drawings [21].

However, in this research the system does not use existing crowdsourcing Web sites, and experimenter and participants are under face to face environment to try a task. Experimenter also instructed the participants verbally to deal with the tasks. Conventionally, almost all of crowdsourcing Web sites that can deal with micro-tasks support only selection formula tasks or text description formula tasks. They can only run independent, parallel tasks but can't run sequential tasks. So the proposed method cannot be contributed the task directly with existing crowdsourcing Web sites. In this paper, we develop the environment that client who requests tasks generates a task in any format by using existing crowdsourced Web sites indirectly. In this environment, in addition to a task page on the crowdsourcing Web sites, a Web server that provides the task (task server) is also used. By inducing workers who is recruited on the crowdsourcing Web sites to the Web page provided by the task server, it is possible to perform sequential tasks. In this research, we discuss the system which cooperates with crowdsourcing Web sites, taking the method of generating drawings by crowdsourced microtasks as an example.

2 Related Work

2.1 The Microtask Crowdsourcing Sites

Today, many crowdsourcing web sites are existing, bad they has plural problems. First, almost of them can only use selection formula tasks or text description formula tasks. So they can only run independent, parallel tasks but can't run sequential tasks (such as to reflect the results of previous task to the next worker's tasks). There are few reports about sequential microtasks. By using APIs, these problems are solved to some extent. Typical example is Amazon Mechanical Turk (MTurk) [1]. MTurk has a huge worker pool and many researches about microtasks have used MTurk. Many systems using MTurk had been proposed as it can clean data, categorize items, get feedback, and moderate content [2]. Yu et al. had used MTurk to generate designs [25], Hara et al. had used it to identify the obstacle on the sidewalk using the Google Street View [10], Komarov et al. had used it to perform evaluation of the user interface [14], and Kawashima et al. had used it to regenerate an 100-dollar bill [12]. Especially, Komarov et al. and Kawashima et al. had used microtasks which is neither selection formula tasks nor text description formula tasks. Greg et al. had run sequential tasks at Mturk [8]. This shows that the MTurk has broad utility.

However, in either case of using Mturk or using other sites, it is impossible to run sequential tasks. In this paper, we proposed a method that prepares external server for the tasks and links with the crowdsourcing sites. It can be used to free task design without restrictions of any crowdsourcing sites.

2.2   Microtasks that Do Not Through the Crowdsourcing Site

Crowdsourcing Web sites are not always necessary to complete microtasks. For instance, Vaish et al. and Truong et al. have developed microtask applications that are able to install on smartphones, and have shown the usefulness [23,24]. Moreover, LaToza et al. have developed the source code generation system by using microtasks, and have found positive result, which success the developing program using the proposed system [15].

However, an issue about the payment to the workers may occur without using crowdsourcing Web sites. Crowdsourcing Web sites like MTurk give unique account for each worker with the function of payment. In other words, if clients do not use these crowdsourcing sites, they have to implement the payment mechanism by themselves. This rests on the client. Notably, Vaish et al. have tried the no-paid microtasks. But the payment to the workers in MTurk is known, which more than $6 per hour is better [19,20]. Martin et al. have mentioned that payment is the most important factor to attract workers [6]. Thus asking workers to contribute microtasks without payment may have ethical issues.

In this paper, we develop the system using an existing crowdsourcing Web site for not to put extra strain and to pay an appropriate compensation to the worker.

2.3   Generating Drawings by Crowdsourced Microtasks

A method of generating a drawing by crowdsourced microtasks have been proposed. The proposed method makes a drawing from a photo. Generally, when we make a drawing, we first draw lines characterizing the object. Anyone can draw lines, and, if a model is displayed, the drawing action may be easier. Therefore, we supposed that we could generate a drawing using a crowdsourcing method in

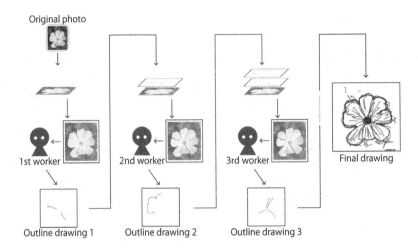

Fig. 1. Method of generating a drawings

which many workers perform the microtask of drawing lines. With this method, clients do not have to make a contract with a creator. To realize this method, we constructed a mechanism to generate one drawing out of many workers tasks. Figure 1 shows the concept of the method we proposed. In this microtask, lines drawn by workers are overlaid to generate one drawing. An original photo (a model) and drawing area (a canvas) are overlaid and displayed to each worker, and the workers draw outlines of the model. After the second workers task is complete, the lines drawn by the previous worker overlay the model. While viewing the overlaid image, the worker adds lines to complete the drawing. Adding lines is the microtask, and workers perform this microtask. Finally, one drawing is completed by combining the drawn lines.

To test the feasibility and validity of this method, Sasaki et al. have had experiments under the face to face environment [21,22]. However, in these experiments, as experimenter had to instruct all the participants how to complete the tasks and let them to contribute the tasks in experimenters presence, it is not practical to operate as a service. In this research, we constructed an environment that workers can contribute the task without experimenters escort. In the previous study, each worker had given 7 s per photo to draw lines [22]. In accordance with the previous research, we give the same 7 s to workers.

3   System Implementation

In the experiment that previous study had carried out, participants are given instruction by the experimenter under the face to face environment. In this study, we use CrowdFlower [5], which is one of crowdsourcing Web sites. The reason why we use CrowdFlower is that we can order a task as a customer from Japan, and the number of the contributors is more than five million [18]. However,

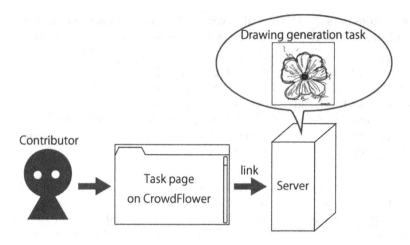

Fig. 2. The concept of the system

CrowdFlower can only run the selection formula or text description task as well as other crowdsourcing Web sites.

Therefore, we prepare the Web server for displaying microtasks and introducing the workers from a task page on the CrowdFlower. Figure 2 shows that the concept of this system. First, we create a task page on CrowdFlower and recruit workers. On the task page, we describe the goal of this task and ask some questions to obtain personal data using questionnaire form. A link to the task server is also described on the page. This makes contributors transit to the page on which they contribute tasks actually. On the task server, we can prepare any kind of executable tasks. In this study, drawing generating system is programed into the task server and set an instruction page for workers derived from CrowdFlower. Additionally, in CrowdFlower it is possible to limit each worker to contribute only once to one task with settings. It is applied to prevent from repetitive contributing in our system.

3.1   Countermeasure for Linking with the Crowdsourcing Sites

On condition that linking with the crowdsourcing Web sites, there are some issues that must be noted. In this section, we describe its contents and solutions. We used CrowdFlower as example in this paper, but of course the countermeasures can be used at most other crowdsourcing sites.

Shutting Out the Invasion from Outsides. In this system, we supposed that contributors come to the task server via task page on CrowdFlower. Especially in generation drawings, when unrelated workers contribute the tasks, a direct (and often negative) effect is given to the result. Thus we must prevent from entering to the task server from outside the CrowdFlower. There is a danger that workers (who have completed the task) share the URL of the task page. So we design that accessing from outside the CrowdFlower is cut off by checking referrer data. This mechanism can stop intrusions to the task server by inputting of the URL directly.

Shutting Out the Access from Other Devices. The generation drawings system can only accept input by mouse cursor. Therefore, it is necessary to cut off access from touch-only tablet devices and smartphone. We design to cut off the access from Android OS and iOS by monitoring the user agent. Therefore, regardless of our system, experimental apparatus are expected to be immobilized in remote asynchronous environment by setting allow or reject devices.

Countermeasure for Malicious Workers. Workers can finish the task without visiting the task server because of the design of this system, resulting in that CrowdFlower will pay the reward to such workers without contributing the generating drawing tasks. However, CrowdFlower can prohibit untrusted contributors to perform tasks. In CrowdFlower, each contributor has a unique ID, and we can check what each contributor have answered. Therefore in the task server, the system displays a unique authorization code to the worker after finishing the tasks, and workers need to input it to the form on the CrowdFlower. The displayed codes are stored in the task server. We can check whether each contributor have finished the task by confirming whether the input codes contributors entered match with the stored codes. If contributor entered the unmatched code, the contributor will not be able to participate in the future task. This makes it be possible to ensure the quality of the task.

Transaction Processing. In the generation drawing system, it is necessary to carry out the transaction processing accurately. If more than two workers draw lines with the same photo at the same time, the system cannot distinguish which drawn lines should be displayed to the next worker. However, we cannot utilize transaction processing function associated with a database management system because our system does not use database. So we design to use lock file to lock the photo and drawn lines for prohibiting other access to the photo while the drawing is processing. After finishing drawing lines, system discards the lock file and another worker can draw lines on the photo.

Countermeasure for the Person Who Left/Abandoned the Task. If a worker leaves without any operation during the task, a lock file for transaction processing will be left, resulting in that other workers cannot draw lines onto the photo. Therefore, if the drawings task is kept by a worker without any operation for a certain time, the system will automatically expel the worker from the task. This is named as kick-out function which can avoid the state of no operation for a long time in the drawing page. In addition, if a worker stopped contributing the task in the middle, the lock file will also be left. In crowdsourcing, it is a known issue that worker abandons the task. This issue should be corrected [13]. To solve this problem, the system is designed to automatically delete the lock file if it continues to exist for a certain time.

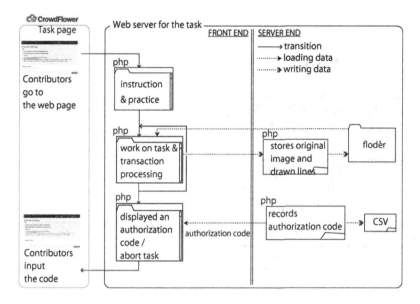

Fig. 3. System design

3.2 Implement

Figure 3 shows that the structure of this system which implement the function expressed in the Sect. 3. To implement this system, we use PHP and JavaScript mainly and do not use database. Contributors follow roughly these three kind of pages: a page for instruction, pages for contributing tasks, and pages for displaying an authorization code. Besides, this system monitors the referrer data and user agent in the instruction page, carries out transaction processing and kick-out workers who leave without any operation in each page for contributing tasks. Contributors go through these three kind of pages and return to the task page on CrowdFlower. After that, worker input the authorization code on the form, which is displayed after finishing tasks.

4 Experiment

We carried out the generation drawings experiments that is described in previous study using the implemented system. Through this experiment, we investigate whether drawings are generated as well as the previous study.

4.1 Procedure

Figure 4 shows the flowchart of this experiment. The experiment starts a task page on CrowdFlower shown in Fig. 5. In this task page, we let all contributors answer some questionnaires (sex, age, and some questionnaires about drawing)

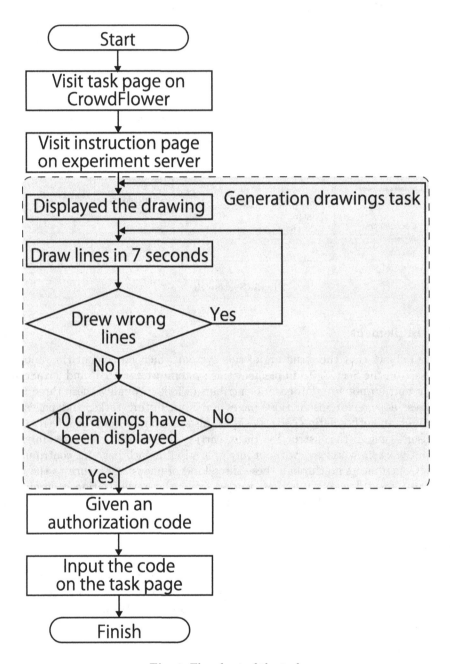

Fig. 4. Flowchart of the task

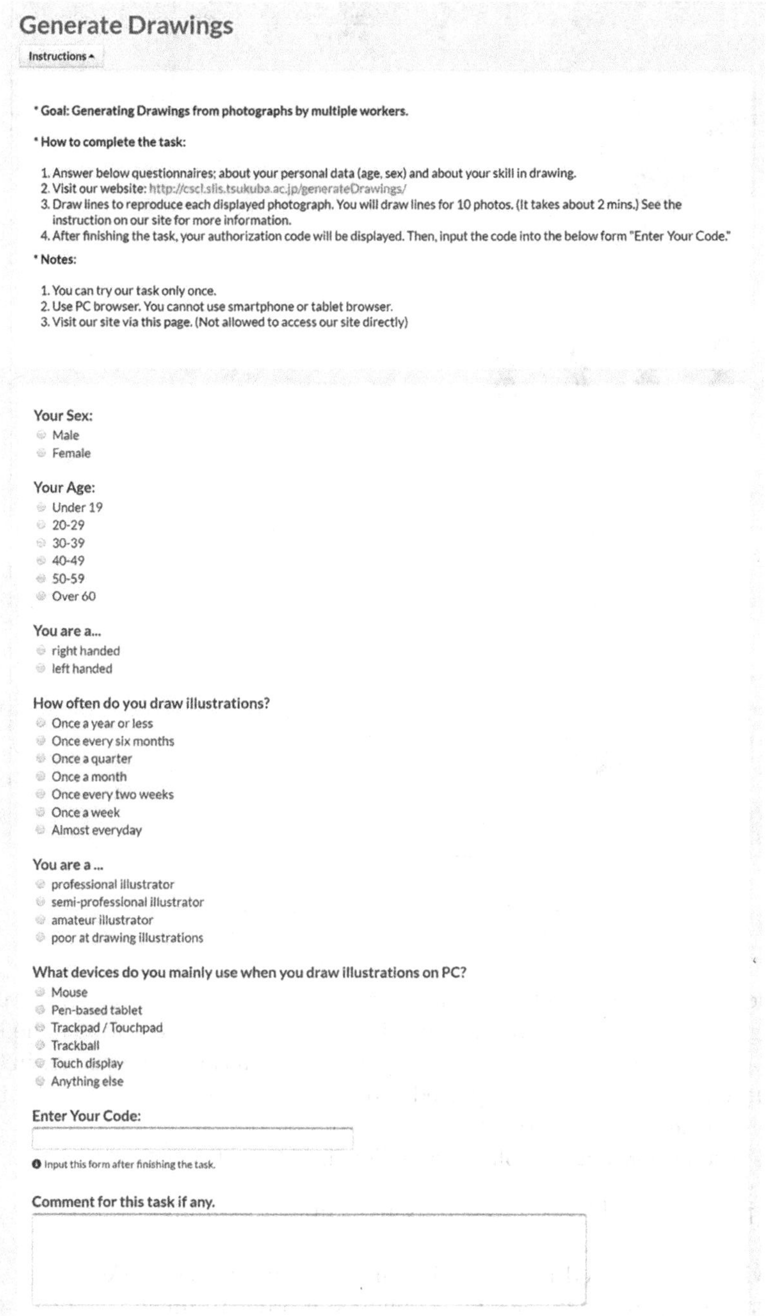

Generate Drawings

Instructions ▲

* **Goal: Generating Drawings from photographs by multiple workers.**

* **How to complete the task:**

  1. Answer below questionnaires; about your personal data (age, sex) and about your skill in drawing.
  2. Visit our website: http://cscl.slis.tsukuba.ac.jp/generateDrawings/
  3. Draw lines to reproduce each displayed photograph. You will draw lines for 10 photos. (It takes about 2 mins.) See the instruction on our site for more information.
  4. After finishing the task, your authorization code will be displayed. Then, input the code into the below form "Enter Your Code."

* **Notes:**

  1. You can try our task only once.
  2. Use PC browser. You cannot use smartphone or tablet browser.
  3. Visit our site via this page. (Not allowed to access our site directly)

Your Sex:
- Male
- Female

Your Age:
- Under 19
- 20-29
- 30-39
- 40-49
- 50-59
- Over 60

You are a...
- right handed
- left handed

How often do you draw illustrations?
- Once a year or less
- Once every six months
- Once a quarter
- Once a month
- Once every two weeks
- Once a week
- Almost everyday

You are a ...
- professional illustrator
- semi-professional illustrator
- amateur illustrator
- poor at drawing illustrations

What devices do you mainly use when you draw illustrations on PC?
- Mouse
- Pen-based tablet
- Trackpad / Touchpad
- Trackball
- Touch display
- Anything else

Enter Your Code:

❶ Input this form after finishing the task.

Comment for this task if any.

Fig. 5. The task page on CrowdFlower

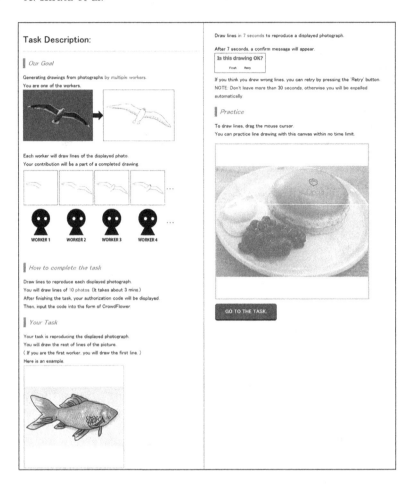

Fig. 6. The task description page

to gather personal data. The questionnaires was selected for investigate worker's drawing skill. After answering the questionnaires, contributors follow the link to the experiment task server and are displayed instruction page shown in Fig. 6. The authentication code is displayed after drawing task 10 times. The task is completed when worker enter it.

The instruction page displays the following content:

- The purpose of this experiment is to complete the line drawing by plural workers.
- Drawing is completed by overlaying lines drawn by each worker.
- It is necessary to draw lines for 10 photos in order to finish this task.
- After finishing to draw lines for 10 photos, an authorization code will be displayed. To finish this task, you need to input the code into the form on CrowdFlower's task page.

- Your task is that looking the displayed photos and drawn lines to complement the insufficient.
- You have a time limit of 7 s to draw lines for one photo.
- After 7 s drawing, you can retry to draw by pressing retry button if you have failed to draw lines.

In the instruction page, we also provide a canvas for practicing. Contributors can practice drawing before starting the tasks. After practicing, contributors go to the page for contribution tasks.

On the contribution task page, a canvas, a photo, and drawn lines are displayed as shown in Fig. 7. On this page, these two items are described; each contributor has 7 s to draw lines per photo, and contributor does not have to be rush. The time limit is measured since the contributor begin to draw the first line. After 7 s, contributors cannot draw lines. If contributors have failed to draw lines, they retry to draw by pressing displayed retry button. 10 photos for generating drawings are displayed at random. Figure 8 shows that the 10 photos used in this experiment, which is also used in the previous study [22]. These photos include clear and unclear outlines, and they have a variety of subjects and compositions. After drawing 10 photos, the system displays an authorization code. Each contributor input the code and comments into the form on task page to finish this experiment.

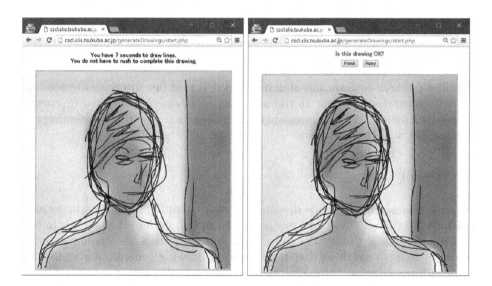

Fig. 7. Display on contributor's browser. Left: A drawing canvas / Right: A confirm window

Fig. 8. Photos used at the experience

4.2 Participants

20 participants worked on at 1 task (drawing lines for 10 photos), 1 task was carried out 6 times, and the total number of contributor is 120. According to FAQ page of CrowdFlower, an example shows that the payment of per 3 answer by 1 contributor is 10 cents [4]. Thus in this study, we decided to pay to a contributor 33 cents (3.3 times of 10 cents) as we regarded drawing 10 photos as answering 10 questions for a contributor.

4.3 Generated Drawings

Advance research by Sasaki et al. have suggested that line drawings are possible to be completed after about 16 times of drawing in case of generated by crowd-sourced microtask [22]. Thus we exploit the drawings up to 16th by rejecting the drawings from 17th to the end.

5 Result

Figure 9 shows generated line drawings in each condition. The experiment was conducted 6 times, 6 drawings was generated per photo for all 10 photos in one experiment. The drawings has been generated with the same quality as prior research. It was confirmed that the microtask drawing generation system that links with the crowdsourcing site operated correctly. According to the results, it was suggested that our method can be used to free task design without restrictions of any crowdsourcing sites.

Original Photos

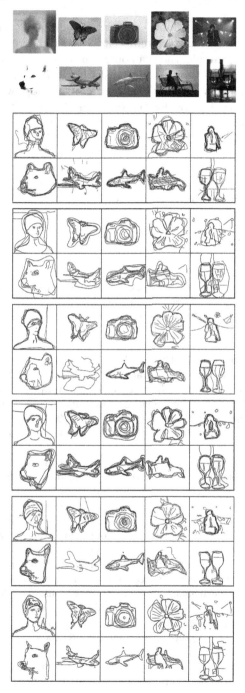

Fig. 9. Generated drawings

6   Conclusion

In this study, we developed a microtask drawing generation system that can link with exiting crowdsourcing sites. Existing crowdsourcing sites has many problem. For example, they can only run the selection formula or text description task, they can only run parallel tasks but can't run sequential tasks, and they has restrictions by APIs. Therefore in this Study, we proposed a method that prepares external server for the tasks and links with the crowdsourcing sites. In order to enable setting free-formatted tasks at exiting crowdsourcing sites. Since the application of this method is not limited to line drawings generation, the increase of various use of microtask crowdsourcing is prospective.

Acknowledgment. This research was partially supported by the JSPS Grants-in-Aid for Scientific Research No. 26330218.

References

1. Amazon mechanical turk. https://www.mturk.com
2. Overview - requester - Amazon mechanical turk. https://requester.mturk.com/
3. Bly, S.A.: A use of drawing surfaces in different collaborative settings. In: Proceedings of the 1988 ACM Conference on Computer-Supported Cooperative Work, pp. 250–256 (1988)
4. Job Costs FAQ CrowdFlower success center. https://success.CrowdFlower.com/hc/en-us/articles/202703165-Job-Costs-FAQ
5. CrowdFlower: make your data useful. https://www.CrowdFlower.com/
6. Martin, D., Hanrahan, B.V., O'Neill, J., Gupta, N.: Being a turker. In: Proceedings of the 17th ACM Conference on Computer Supported Cooperative Work & Social Computing (CSCW 2014), pp. 224–235 (2014)
7. Patterson, D.: Technical writing: lines & spots. SIGDOC Asterisk J. Comput. Doc. **2**(10), 8–10 (1976)
8. Little, G., Chilton, L.B., Goldman, M., Miller, R.C.: TurKit: human computation algorithms on mechanical turk. In: Proceedings of the 23nd Annual ACM Symposium on User Interface Software and Technology (UIST 2010), pp. 57–66 (2010)
9. FlockDraw - free online drawing tool - collaborative group whiteboard. http://ockdraw.com/
10. Hara, K., Le, V., Froehlich, J.: Combining crowdsourcing and google street view to identify street-level accessibility problems. In: Proceedings of the SIGCHI Conference on Human Factors in Computing Systems, pp. 631–640 (2013)
11. Ishii, H., Kobayashi, M., Grudin, J.: Integration of inter-personal space, shared workspace: clearboard design and experiments. In: Proceedings of the 1992 ACM Conference on Computer-Supported Cooperative Work, pp. 33–42 (1992)
12. Kawashima, T., Koblin, A.: Ten thousand cents. In: ACM SIGGRAPH ASIA 2008 Artgallery: Emerging Technologies, p. 18 (2008)
13. Kucherbaev, P., Daniel, F., Tranquillini, S., Marchese, M.: ReLauncher: crowdsourcing micro-tasks runtime controller. In: Proceedings of the 19th ACM Conference on Computer-Supported Cooperative Work & Social Computing, pp. 1609–1614 (2016)

14. Komarov, S., Reinecke, K., Gajos, K.Z.: Crowdsourcing performance evaluations of user interfaces. In: Proceedings of the SIGCHI Conference on Human Factors in Computing Systems, pp. 207–216 (2013)
15. LaToza, T.D., Ben Towne, W., Adriano, C.M., van der Hoek, A.: Microtask programming: building software with a crowd. In: Proceedings of the 27th Annual ACM Symposium on User Interface Software and Technology, pp. 43–54 (2014)
16. Lee, Y.J., Lawrence Zitnick, C., Cohen, M.F.: ShadowDraw: real-time user guidance for freehand drawing. ACM Trans. Graph. **30**(4), 10 (2011). Article 27
17. Limpaecher, A., Feltman, N., Treuille, A., Cohen, M.: Real-time drawing assistance through crowdsourcing. ACM Trans. Graph. **32**(4), 8 (2013). Article 54
18. RealWorld start a business tie-up with CrowdFlower — Press release by RealWorld. Inc. http://prtimes.jp/main/html/rd/p/000000010.000007199.html
19. Salehi, N., Irani, L.C., Bernstein, M.S., Alkhatib, A., Ogbe, E., Milland, K.: We are dynamo: overcoming stalling and friction in collective action for crowd workers. In: Proceedings of the 33rd Annual ACM Conference on Human Factors in Computing Systems, pp. 1621–1630 (2015)
20. Fair payment - WeAreDynamo Wiki. http://wiki.wearedynamo.org/index.php?title=Fair_payment
21. Sasaki, K., Hirata, A., Inoue, T.: Investigation of the illustration generated by crowdsourced microtasks. IPSJ Trans. Digit. Content **4**(1), 37–45 (2016)
22. Sasaki, K., Hirata, A., Inoue, T.: A basic drawing generation method by crowdsourced microtasks. IPSJ Trans. **57**(1), 260–269 (2016)
23. Truong, K.N., Shihipar, T., Wigdor, D.J.: Slide to X: unlocking the potential of smartphone unlocking. In: Proceedings of the SIGCHI Conference on Human Factors in Computing Systems, pp. 3635–3644 (2014)
24. Vaish, R., Wyngarden, K., Chen, J., Cheung, B., Bernstein, M.S.: Twitch crowdsourcing: crowd contribution in short bursts of time. In: Proceedings of the SIGCHI Conference on Human Factors in Computing Systems (CHI 2014), pp. 3645–3654 (2014)
25. Lixiu, Y., Nickerson, J.V.: An internet-scale idea generation system. ACM Trans. Interact. Intell. Syst. **3**(1), 2: 1–2–2: 1–24 (2013)

Proposal of an Architecture and Implementation of a Triage Support System

Ryuga Kato[✉], Kento Izumida, Hiroshi Shigeno, and Ken-ichi Okada

Graduate School of Science and Technology, Keio University, Kanagawa, Japan
{kato,izumida,shigeno,okada}@mos.ics.keio.ac.jp

Abstract. At the time of disaster, medical resources are limited. To save the injured person as many as possible, triage is important. Recently, the concept of triage in emergency medical care at the time of disaster has attracted widely in Japan. In order to perform emergency lifesaving activities at an real disaster spot quickly and accurately, it is essential to do triage training frequently. Many systems have been developed to support medical activities at real spot and triage training. However, current systems are designed either for training only or for usage in real situations only. In this study, we propose an architecture and implementation of a triage support system. We designed the system so that the users can select different modes, and implemented a prototype system. The evaluation shows that our system can be used in different situations and the operation of the system can be done without any problems.

Keywords: Triage · Architecture · Tablet · HMD · Beacon · Training

1 Introduction

When a large-scale disaster occurs, medical resources such as personnel and equipment become limited. In such situations, triage becomes important. By performing triage, an act of deciding the priority of treating patients by severity of their condition, efficient use of the resources can be achieved. After triage, the patient needs to be transported to a hospital quickly and receive appropriate treatment there.

Many systems have been developed to assist medical activities in emergencies. Some examples are: a system in which patients' vital signs can be monitored in real time and a system which visualizes the patients' location. There are also systems that support triage training, since training played a key role in acquiring the skills and knowledge necessary to perform triage. However, current systems are designed either for training only or for usage in real situations only. Therefore, users cannot get used to the system during training, and may lose time in figuring out how to use the system in actual disasters. Moreover, how to input information into the system and look at the already inputted information is restricted in current systems, so the usability is not high.

In this paper, we propose an architecture and implementation of a triage system. To solve the issues stated above, we designed the system so that the users

© Springer Science+Business Media Singapore 2016
T. Yoshino et al. (Eds.): CollabTech 2016, CCIS 647, pp. 246–261, 2016.
DOI: 10.1007/978-981-10-2618-8_20

can select different modes, such as "Table-top Training" and "Disaster", according to the situation. These modes can be created easily using the base system, which includes the minimum necessary functions to perform triage. In addition, we implemented a prototype system according to the architecture using a tablet terminal and monocular HMD. After conducting an evaluation experiment, we found that our system can be used in different situations and the operation of the system can be done without any problems.

The rest of this paper is organised as follows: First, we describe the works related to our research and their issues, about disaster relief. Next, we show our proposal for solving the issues, and provide the details of our proposal. Furthermore, we show the evaluation experiment and discuss the result of the experiment. Finally, we present the main conclusions and future work.

2   Disaster Relief

2.1   Triage in Emergencies

When disasters such as an earthquake occur, the neighboring environment instantly becomes far different from the daily life and medical resources also become limited. In such situation, triage plays an important role in life saving activities. Triage is the activity to determine priorities for patients' treatment based on the severity and urgency. In Japan, health care workers perform triage based on START (Simple Triage and Rapid Treatment) method [1]. Injured persons are categorized based on their vital signs into the following four: Red (immediate), Yellow (delayed), Green (minor) and Black (dead). These four colors correspond to triage tags which are used to visually indicate each injured person's condition [2]. A health care worker writes necessary information about the injured person on a paper tag, and attaches to the patient. In addition, they do activities while keep in touch with others such as emergency headquarters.

Mass casualty incidents don't occur frequently. But, it is essential that training is performed frequently and health care workers are equipped with the necessary skills and knowledge to be able to deal with an incident whenever it occurs. There are various training methods. One of the methods is the disaster drill using real people as a role of patient. People act based on the information given on paper. Trainee perform triage by looking at vital signs written on paper. Through this type of training, trainee can experience how to actually move around and practice the actual actions. In Japan, this type of training is conducted widely in hospitals and local governments. The other type of training is desktop simulation. The Emergo Train System (ETS) is this type of training. ETS focuses on optimal staff assignment by moving magnets that represent patients and health care workers on a whiteboard [3]. By repeating the desktop training, trainees can acquire knowledge about how to manage the resources.

In order to master the process of triage, it is important for health care workers to perform the training repeatedly. However, there are some problems of the high cost and long time required for training. Desktop trainings seem to be cost-efficient, but the training environment is completely different from the real disasters and so they lack in reality.

2.2 Related Work

In order to solve these issues, many research has been done and many systems also have been developed. These systems are largely divided into two types: the system supporting a construction of the training environment and the system supporting an activity in the real spot.

There are systems to train triage skills, such as a system which contains a disaster simulation using Virtual Reality for educating health care workers [4,5] and there is a system which also use head-mounted displays (HMD) [6]. Other systems which generate virtual patients and allow the trainee to use Kinect to control avatars [7], and which allow doctors to discuss about a patient simultaneously by using a tabletop interface [8] have also been developed.

Many systems that support life saving activities at the real spot have also been developed. In the USA, the experiment about understanding the positions of patients with the active RFID [9] in Wireless Internet Information System for Medical Response in Disasters (WIISARD) project. In the CodeBlue project which is conducted by Harvard University and Boston University, a system which collects biological information of a patient using various sensors, and supports the medical service at the time of the disaster has been developed [10]. Other researches have also been conducted, a study on network to communicate biological information efficiently [11] and a study that gathers information of patients with the small terminals such as PDAs [12].

As stated above, many systems have been developed. However, current systems are designed either for training only or for usage in real situations only, and it takes so much time and labor to get used to the system. Therefore, users cannot get used to the system during training, and may lose time in figuring out how to use the system in actual disasters.

3   Requirements of an Architecture of a Triage Support System

In order to provide the maximum performance, it is important that the system for training is usable in the disaster spot. However, triage support systems are developed separately now, and there is no system which is usable in both a disaster spot and training. Most of training systems often become the system depending on a specific purpose, and it is necessary to set up software and hardware for each training system. When developing a system according to a purpose, not only development efficiency becomes low, but also takes time for users to learn how to use the system in each system. Therefore, it is necessary to develop the system that can be used in common for any scene.

3.1 Classification of the Function According to the Situation

The function required for a triage support system varies according to activity contents or training contents. For example, when people perform training in individual, the function that makes a scenario for training automatically is required. When people act on an actual disaster spot, the function to send a message to coordinate with other people is required. On the other hand, there is the function that is required in any situation, for example, the function to input the triage result or the function to show the information of an injured person.

In order to develop the system which is usable in any situation efficiency, it is important that each of functions are not collectively controlled but classified by function. By classifying the functions required to use commonly from the functions not required to use commonly, the developing efficiency can be improved. In this study, the set of functions that are necessary in all situations is called "a basic system" and the set of functions that are necessary according to the situation is called "additional functions".

3.2 Making the Mode

In order to make the system which is usable in various situation, it is necessary for appropriate functions to be prepared according to each situation. The system must present functions suitable for respective situations to a user to use the system appropriately. Therefore, it is important that additional functions are summarized according to the situation. In this study, we call the thing which is a combination of a basic system and additional functions according to respective situations "a mode". By presenting modes instead of functions, it becomes able to prevent users from confusion.

3.3 Cooperation Between Software and Hardware

When emergency service workers perform lifesaving activity at the disaster spot, there are many activities using both hands such as triage and first aid. The tablet terminal is a mobile device that has spread widely, but people must make operation of the tablet terminal in both hands. Therefore, during activities using both hands, it is difficult to use the mobile device like a tablet terminal. The wearable device, such as a monocular HMD, which people can operate in one hand or hands-free is suitable for the work using both hands. However, it is hard to display much information at a time on a monocular HMD. The device which has a big screen is suitable to show a list of patient or information or a map.

Thus, it is important for each hardware to be mounted with functions suitable for characteristics of the hardware. For example, an input function of triage results should be implemented in the device which people can operate in one hand or hands-free, and a function of displaying information of patient should be implemented in the device which has a big display. In this way, by using a device properly according to the situation, the system can utilize the strength of each hardware, and users become able to work efficiently.

4   Implementation

We have built the prototype system based on a proposal architecture taking into account the following three points needed in a triage support system as stated in Sect. 3: classification of the function, making the mode, and cooperation between software and hardware.

4.1   System Configuration

Beacons, which represent the virtual patients, are placed around in the training room. We used Beacons produced by Aplix Corporation [13]. As shown in Fig. 1, the user wears monocular HMD (Vuzix M100 smart glass) [14] on the head and has a Nexus7 [15] in hand to detect the Beacons and display the information. The program to output information is developed in Java, JavaScript, PHP.

As stated in Sect. 3, each mode consists of a combination of basic system and additional functions. We divided the constitution of the system into the part which called a basic system and the part which called additional functions. Since a basic system is the collection of functions required commonly, they are called directly. On the other hand, as the additional functions vary with each mode, a list of additional functions, which is defined the relationship between the mode and the additional function, is called first. By calling the required functions with this list indirectly, the time of program creation can be saved even if a new function and make modifications are added.

Basic System Configuration. Figure 2 shows the overall configuration of a basic system. A basic system is a collection of functions required in every situation. Specifically, a basic system consists of three functions: to input the result

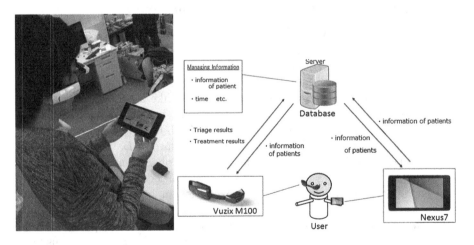

Fig. 1. A manner of using our system   **Fig. 2.** Basic system configuration

of triage, to input the information of a patient being transported, and to display the information of patients.

We implemented these functions in both a tablet terminal and a monocular HMD. Since it is necessary to use both hands to confirm the status of a patient when health care workers perform triage and decides who should be transported, we allowed users to input the information by a monocular HMD which users do not need to hold by hand. In addition, we allowed users to input complex information such as a name or an address that users cannot input in monocular HMD by a tablet terminal. The all data which users input are managed in a database, and users can see them with a tablet terminal or a monocular HMD. Since it is hard to display many information on a small screen such as a monocular HMD, detailed information of a patient allows users to see on the tablet terminal which has a big screen. In order to see information of patients instantly, we implemented that simple information can be displayed on a monocular HMD.

Desktop Training Mode. Figure 3 shows the overall configuration of desktop training mode. This mode consists of a basic system and the function of the scenario for training, and the purpose is to learn about the triage and how to use the device. The training scenario is managed in a database beforehand, and the information of a virtual patient can be displayed on the computer at the time of training. Users perform the desktop training using three devices: PC, a tablet terminal, and a monocular HMD.

Field Mode. A field mode is the system which supports cooperative work at the real spot. It consists of a basic system and additional functions, such as making a message, inputting the information of a location, and recording the logs of user's activities. A monocular HMD and a tablet terminal have a built-in GPS receiver, and can obtain user's current location information at constant intervals. Using user's current location information, the system makes an activity

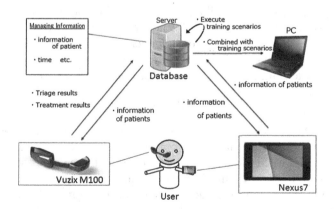

Fig. 3. Desktop training mode configuration

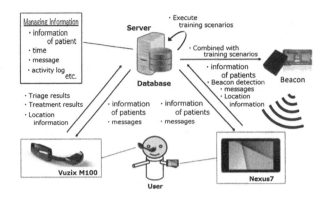

Fig. 4. Actual training mode configuration

log of the user automatically. The transmission of a message can be done with a tablet terminal, and checking received messages can be done with both a tablet terminal and a monocular HMD.

Actual Training Mode. Figure 4 shows the overall configuration of an actual training mode. In this mode, users can train the process of triage with walking around training environment. To provide the training close to real activities, we add the function of the scenario for training to a field mode. Before training begins, Beacons are laid out around the training environment. Each Beacon is combined with the information of a virtual patient. As the trainee moves closer to a Beacon, information about the virtual patient corresponding to the Beacon shows up.

4.2 Screen Design and User Interface

The flow of using our system is following. This prototype system assumes that the QR code is printed on a paper tag. If a new patient is discovered, a healthcare worker attaches QR code printed on a paper to the patient. The user scans the QR code and inputs the information of the patient. All screen designs are integrated under a common design. From this, many users become able to operate our system with ease.

Monocular HMD. When a user log in to our system, a user will be presented with an initial screen that has three options: Desktop training Mode, Actual training Mode, and Field Mode. After selecting a mode, the menu screen appears based on each mode as shown in Fig. 5. For example, in the actual training mode, there are five buttons: to input the result of triage, to input the information of the patient whose condition is changed suddenly, to input the information of who to transport, to confirm the information of patients, and to check all messages.

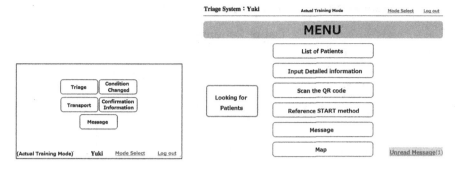

Fig. 5. The menu screen of a monocular HMD   **Fig. 6.** The menu screen of a tablet terminal

When the user select "Triage" button, the system switches camera automatically. By scanning the QR code which is attached to the patient, the screen to input the result of triage appears. When the user performs triage and chooses the triage category, the information of the patient is saved to the database automatically. Similarly, when patient's condition change suddenly, the user performs triage again and inputs a necessary information.

If the user chooses the patient who should be transported to hospital, the user selects "Transport" button and the screen to input the information of the transported patient appears. Since the patient ID that has been performed triage is displayed by the drop down list, the user select the patient ID and complete inputting information. When the user select "Confirmation Information" button, the system switches camera automatically. The user scans the QR code which is attached to the patient, the information of the patient is displayed on the screen. In addition, when the user select "Message" button, a list of messages is displayed on the screen. In order to reduce learning time about how to use this prototype system, the input method is not using gesture input, but using a physical key. Thus, by minimizing displaying and inputting to a monocular HMD, the user can operate intuitively and quickly.

Tablet terminal. As stated above, when a user log in to our system, a user will also be presented with an initial screen that has three options: Desktop training Mode, Actual training Mode, and Field Mode. After selecting the mode, the menu screen appears based on each mode as shown in Fig. 6. For example, in the actual training mode, there are six buttons: to check a list of patients, to input the detailed information of the patient, to scan the QR code, to display the flowchart of START method, to check all messages, and to display a map. When the user select "List of Patients" button, a list of patients is displayed on the screen as shown in Fig. 7. The category column is painted in a color depending on the triage category, and is visually intelligible. When a user pushes patient ID, a user can see the detailed information of the patient as shown in Fig. 8. In this page, the information of the patient is displayed in the upper part, and the

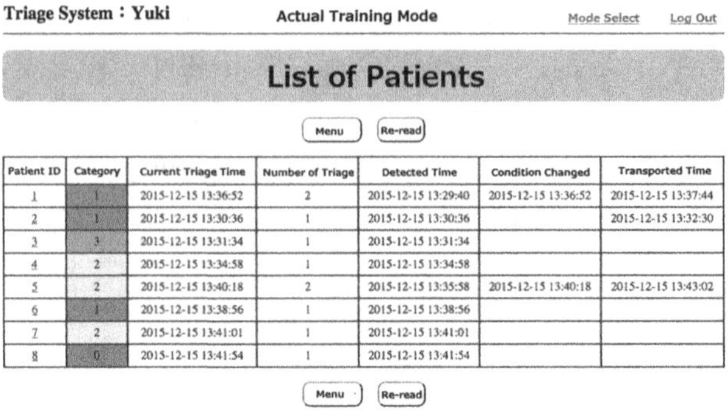

Triage System : Yuki   **Actual Training Mode**   Mode Select   Log Out

List of Patients

[Menu] [Re-read]

Patient ID	Category	Current Triage Time	Number of Triage	Detected Time	Condition Changed	Transported Time
1	1	2015-12-15 13:36:52	2	2015-12-15 13:29:40	2015-12-15 13:36:52	2015-12-15 13:37:44
2	1	2015-12-15 13:30:36	1	2015-12-15 13:30:36		2015-12-15 13:32:30
3	3	2015-12-15 13:31:34	1	2015-12-15 13:31:34		
4	2	2015-12-15 13:34:58	1	2015-12-15 13:34:58		
5	2	2015-12-15 13:40:18	2	2015-12-15 13:35:58	2015-12-15 13:40:18	2015-12-15 13:43:02
6	1	2015-12-15 13:38:56	1	2015-12-15 13:38:56		
7	2	2015-12-15 13:41:01	1	2015-12-15 13:41:01		
8	0	2015-12-15 13:41:54	1	2015-12-15 13:41:54		

[Menu] [Re-read]

Fig. 7. The list of patients (Color figure online)

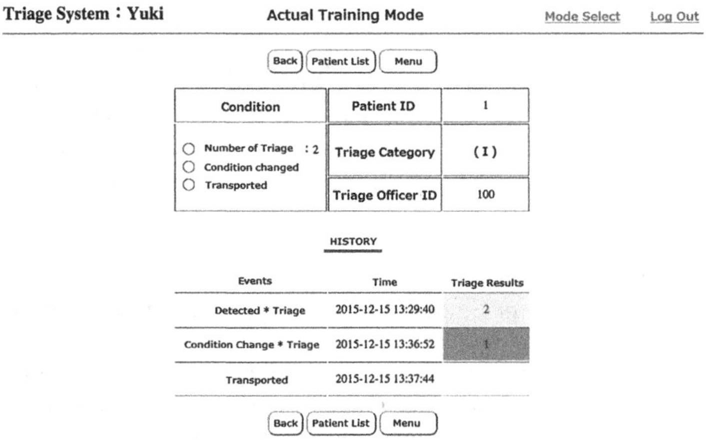

Triage System : Yuki   **Actual Training Mode**   Mode Select   Log Out

[Back] [Patient List] [Menu]

Condition	Patient ID	1
○ Number of Triage : 2 ○ Condition changed ○ Transported	Triage Category	(I)
	Triage Officer ID	100

HISTORY

Events	Time	Triage Results
Detected * Triage	2015-12-15 13:29:40	2
Condition Change * Triage	2015-12-15 13:36:52	1
Transported	2015-12-15 13:37:44	

[Back] [Patient List] [Menu]

Fig. 8. The detail information of a patient (Color figure online)

information of treatments provided for the patient is displayed in chronological order in the lower part. When a user select "Input Detailed Information" button, the screen to input detailed information of the patient appears. Since it takes much time to input the letter in HMD, we implemented the inputting the letter information such as a name and an address for a tablet terminal. The detailed information that a user input to a tablet terminal is linked to the data that the user already input to a monocular HMD. When a user select "Scan the QR code" button, the system switches camera automatically. By scanning the QR code which is attached to the patient, the information of the patient is displayed on the screen.

If the user forget the flow of START method, by selecting "Reference START method" button, the flowchart of START method is displayed on the screen. With this function, the user can perform triage while confirming START method. When a user select "Message" button, a list of messages is displayed on the screen. In a tablet terminal, a user can perform not only checking messages but also sending message. In addition, when a user select "Map" button, a user can confirm the location of patients that are performed triage. If there are patients that is performed triage around the current location, the location of patients is displayed on the map as a colored marker. The color of the marker is the same as a triage category of the patient. When a user push the marker, a user can see detailed information of the patient.

4.3   Execution of Training Scenario

Desktop training mode. In the desktop training mode, people learn about triage method while sitting at a computer. The training scenario, including the condition information of virtual patients, needs to be prepared in advance. The system obtains training scenario from the database, and the image and information of virtual patient are displayed on a computer. A trainee perform triage and input the result of triage to a monocular HMD while watching the display of a computer. When a trainee has finished performing triage to five patients, correct answer explanation is displayed on a computer. By performing desktop training mode repeatedly, the user gets familiar with both triage and operation of the system.

Actual training mode. In the actual training mode, people can train the process of triage with walking around training environment. The training scenario, including information of the patient whose condition changes and the time of ambulance arrival, needs to be also prepared in advance. Before training, Beacons are laid out around the training environment depending on the number of virtual patients.

Fig. 9. Displaying virtual patients

When a user select "Looking for Patients" button, the screen as shown in Fig. 9 appears. In this screen, eight virtual patients are displayed, since the system detect eight Beacons. The image size of virtual patient changes based on the distance between a tablet terminal and Beacon. Since each Beacon correspond with the information of one virtual patient, as a user approaches specific Beacon, the image size correspond with the Beacon becomes bigger. When a user approaches closest distance, it is displayed "Able to triage". By selecting the displaying, the image of virtual patient and the information of the patient are displayed on the screen of a tablet terminal. The trainee perform triage and input the result of triage to a monocular HMD while watching the display of a tablet terminal. The event such as an ambulance arrival and sudden condition changing occurs based on a training scenario, and these events are notified to a trainee as a message. When a trainee has discovered all Beacons and finished dealing with all events, the training finished.

5   Evaluation

In order to confirm the usefulness of our prototype system, we conducted an evaluation experiment with students as the first step. During the experiment, we focused on two points: whether a user can operate our system in both desktop training and actual training without any problems, and usability.

5.1   Experiment Description

We conducted an evaluation experiment with 20 participants. All participants were university or graduate school students not professional in triage. Therefore, before the experiment, they studied about the basic knowledge necessary to perform triage and what to do when events such as an ambulance arrival occurs. The participants were divided into two groups, each comprising 10 participants. One group use our system, the other use paper tags, that is, traditional method. Before an experiment, they performed desktop training and studied about the basic knowledge about triage. The group that uses our system had a tablet terminal and monocular HMD, and switched the system to desktop training mode. The other group had paper tags and a pencil. Both group performed desktop training, sitting in front of a computer. The information of virtual patient is displayed on the computer, and the participants performed triage based on it. When performing triage, the group using proposal system used monocular HMD to input the result of triage, the group of traditional method wrote the result of triage on a paper tag. After triage to all virtual patients, the participants checked and confirmed what they mistake. We explained them, they could try desktop training until they are satisfied.

After desktop training, the participants performed actual training. The group using proposal system had a tablet terminal and wore monocular HMD, and switch the system to actual training mode. Further, they performed the training carrying paper tags which the QR code is printed. The group of traditional

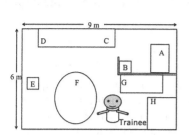

Fig. 10. Experiment room   **Fig. 11.** Example of paper tags

method performed the training carrying normal paper tags. The experiment room was set up as shown in Fig. 10, and the alphabets represent where Beacon was and the corresponding patient ID. The oval and squares represent desks, and Beacons were placed on the desk. During the training, the patient walked freely around the room with performing triage one by one. When events occurred as described below, participants handled them as soon as possible. The group using proposal system received the notifications popping up onto the screen of a tablet terminal, and the group of traditional method was communicated the notifications by the experimenter.

- Sudden change of patient's condition: Patients need to go to the virtual patient whose condition changed suddenly as soon as possible. Participants stand in front of the Beacon and perform triage again.
- Ambulance arrival: Patients need to choose which patient to send to the hospital. Status of the virtual patient can be seen by walking towards a Beacon, for example, whether he/she had already been triaged, or whether his/her condition had suddenly changed before. After checking the information of the patients, the patients decided who should be transported immediately. When deciding the patient, the group using proposal system inputted the patient ID into the system, the group using traditional method filled the time that the patient was transported on the paper tag.

When all patients had been triaged and all events had finished, the participant prepared the report of the patients. The group using proposal system made the report by referring the data that they inputted into the system, and the group of traditional method made the report by referring the paper tag that they wrote.

In order to prevent from making a difference in required time and an accuracy rate, the system set the fixed values for biometric information of virtual patients. In this experiment, there were eight patients: three red tags, three yellow tags, one green tag, and one black tag. The condition of one yellow tag and one green tag patient suddenly changed, and the event of transport availability occurred three times. In order to confirm whether there is a difference in comparison with our prototype system and traditional method, we decided to use (1) Required time, (2) Accuracy rate, and (3) Questionnaire about our system as evaluation criteria.

5.2   Results

The result of triage. The result of triage is as shown in Table 1. We compared both group, the group using our system and the group of traditional method. The required time means the average time per patient it took the participant to perform triage, and the accuracy rate means whether the participant determine the triage category accurately. The "$\pm$" represents the standard deviation.

Table 1. The result of triage

	Proposal system	Traditional method
Required time (sec)	26.6 ± 6.4	32.8 ± 4.0
Accuracy rate (%)	88.0 ± 10.3	88.5 ± 9.4

We did a t-test about the result of required time, and there was statistically significant ($P < 0.05$). It is thought that this was mainly due to the difference of recording method. If he/she records the information of patient in a paper tag, he/she must write date, time and name of triage officer to a paper tag each time. But, by using our system, it is not necessary to input such data each time, that is because the system inputs such data automatically. On the other hand, the result of accuracy rate was not statistically significant. It is thought that this was because both group performed the same desktop training before the actual training. This shows input error rarely occurs when using our system.

Table 2. The result of patient transportation decision

	Proposal system	Traditional method
Required time (sec)	35.7 ± 6.6	25.1 ± 7.2
Accuracy rate (%)	100.0 ± 0.0	79.7 ± 23.6

The result of patient transportation decision. The result of patient transportation decision is as shown in Table 2. We compared both group, the group using our system and the group of traditional method. The required time means the average time per patient it took the participant to decide and record who should be transported, and the accuracy rate means whether the participant

Table 3. The result of the report

	Proposal system	Traditional method
Required time (sec)	391.5 ± 71.2	484.6 ± 51.9
Accuracy rate (%)	100.0 ± 0.0	88.0 ± 10.3

Table 4. The result of questionnaire

Question	Proposal system	Traditional method
Did you get familiar with the system in desktop training?	5.0	-
In actual training, were you able to work in the same way as in desktop training? **	1.0	-
Do you think our system is usable in the real spot?	4.4	-
Was it easy to use a monocular HMD and a tablet terminal?	4.1	-
Was the making of the report easy?	4.9	3.4

**: Participants answered on a scale of 0 (No) to 1 (Yes).

determine who should be transported accurately. The "±" represents the standard deviation.

We did a t-test, the result of the required time was statistically significant (P < 0.01), and the result of accuracy rate was also statistically significant (P < 0.05). It is thought that an accuracy rate of the group using our system became higher, that was because they can decide who should be transported while looking the data of patients display on a tablet terminal. It is also thought that the accuracy rate of the group of traditional method became lower, that was because they decided who should be transported by memory without checking the information of a paper tag. As a result, the group using our system took more time than the group of traditional method.

The result of a report. In Table 3, the result of a report is shown. We compared both group, the group using our system and the group of traditional method. The required time means the amount time that it took to finish making the report of patients, and the accuracy rate means whether the participant made the report accurately. The "±" represents the standard deviation.

We did a t-test, the result of the required time and accuracy rate were statistically significant (P < 0.01). The group using our system transcribe the data which the system compile information of patients automatically. As a result, an accuracy rate became higher and required time became shorter. On the other hand, the group of traditional method needed to collect paper tags and make the report with confirming the information of a paper tag. As a result, required time became longer. It is thought that recording omissions and mistakes cause an accuracy rate to decrease. As shown in Fig. 11, there were some recording omissions and mistakes, and some participants made the report with incorrect information. This shows that it becomes possible to reduce mistakes by recording the information of patients as data in triage.

Questionnaire. The result of questionnaire are as shown in Table 4. Participants answered the questionnaire on a scale of 1 to 5. 5 is the best score and 1 is the worst score. In the question 2, participants answered on a scale of 0 (No) to 1 (Yes). All questions achieved high scores, and it can be said there is no problem with operability of our system. In the comment field, there are some opinions. For example, "The operation of this system is easy to understand", "I could concentrate in doing triage since the system compile the information automatically", and "Since this system can be used in both desktop training and actual training, I got familiar with the system right away".

From these results, it can be said that our prototype system based on proposal architecture has high operability and users can use in various situations.

6   Conclusion

In the event of disaster such as an earthquake, medical resources become limited. To maximize the limited resources, priorities for patients' treatment based on the severity and urgency as well as their transportation, the selection of hospitals, and medical treatment need to be determined, that is called triage. In order improve the skills and be ready for the disasters to come, frequent training is essential. Recently, many systems have been developed to assist medial activities in emergencies. However, most of the current training system are far apart from the system to use in the real spot. Most of systems are designed either for training only or for usage in the real spot only. So, users cannot get used to the system and they cannot maximize their skills which they have cultivated in the training.

In our study, we propose an architecture of a triage system and developed a prototype system based on the architecture. We made plural modes to support using the system depending on the situation, and created functions that became necessary for the situation in each mode. Users work with a monocular HMD and a tablet terminal. Multiple devices can be used separately by each task.

Through the evaluation experiment, we were able to see that the participants could work about triage and decision of patient who should be transported quickly and precisely by using our system compared to traditional method which uses paper tags. In addition, we confirmed that our system could be used in both desktop training and actual training and there is no problem with the operability of our system. As future work, we hope to do further evaluation experiments targeted at experts, and make sure whether professionals can use our system as well. In addition, We want to implement more additional functions such as voice input or gesture input. It is thought that it is possible to get used to both triage activities and operation of devices, and this would make the activities of healthcare workers more efficient.

References

1. Simple Triage and Rapid Treatment, DisasterMedical Assistance Team. http://www.dmat.jp/index.html
2. Critical Illness and Trauma Foundation, Inc., The Triage Tag. http://citmt.org/Start/tag.html
3. Emergo Train System. http://www.emergotrain.com/
4. Kizakevich, P., Furberg, R., Hubal, R., Frank, G.: Virtual reality simulation for multicasualty triage training. In: Interservice/Industry Training, Simulation, and Education Conference (I/ITSEC), pp. 1–8 (2006)
5. Rui, Y., Bin, C., Fengru, H., Yu, F.: Using collaborative virtual geographic environment for fire disaster simulation and virtual fire training. In: 2012 20th, International Conference Geoinformatics (GEOINFORMATICS), pp. 1–4 (2012)
6. Vincent, D.S., Sherstyuk, A., Burgess, L., Connolly, K.K.: Teaching mass casualty triage skills using immersive three-dimensional virtual reality. Acad. Emerg. Med. **15**(11), 1160–1165 (2008)
7. Bartoli, G., Bimbo, A.D., Faconti, M., Ferracani, A., Marini, V., Pezzatini, D., Seidenari, L., Zilleruelo, F.: Emergency medicine training with gesture driven interactive 3D simulations. In: ACM workshop on User Experience in e-Learning and Augmented Technologies in Education (UXeLATE 2012), pp. 25–30, October 2012
8. Zadow, U.V., Buron, S., Harms, T., Behringer, F., Sastmann, K., Dachselt, R.: SimMed: combining simulation and interactive tabletops for medical education. In: CHI 2013, pp. 1469–1478 (2013)
9. Lenert, L., Chan, T.C., Griswold, W., Killeen, J., Palmer, D., Kirsh, D., Mishra, R., Rao, R.: Wireless internet information system for medical response in disasters (WIISARD). In: AMIA Annual Symposium Proceedings (2006)
10. Malan, D., Fulford-Jones, T., Welsh, M., Moulton, S.: CodeBlue: an ad hoc sensor network infrastructure for emergency medical care. In: International Workshop on Wearable and Implantable Body Sensor Networks, pp. 203–216 (2004)
11. Selavo-MattWelsh, L., Tia Gao, M.S., Massey, T.: Participatory user centered design techniques for a large scale ad-hoc health information system. In: Proceedings of the 1st ACM SIGMOBILE International Workshop on Systems and Networking Support for Healthcare and Assisted Living Environments, pp. 43–48 (2007)
12. Tzengb, Y.-M., Houc, I.-C., Sangb, Y.-Y., Changa, P., Hsub, Y.-S.: Development and pilot evaluation of user acceptance of advanced massgathering emergency medical services pda support systems. In: Proceedings of the 11th World Congress On Medical Informatics (2004)
13. Aplix Corporation. http://www.aplix.co.jp/product/mybeacon/
14. Vuzix, "M100 Smart Glasses". https://www.vuzix.com/Products/M100-Smart-Glasses
15. Asus, "Nexus 7". https://www.asus.com/jp/Tablets/Nexus72013/

Author Index

Printed in the United States
By Bookmasters